Artificial Intelligence

&

Machine Learning

in

Marketing

I0462039

A book that explains how technology is an enabler in marketing practice

By
Dr James Seligman

The Author

James Seligman was the Director responsible for the Masters in Marketing Management at the School of Management, Faculty of Management and Law, University of Southampton. An innovative 12-month international program, which uses the new DNA model of marketing theory and practice modules developed by the Marketing subject group. He joined Southampton University in 2008 and retired in late 2015. The MSc in Marketing Management degree has wide commercial support as it produces students who are trained for today's marketing challenges and considers technology as an enabler in modern marketing.

He has a Masters in Marketing and three undergraduate degrees in Business Administration, Educational Studies, and Psychology. His PhD is on Customer Experience and Technology.

As a Principal Fellow, he was also engaged in educational development and the student experience. The author of several books and journal articles, James research interests lie in the marketing of education, CRM and CEM, as well as the wider marketing characteristics of Brand, Strategic Marketing Intelligence, Analytics, Integrated Marketing Communications, Value Propositions, and Customer Insight. His most recent research has been on CEM and technology, Artificial Intelligence and Machine Learning in Marketing.

Prior to joining Southampton, he was a Curriculum Area Manager and Business Development Director, Lecturer, entering Higher Education ten years ago. Before this time, he had a successful thirty-year commercial career as an international senior executive with Coca-Cola, Pepsi, Beecham, Timberland, Commonwealth Games, and Speedo International group of companies.

Copy Right

Library of Congress – in – Publication Data

James Seligman, Southampton University, Hampshire,

England. Artificial Intelligence and Machine Learning, the

Future of Marketing, James Seligman Includes in text and

bibliographical references

ISBN:
ISBN:

Preface

The exponential growth of information has inspired companies to gather and process information in a systematic approach. This in turn has led to changes within companies and marketing information. From the operational point of view, decision-making processes and mid-level managers are under frequent pressure of *catching up* with new technologies and methods. From the strategic point of view, we are observing a *dramatic shift* from the focus of creating *competitive advantages* through tangible and intangible assets as Davenport (2007) states, "competing on knowledge and analytics". Today's business professionals are destined to make their marketing decisions in *multifaceted and data-rich external and internal environments*. The use of analytical and quantitative methods is not regarded as the skill of scientists and researchers anymore. Marketing job descriptions require knowledge not only of analytical methods but also as of artificial intelligence and machine learning that until recently were used only in laboratories and research institutions.

This trend is translated into the world of marketing by the marketing engineering approach. This method emphasizes the need to use analytical methods in order to produce efficient decision-making in the marketing departments of organisations. However, the focus now lies more on 'using a predefined number of methods and attaining the skills to use them'. However, as higher management emphasizes the need to educate marketing managers and teach these new methods and skills, there are limited textbooks in this direction that marketing students and practitioners can reference.

Especially in marketing, most theory and practice methods are based mostly on *statistical and econometric techniques*. These procedures have been around a long time and later adapted to suit the needs of the marketing professional. However, their extensive use has been *influenced* by the fact of the explosive growth of information technologies (IT) in the last decade. Apart from providing the basis for improving the analytical capabilities of companies, IT has created a growing stream of alternative analytical methods, marketing capabilities that compete with the much of historic marketing theory and practice.

These alternative methods fall under the broad category of artificial intelligence and machine learning. According to Coppin (2004) artificial intelligence involves using methods based on the intellectual behaviour of humans and animals to solve complex problems. The roots of artificial intelligence, date back to philosophers of Aristotle and Socrates. As Coppin (2004) states, Plato wrote that his teacher Socrates intended to create an algorithm of describing the behaviour of people and judging whether it was good or bad. Artificial intelligence continued to evolve, and today represents a field of growing importance in academia and industry.

Artificial intelligence covers a broad scope of methods and mainly Artificial Neural Networks, Fuzzy Logic and Genetic Algorithms.

Their applications have been widely used in the production industry and in the past decade especially in the field of finance.

It is not until recent decades that AI and ML have entered other business-related spheres, and the number of publications point out in this direction. However, the main criticism of these methods has been their highly computational complexity and often the difficulty understanding AI and ML by marketing professionals as compared to industrial engineers, finance IT professionals familiar with this technology. Their widespread use though out marketing, including international marketing has not yet been fully addressed.

This book endeavours to enlighten marketing educators, students and practitioners to the fields of AI and ML concepts, practices demonstrating the theory and practice of the areas in marketing context.

Objectives

The book objectives are to provide a broad delivery of information on the fields of artificial intelligence (AI) and machine learning (ML) to educators, students and practitioners of marketing. By explaining AI and ML terminology and its applications including marketing, the book is designed to inform and educate. Marketing use of AI and ML has exploded in recent decades as marketers have seen the considerable benefits of these two technologies. It is understood and explained that AI deals with 'Intelligent behaviour' by machines rather than natural intelligence found in humans and animals, it is the machine mimicking ' cognitive functions' that humans associate with the mind in learning, expression and problem solving and much more.

ML on the other hand is a field of computer science that gives computers the ability to learn without being explicitly programmed. Evolved from the study of pattern recognition and computational learning theory in artificial intelligence, machine learning explores the study and construction of algorithms that can learn from and make predictions on data Kohavi (1998). Such algorithms overcome following strictly static program instructions by making data-driven predictions or decisions, through building a model from sample inputs (Dickson, 2017).

SECTION ONE

Artificial Intelligence

Contents

Contents

SECTION TWO

MACHINE LEARNING

Contents

SECTION ONE

Artificial Intelligence

Introduction

Artificial Intelligence has a rich history. Artificial intelligence (AI), also machine intelligence, (MI) is Intelligence displayed by machines, in contrast with the *natural intelligence* (*NI*) displayed by humans and other animals. In computer science AI research is defined as the study of "intelligent agents": any device that perceives its environment and takes actions that maximize its chance of success at some goal.

Chapter Learning Outcomes

☐ The evolution of Artificial Intelligence (AI) as a science.

☐ The role of (AI) in marketing today.

☐ Major goals themes and practices of (AI) in marketing.

☐ The role of Reach technology as an enabler in modern marketing.

☐ Having successfully completed the module, you will be able to:

☐ 1. Critically assess the use of (AI) basics in marketing.

☐ 2. Assess the history of (AI).

☐ Having completed the module, you will be able to:

☐ 1. Understand the basics of (AI) and it's uses.

• 2. Manage tasks in a group and as an individual.

Critical thinking

Having successfully completed this topic, you will be able to: 1. Critically evaluate the role of (AI) within an organization. 2. Measure the fundamental elements of (AI) and effect.

OBJECTIVES

Literature frameworks that (AI) has been around in some shape or form for many centuries, and in its basic form enabled the automation of tasks and thinking by using machines.

1 History

The history of AI is a fascinating one and reaches back to the time of the ancient Greeks who debated concepts of machines with intelligence found in Greek mythology. Intelligent items appear in literature down the centuries with mechanical devices showing a degree of intelligence, With introduction of computers following 1945 armistice it is now achievable to create programs that allow intellectual task used in a variety of ways to solve problems or provide information, the computation breakthroughs are real and significant.

In the fourth century Aristotle put together what is named syllogistic logic, the first formal deductive reasoning system, and in the thirteenth century Spanish theologians invented machines to discover nonmathematical truths through combinatorics. Even more surprising was an Arab inventor who made the first programmable humanoid robot fuelled by water flow. In the fifteen-century printing was first used, and we saw the introduction of clocks, a modern measure of time and mechanicals animals and toys. In the seventeenth century, Descartes maintained humans and animals were just multifaceted machines. Pascal also invented the first mechanical digital calculating machine that encouraged other devices using a mechanical format such as the 'Turk' in the eighteenth century. The nineteenth century saw an upsurge of devices such as the programmable jacquard look with punch cards, calculating machines, the analytical engine, a binary algebra (laws of thought) and modern proposition logic by Gottleb Frege.

In the twentieth century, AI started to pick up speed with some wonderful innovations and thinking. Russell and Whitehead revolutionized formal logic, and Quevedo built the chess machine using electo-magnets under the board. Mc Cullock and Pitts published a book on calculus and ideas, placing the base for neural network thinking regarding computing machinery and intelligence, which provided the base for McCarthy in 1956 to coin the term, 'Artificial Intelligence.' In the 60's the first game – playing programs emerged. Lisp language was launched followed by Masterman's sematic nets for machine translation and Slagle's integration program SAINT which solved calculus problems. Evand program ANALOGY that demonstrates that computers can solve analogy problems. Bobstrow also argued that computers could comprehend lateral language as well as answer algebra word problems.

In 1967 the Dendral program saw the first successful knowledge-based program in mathematics which paralleled innovation such as Engebarts' mouse, the SRI Robot (Shakey), interactive program SCHOLAR and ARCH, PROLOG, MYCIN, FRAMES, VERSION SPACES,INTERNIST, CHI, neural networks algorithms.

The 1990's was an Idyllic Period for AI, with expressions on machine learning, intelligent tutoring, case-based reasoning, multi agent planning, scheduling, uncertain reasoning, data mining, natural language understanding and translation, vision, virtual reality, games and other topics. It could be said that the 2,000's we have seen AI theory *turn into practice* with robotics, automated cars and trains, PC's, Laptops, mobile devices, internet, social forums, text, Video links, software programs, satellites, space discovery, home appliances that think and operate without humans.

Revision

- Outline the objectives of (AI)
- Explain providing examples of (AI) applications/goals
- Name some (AI) applications in marketing today, show examples

2 Goals

Introduction

The goals of (AI) are to reproduce human thinking and reasoning which solves problems. To do this (AI) needs to be planned and data inputted so that it can operate efficiently. The ability of (AI) means it has wide applications and this chapter these goals are considered with a link to marketing.

Chapter Learning Outcomes

☐ The role of reasoning and problems solving.

☐ The planning and learning capability.

☐ The use of (AI) in natural language processes and perception.

☐ Debate on motion and manipulation, social intelligence and creativity.

☐ Having successfully completed the module, you will be able to:

☐ 1. Critically assess the goals of (AI) basics in marketing.

☐ 2. Assess the applications of (AI) in today's world.

☐ Having completed the module, you will be able to:

☐ 1. Understand the variety of (AI) applications and their uses.

• 2. Be able to explain the principal goals if (AI).

Critical thinking

Having successfully completed this topic, you will be able to: 1. Critically evaluate the variety of roles of (AI). 2. Understand and explain elements of (AI) to management.

OBJECTIVES

The goals of (AI) are boundary less as machines mimic cognitive functions such as learning, and problem solving and take on increased capacity. The chapter explores (AI) development to date.

Artificial Intelligence (AI) or Machine Intelligence (MI) is now understood as an intelligent behaviour by machines more exactly than human and animal intelligence that come from a living brain. AI is the investigation of intelligence signals that considers information and takes some form of action to deliver a result, a conclusion; it is a *machine mimicking human thought and behaviour* along learning and problems solving positions. However, it is argued the scope of AI goes beyond the purposes of the human mind as will be seen with 'AI innovation.' As a subject, AI was founded as an academic discipline in 1956,and has expanded once statistical approaches became fruitful in machine learning and, traditionally followed *reasoning, knowledge, planning, learning, language processing, perception, and manipulation* to change and move objects. It's objectives contrast in academic literature, however it is reasonable to say GENERAL INTELLIGENCE is the future including items such as *computational intelligence, statistical methods, search and optimization, neural networks, methods based on probability, economics and methods based statistics* in detail whatever that can use computer ability and data in our theoretical grasp. Humans will use AI to make their *lives easier* inventing technology that empowers computers and machines to work artificially that delivers intelligence across a background of planning, learning, problem-solving, speed, accuracy, complexity.

AI technology is a passionate topic in marketing; now however AI is a comprehensive term covering a wide range of different technologies. Artificial intelligence denotes any technology that seeks to caricature human intelligence, which covers a colossal range of capabilities such as *voice and image recognition, machine learning techniques and semantic search.*

Marketers like to examine the latest exciting technologies and debate AI for *image recognition, speech recognition, preventing data leaks, or even targeting drones at remote communities.* All these techniques are 'AI' based on the reason that they involve computer intelligence, however this has been fragmented into 3 different types of technology - *Machine Learning Techniques, Applied Propensity Models, and AI Applications.* 1.Machine learning techniques engage using algorithms to 'learn' from historical data sets, which can then generate propensity models. 2. Applied propensity models are when these propensity models are put to function predicting given events- such as scoring leads based on their probability to convert. 3. AI applications are other forms of AI, which do tasks one would typically associate with a human operator such as answering customer questions or writing new content. Each different application has major consequences for marketers, but the applications have different roles to play across the customer journey.

Some are better for attracting customers, whilst others are useful for conversion or re-engaging past customers. That's why we have divided the techniques across the RACE framework of reach, act, convert and engage.

Reach - Attract visitors with a range of inbound techniques.
Reach involves using measures such as content marketing, SEO and other 'earned media' to passage visitors to a site and lead them on the buyer's voyage. AI & applied propensity models can be operated at this point to attract more visitors and provide individuals that do reach your site with a more attractive experience.

1. AI generated content
This is a truly interesting area for AI. AI cannot write an opinion column or a blog post on industry-specific best practice advice, but there are certain areas where AI generated content can be valuable and help draw visitors to your site.
For functions AI content writing programs can pick rudiments from a dataset and arrange a 'human sounding' article. An AI writing program called 'WordSmith' produced 1.5 billion pieces of content in 2016 and is expected to grow further in acceptance.
AI writers are valuable for reporting on regular, data-focused events. Examples include quarterly earnings reports, sports matches, and market data. If one operates in a pertinent niche such as product services, then AI generated content could form a useful component of your content marketing strategy. The positive news is that automated insights, the firm behind Wordsmith, has proclaimed a free beta version of its AI writing application, so you can try out the technology and see if it could be useful to your brand.

2. Smart Content Curation
AI powered content curation allows one to enhance engagement with visitors on a site by presenting them content relevant to them. This technique is most commonly found in the 'customers who bought X also bought Y' section on many sites but can also be useful to blog content and personalizing site messaging. It's also a good technique for subscription businesses, where the more someone uses the service, more data the machine learning algorithm must use, and the better the recommendations of content become. Think of Netflix's recommendation system being able to consistently recommend you a show you would be interested it.

3. Voice search
Voice search is another AI technology, but when it comes to using it for marketing, it's about utilizing the technology developed by the major players (Google, Amazon, Apple) rather than acquiring your own capability. Voice search will change future SEO strategies, and brand marketers will need to keep up. A brand that spikes voice search can leverage big gains in natural traffic with high purchase intent thanks to increased voice search traffic due to AI driven virtual personal assistants.

4. Programmatic Media Buying

Programmatic Media buying can use propensity models created by machine learning algorithms to more efficiently target ads at the most relevant customers. Programmatic ads need to get cleverer in the wake of Google's recent brand safety scandal. It was revealed ads placed programmatically through Google's ad network were appearing on terrorist's websites. AI can help here by recognizing questionable sites and removing them from the list of sites, ads can be located upon.

Act - Draw visitors in and make them aware of your product

5. Propensity modeling

As already stated, propensity modeling is the objective of a machine learning project. The machine learning algorithm is served large quantities of historical data, and it operates this data to invent a propensity model, which (in theory) is expert in making accurate predictions.

6. Predictive analytics

Propensity modeling can be practical to several different areas, such as predicting the likely hood of a given customer to switch, predicting what price a customer is likely to convert at, or what customers are most expected to make repeat purchases. This application is called *predictive analytics*, because it uses analytics data to make predictions about how customers behave. The significant thing to remember is that a propensity model is *only as good as the data provided* to create it, so if there are mistakes in the data or a high level of chance, it will be unable to make precise predictions.

7. Lead scoring

Propensity models made by machine learning can be exercised to score leads based on principles so that your sales team can establish how 'warm' a given lead is, and, if they are value devoting time to. This can be particularly important in B2B businesses with consultative sales processes, where each sale takes a substantial amount of time on the part of the field sales team. By contacting the most relevant leads, the sales team can save time and distillate their energy where it is most effective. The insights into a leads propensity to buy can also be used to target sales and discounts where they are most effective.

8. Ad targeting

Machine learning algorithms can run through immense amounts of historical data to establish which ads perform greatest, on which people and at what period in the buying process. Operating this data, they can serve customers with the most effective content at the right time. By using machine learning to repeatedly optimize thousands of variables one can achieve more active ad placement and content than traditional methods.

Convert - nudge interested consumers into becoming customers

9. Dynamic pricing
All marketers know that sales are effective at moving more merchandise. Discounts are particularly powerful, but they can also harm your bottom line. If you make twice as many sales with a two-thirds smaller margin, you have made less profit than you would have if you did not have a sale. Sales promotions are genuine because they get people to buy your product that previously would not have considered them able to justify the cost of the purchase. But they also mean people that would have paid the higher price pay less than they would have. Dynamic pricing can avoid this problem, by targeting only special offers only at those likely to need them.

Machine learning can develop a propensity model of which stances show a customer is likely to need a proposition to convert, and which are probable to convert without the need for an offer. This means you can *increase sales whilst not reducing your profit margins by much, thus maximizing profits.*

10. Web & App Personalization

Using a propensity model to predict a customer's phase in the buyer's journey can let you help that customer, either using an app or on a web page, with the most relevant content. If someone is still new to a site, substance that informs them and keeps them interested will be the most real, whilst if they have visited many times and are obviously interested in the merchandise then more in-depth content about a value benefits will perform even better.

11. Chatbots

Chatbots copycat human intelligence by being able to interpret consumer's queries and complete orders for them. You might think chatbots are enormously difficult to develop and only giant brands with immense budgets will be able to develop them. But in fact, using open chatbot development platforms, it is comparatively simple to create your own chatbot without a developer.

Facebook is attracted in enabling the development of chatbots for brands. It wants to make its Messenger app the 'go-to place' for individuals to have conversations with brand's virtual representatives. The good news for brands is that this means they can use some of Facebook's powerful bot development tools. Using the lessons they've learned from the beta tests of 'M' (Facebook Messenger's own chatbot), Facebook has established the wit.ai bot engine which allows you to train bots with sample conversations and have your bots repeatedly learn from interrelating with customers.

12. Re-targeting

A great deal like with ad targeting, machine learning can be used to ascertain what content is most likely to bring customers back to the site based on historical data. By building a precise prediction model of what content mechanism is best to win back different types of customers, machine learning can be used to optimize and retarget ads to make them as effective as possible.

Engage - Keep your customers returning

13. Predictive customer service

It's much simpler to make repeat sales to your existing customer center than it is to attract new customers. So, keeping your existing customers content is also key to your bottom line. This is chiefly true in subscription-based business, where a high churn rate can be enormously costly.

Predictive analytics can be used to work out which customers are most likely to unsubscribe from a service, by evaluating what characteristics are most common in customers who do unsubscribe. It's then conceivable to reach out to these customers with offers, prompts or assistance to prevent them from churning.

14. Marketing automation

Marketing automation procedures generally involve a series of guidelines, which when activated initiative interactions with the customer. But who decided these rules? Generally, a marketer who is essentially predicting what will be most effective. Machine learning can run through billions of themes of customer data and establish when are the most effectual times to make contact, what words in subject lines are most active and much more. These insights can then be applied to boost the effectiveness of your marketing automation efforts.

15. 1:1 dynamic email

In a comparable manner to marketing automation, applying insights produced from machine learning can establish particularly effective 1:1 dynamic e-mail. Predictive analytics using a propensity model can ascertain a subscriber's propensity to buy certain groupings, sizes and colors through their preceding behavior and displays the most relevant merchandises in newsletters. The product stock, deals, pricing is appropriate at the time of opening the email.

However, AI goes further in my experience, consider a framework for a hybrid intelligent system in support of marketing strategy development has been proposed by Li and Li et al (1997), with five objectives:

1. To help strategic analysis
2. To couple strategic analysis with managers' judgement
3. To integrate the strengths of diverse support techniques and technologies
4. To combine the benefits of different strategic analysis models
5. To help strategic thinking

2.1 Reasoning, problem solving

In AI, algorithms reproduce the steps of human reasoning to solve an issue and provide a logical deduction. In marketing it can also discover *uncertainty, form, correlation, and patterns from probability to economics*. In today's processor age the issues for the public and marketing organizations is the propensity of 'too much data' that makes reasoning all more challenging. One way that AI representations differ from computer programs in traditional languages is that an AI *representation characteristically stipulates what needs to be computed,* not how it is to be computed. One may stipulate that the proxy (substitute) should find the most probable merchandise for customer's needs, or state that a robot should pick and choose an item for a customer, but *not give instructions* on how to carry out the task. A great deal of AI *reasoning* involves searching through the area of possibilities to determine how to complete a task.

In determining what and proxy will do, there are three facets of computation that must be characterized:
(1) The calculation that goes into the design.
(2) The working out that the proxy can do afore it detects the world and needs to act.
(3) The computation that is done by the proxy as it is proceeding.

Design time reasoning is the analysis that is accepted to design the proxy in other words the marketing teams' input. The designer/inputter/ marketer, not the proxy system itself, carries it out. Offline calculation is the calculation done by the proxy before it must proceed. It can include compilation and learning. Offline, the proxy takes contextual knowledge and data and accumulates them into a practical form called a 'knowledge base' something marketers comprehend. Contextual knowledge can be given either at design time or offline.

Online 'working out' is the estimation done by the proxy between examining the environment and acting in the setting. A section of information obtained online is called an 'opinion.' A proxy naturally must use both its knowledge base or history and its computed readings to determine what to do. In marketing there is a major reliance on history to project what is going on and the future.

Reasoning in AI can take up time and vast system space subject to the task, the size of memory of the system used can cause problems, thus the marketing task .

Problem solving has two forks, in *psychology*, problem solving refers to *a state of desire* for reaching a definite goal from a present condition that also is not directly moving toward the goal, is far from it, or needs more complex logic for finding a missing description of conditions or steps toward the goal. In *computer science* and in the part of artificial intelligence that deals with algorithms, problem solving encompasses several techniques known as *algorithms, heuristics, root cause analysis*, etc. Artificial Intelligence is simply about machines sensing, reasoning, acting, and behaving like human beings. It takes marketing computing into areas where it has never been before.

Through computing marketers primarily solve problems, which I call inside-out problems -- meaning someone gave you a very good expression of the problems. Generally, these are *nice equations*. Newton gave us some equations. Einstein gave us some equations. Schroedinger gave us some equations. What do we do with those problems? We start from outside-in. Meaning, *we do not know what the foundational equations are.*

All you know is, observations. Input-output. And 99 per cent of the problems in the world are that kind of problem. Areas like teaching, farming, health, education, and politicking, marketing decision-making in general.

The steps that are required to build a marketing system to solve a problem are:

1. Problem Definition that must include precise specifications of what the initial situation will be as well as what final situations constitute acceptable solutions to the problem.

2. Problem Analysis, this can have immense impact on the appropriateness of varies possible techniques for solving the problem.

3. Selection of the best technique(s) for solving the problem.

The difference between humans and AI is that humans act intuitively to a problem based on their knowledge and experience, versus machine *step-by-step deduction using models*. The key issue here in AI is *input equals output,* as it is said *garbage in = garbage out!*

2.2 Knowledge representation

What is a knowledge representation? The notion can best be understood in terms of five separate roles it plays, each central to the task at hand:

- A knowledge representation (KR) is most fundamentally a substitute, an exchange for the object itself, used to enable an entity to decide significances by thinking rather than acting, i.e., by analysis rather than acting in it.

- It is a recognized structure of ontological promises, i.e., *an answer to the proposed question*: In what conditions should I think about an item.
- It is a detached theory of intelligent thinking, expressed in terms of three components: (i) the statement's axiom comprehension of intelligent reasoning; (ii) the set of corollaries the representation supports; and (iii) the set of implications it recommends.
- It is a vehicle for sensibly effective computation, i.e., the computational ambiance in which thinking is accomplished. One influence on this pragmatic efficiency is provided by the route a representation provides for organizing information to facilitate making the recommended inferences.
- It is a medium of human expression, i.e., a language in which we say things about an item.

Understanding the 'parts' and acknowledging their diversity has several useful consequences in marketing. First, each part is rather dissimilar from a *representation*; each leads to an inspiring and set of properties we want a representation to have. Second, we consider the roles and provide a structure useful for symbolizing a wide variety of 'representations' most useful in marketing scenarios.

The basic "mind set" of a representation can be secured by our understanding how it considers each of the roles, and that doing so reveals essential 'similarities and differences'. The marketing scenarios can be mixed and useful in building the best course of action in a marketplace.

Third, we reflect that some previous divergences about representation are practically unscrambled when all five roles are given appropriate thought. Revisiting and scrutinizing the early influences concerning frames and logic can explain this. In the end, by marketers viewing *representations* in this method it has importance for both research and practice. For research, this judgment delivers one direct answer to a question of basic meaning.

Supposing a comprehensive view on what's significant about a representation, one makes the case that one noteworthy part of the representation endeavour is *capturing and representing the wealth of the natural world*, it is obtaining inadequate notice. This appraisal can also advance practice by prompting experts about the inducements that are the valuable bases of strength for a variety of representations. Consequently, knowledge representation can be 1) a surrogate, 2) a set of ontological commitments, 3) a fragmentary theory of intelligent reasoning, 4) a medium of efficient computation and human expression.

2.3 Planning

Around marketing planning, the belief is that you are given some description of a starting proxy or states; a goal state or states; and some established of possible actions that the proxy could take. *And you want to find the order of actions that get you from the start state to the goal state.* Planning is a crucial aptitude for intelligent systems, enlarging their individuality and dexterity through the building of sequences of activities to achieve their goals. It has been a sphere of research in artificial intelligence for over three periods. Planning procedures have been valuable in a diversity of everyday jobs including robotics, process planning, web-based evidence collecting, and self-directed agents and marketing problem solving. Planning includes the appearance of actions and models, analysis about the effects of actions, and processes for competently searching the space of 'possible' plans. Planning is the procedure of producing (possibly partial) representations of *future behaviour* preceding the use of such plans to control that conduct, in other words it is frontward looking. The consequence is usually a range of actions, with sequential and other restrictions on them, for implementation by some agent or agents. As a key element of human intelligence, planning has been examined since the original days of AI and cognitive science. Planning research has led to many valuable instruments for real-world applications and has assented important insights into the organization of behaviour and the character of reasoning about actions. (Tate, 1999).

Because of a present marketing state, there is a set of conceivable actions, a description of the objective conditions, which the plan converts the *current state into a goal state.* With a road map for example, and several trucks, and airplanes, one can plan to transport things from their 'start' to their 'goal' journey's end. Problem solving by search is a further example, and is where we explain a problem by a 'state space' and then apply a program to search through this space in action planning, we specify the problem declaratively (using logic) and then answer it by a general planning algorithm.

Program synthesis for example, is where one creates a program(s) from a set of conditions, or examples; in action planning one may want to decode just one instance and we have only extremely simple action composition (i.e., sequencing, perhaps restricted and repetition). Scheduling is where all tasks are known in advance and we only must set the time intervals and machines instead (we must find the right actions and to sequence them of course), there are interaction with these areas!

Domain individuality planning for example, leads with a statement specification of the planning problem and one uses a domain-independent planning system to answer the planning problem. Domain-independent planners are usually generic problem solvers for marketing issues.

They are operative for evolving systems and those where functioning is not significant in running time and should be comparable to specified solvers. *Solution quality* should be satisfactory at least for all the problems we worry about in business. Planning for *logical interference* can be elegantly formalized with the help of the *situation calculus* using the initial state, operators and gaol conditions. The positive proof of the existential query (computed by an automatic theorem test) produces a plan that does what is desired, it can be in most cases quite inefficient. Research in *domain-independent planning* has shaped the majority of AI research in planning to date. The widespread history of these efforts has led to the detection of many persisting problems as well as to certain standard solutions. For example, *Operator schemata* characterize actions. (The terms 'action and event' are often used inter- changeably in the AI planning literature and are here.) Schemata predominantly explain movements in terms of their preconditions and effects. Plans are developed from these operator schemata. Each operator schemata exemplifies a *class of possible actions* by including a *set of variables* that can be replaced by coefficients to derive operator examples, that label individual movements. The language of Strips operators is regularly used throughout the AI planning literature (Fikes, Hart, and Nilsson 1972a, 1972b). These operators, first used in the early planning program Strips, which define an action with three elements: *a precondition formula, an add-list, and a delete-list.* An operator's *precondition formula* (simply, the operator's preconditions) provides facts that must 'grip 'before the operator can be applied. The add- list and delete-list are used jointly to replicate *action incidence*. If an operator's preconditions grip in a state, then the operator can be applied. Applying an operator means acting on it add-list and delete-list to produce a new state that provides variables/options.

As understood from the previous discussion, planning is fundamentally a search problem. The program must navigate a theoretically large marketing search space and find a plan that is appropriate in the initial state and produces a solution to the objective when run. This search can be quite problematic because the *search space* can contain many connections between different states or partial plans. These interactions lead to an astonishing amount of intricacy; for example, "establishing the existence of a precondition in a partially ordered plan can require exponential computation" (Chapman 1987), and the problem of "finding an optimal plan in even a simple blocks world domain has recently been shown to be NP-hard" (Gupta and Nau 1990).

The answering of such *conjunctive goal plans* has been the foundation of much of the modern planning research. Two somewhat orthogonal approaches have been taken toward dealing with this problem: *ordering the various goals by levels of importance and analysing and avoiding the interactions caused by interactions between conjunctive goals.* The use of levels to partially overcome this problem (it is not a complete solution) was introduced in Abstrips (Sacerdoti 1973) and Lawaly (Siklossy and Dreussi 1975).

These systems split the goals into stages of importance or importance with the abstract and general goals being worked on first and the concrete or detailed levels being filled in later. In other words, *layering* is used.

The first systems to control planning problems simply assigned suitable operators to apply to a problem by reflecting the differences between the *goal state and the initial state* and looking for operators that were recognized to remove such differences. GPS (Newell and Simon 1963), for example, directly associated the operators for the problem with the variances they could decrease. Thus, an operator such as PAINT(Robot,x) would be associated with achieving the fact PAINTED(x).

Strips (Fikes and Nilsson 1971) used this theme of *differences*, as well as thoughts from the situation calculus (McCarthy and Hayes 1969) and Green's (1969) QA3 program, to make the theory that the initial model would only be changed by a set of additions to, and deletions from, 'the statements modelling of the state'— everything else continued untouched. (This assumption is sometimes called the Strips assumption.) Strips then described an operator as having an add-list, a delete-list, and a preconditions method (to define the applicability or sub gaoling conditions).

Operators were chosen based on the identification of goals that corresponded statements on the add-lists (those statements the operator could add to the current state). The consideration in most of the research on planning has been on generating plans from the start, *not learning from experience*. Therefore, much of the predictable work in marketing planning has been *historic*; that is, asked to solve the same puzzle again, the 'planner' functions no sounder than it did the first time. Lately, because of the improvements being made in machine learning and the new work on 'case-based reasoning', designing planning systems that learn from experience, has become an important marketing option.

Planning systems have been a vigorous AI research topic for nearly 30 years. Several solutions have been established during this period that still form an essential part of many of today's AI marketing planning systems. In this section, I have tried to broadly cover the major ideas in the field of AI planning and attempted to show the direction in which current research is going. Such a task is certainly not ending, and thus, any finite document in time, must be incomplete.

2.4 Learning

Machine learning is a grouping of artificial intelligence (AI) that authorizes software applications to turn out to be more exact in predicting outcomes without being noticeably programmed. ... Machine learning algorithms are frequently categorized as being *supervised or unsupervised*. Marketing dashboards for instance are continuously being updated with fresh data from the marketplace, the machine collects the raw data, calculates and delivers an up to date representation.

Supervised algorithms oblige humans to provide both input and desired output, in addition to supplying feedback about the correctness of predictions during exercise. Once training is finished, the algorithm will apply what was studied to new data. *Unsupervised algorithms* do not need to be taught with desired outcome data. In its place, they use an *iterative approach* called deep learning to appraise data and arrive at conclusions. *Unsupervised learning algorithms* are used for more difficult processing tasks than supervised learning systems.

The processes involved in machine learning are comparable to that of data mining and predictive modelling in marketing. Both require searching through data to look for patterns and adjusting program actions suitably. Numerous people are acquainted with machine learning from window-shopping on the Internet and being 'observed ads' connected to their buying. This happens because reference engines (SEO) use machine learning to modify online ad delivery in real time. Outside personalized marketing, extra common machine learning uses comprise, *fraud detection, spam filtering, network security threat detection, predictive maintenance and building news feeds*. Artificial intelligence will *influence our future more dynamically than any other innovation this century*. Any marketer who does not understand it will soon find they are being left behind, existing in a world full of technology that feels more and more influential. The *rate of quickening* is now beyond acceptance. After a couple of mishaps over the past four decades, speedy progresses in data storage and computer processing power have changed the AI environment in more recent years. In 2015 for example, Google trained a conversational agent (AI) that could not only convincingly interact with humans such as a tech support helpdesk, but also debate ethics, express opinions, and answer general facts-based questions. The same year, DeepMind founded an agent that exceeded human-level functioning at 49 Atari games, receiving only the pixels and game score as inputs. Quickly after, in 2016, DeepMind outmoded their individual success by releasing a new state-of-the-art gameplay method called A3C.

In the interim, Alpha Go overpowered one of the best human players at Go — an astonishing achievement in a game controlled by humans for two decades after machines first conquered chess. Many experts could not understand how it would be possible for a machine to understand the full range of distinctions and complication of this ancient Chinese war strategy game, with its 10 possible board positions.

Deep Learning is a subfield of machine learning concerned with algorithms enthused by the assembly and task of the brain called *artificial neural networks*.

In adding to scalability, another often declared benefit of deep learning models is their aptitude to achieve automatic feature withdrawal from raw data, also called 'feature learning.' Deep learning algorithms pursue unknown structure in the input distribution in order to determine good representations, often at multiple levels, with higher-level learned structures defined in terms of lower-level features. Deep learning outclasses on problem domains where the inputs (and even output) are analogue. Denoting, they are not a few quantities in a tabular format but instead are images of pixel data, documents of text data or files of audio data.

Modern state-of-the-art deep learning is focussed on training deep (many layered) neural network models using the back-propagation algorithm.

The most general techniques now are: 1) Multilayer Perceptron Networks, 2) Convolutional Neural Networks,3) Long Short-Term Memory Recurrent Neural Networks. To explain:

A multilayer perceptron (MLP) is a class of *feed forward* artificial neural network. An MLP consists of at least three layers of nodes. Except for the input nodes, each node is a neuron that uses a nonlinear activation function.

MLP utilizes a supervised learning technique called back propagation for training. It's multiple layers and non-linear activation distinguishes MLP from a linear perceptron. It can distinguish data that is *not linearly separable* (Rumelhart,1986). Multilayer perceptron's are sometimes colloquially referred to as "vanilla" neural networks, especially when they have a single hidden layer.

Convolutional neural network (CNN, or ConvNet) is a class of deep, feed-forward artificial neural networks that has successfully been applied to analysing visual imagery. CNNs use a variation of multilayer perceptron's designed to require minimal pre-processing (Yan,2013) They are also known as shift invariant or space invariant artificial neural networks (SIANN), based on their shared-weights architecture and translation invariance characteristics (Zhang, 1990).

Convolutional networks were inspired by biological processes (Matusugu, 2003) in which the connectivity pattern between neurons is inspired by the organization of the animal visual cortex. Individual cortical neurons respond to stimuli only in a restricted region of the visual field known as the receptive field. The receptive fields of different neurons partially overlap such that they cover the entire visual field.

Long short-term memory (LSTM) is a recurrent neural network (RNN) architecture that remembers values over arbitrary intervals. Stored values are not modified as learning proceeds. RNNs allow forward and backward connections between neurons. An LSTM is well-suited to classify, process and predict time series given time lags of unknown size and duration between important events.

Relative insensitivity to gap length gives an advantage to LSTM over alternative RNNs[, hidden Markov models and other sequence learning methods in numerous applications (Greff et al, 2015).

2.5 Natural language processing

Natural language processing (NLP) is a field of computer science, artificial intelligence and computational linguistics concerned with the connections between computers and human (natural) languages, and, in specific, concerned with programming computers to positively process large quantities of data. Experiments in natural language processing usually *include natural language understanding, natural language generation (frequently from formal, machine-readable logical forms), connecting language and machine perception, dialog systems, or some combination thereof*. The prospect for this procedure in marketing is enormous particularly in the automation of CRM and CEM systems for a call centres badly run by machines that use (NLP).

Instances of natural language processing systems in artificial intelligence are as follows

- *Communication*: Abundant **communication applications** such Facebook Messenger is present-day using **artificial intelligence**. Facebook announced its M service that suggests to become your personal assistant: 'M can do anything a human can.' When you demand something that M cannot do on its own, it sends a communication to a Facebook worker and, as they work with the software, the AI begins to absorb. **Another application of natural language processing is Skype Translator**, which offers 'on-the-fly' translation to translate live speech in real time across a number of languages. Skype Translator uses AI to aid and allow conversation among people who speak different languages. Minus language barriers, **persons can communicate using the language** they are easy with, which will in performance speed up a range of business procedures. This means marketing messages could be released in real time in various languages.
- *Faster diagnosis*: **Examples of natural language processing systems in artificial intelligence are also in hospitals that use natural language processing to assign a specific diagnosis** from a physician's shapeless notes. For example, NLP software for cancer imaging and reports support the extraction and analysis of data for clinical decisions, as a study published in Cancer affirms. The software is able to verify cancer risk more competently, decrease the need for unnecessary biopsies and simplify faster handling through earlier diagnosis. According to the study, artificial intelligence reviewed 500 charts in a few hours, saving over 500 physician hours. "Accurate review of this many charts would be practically impossible without AI," the author Stephen T. Wong (2017) said.

- **Customer Review**: Natural language processing in artificial intelligence applications **causes easy to collect product reviews from a website and comprehend what consumers are really revealing** as well as their feeling in reference to a specific item. Establishments with a large volume of reviews can truly understand them and use the data collected to *recommend new products or services based on customer preferences.*
- This application aids companies to find relevant information for their business, improve **customer satisfaction, propose more pertinent products or services** and better and understand the customer's needs.
- **Virtual digital assistants**: due to smartphone, virtual digital assistant (VDA) technologies (automated software applications or platforms that support the human user by interpretation of natural language) are presently the most well-known kind of artificial intelligence. Various marketing teams and companies are empathetic to the significance of the VDAs for their businesses and are endowing noteworthy resources to stay up to date. According to a study published by Research and Markets(2017), "VDA users will grow from 390 million in 2015 to 1.8 billion worldwide by 2021, while enterprise VDA users will rise from 155 million in 2015 to 843 million over the same period." VDAs are capable to support the consumers with transaction activities or optimize the call centre operations to present a better customer experience and decrease the operational costs. One will progressively see these applications in other machines such as PCs programs, smart home systems, and automobiles and in the business marketplace.

If these simple examples of natural language processing applications in artificial intelligence, **the following** Artificial Intelligence software **and applications will advance our aptitude to** *convert unstructured data into valuable business insight and make smart automated decision-making* part of our normal processes. At hand is a process for representing the words of a language that is evidencing very useful in many NLP tasks, such as *sentiment analysis* and machine translation. The depictions are known as *word embedding's,* and they are mathematical representations of words that are skilled from millions of instances of word usage in order to *capture meaning.* Capturing 'relationships' *between the words* does this. When hearing about how 'vectorized' representations of words and sentences composition, it can be attractive to reason they really are encapsulating meaning in the appreciation that there is some *understanding happening.* But this would be a major mistake. The representations are resulting from examples of language use. *Meaning drives our use of language, and therefore, the derived representations naturally reflect that meaning.* Consequently, the AI systems learning such representations have *no direct access to actual meaning.* For everybody wanting to construct a 'conversational AI today', such restrictions are still unconditionally essential. Both Amazon's Lex and IBM's conversation service function by allowing the developer to specify *the constraints* within which their app should work. The app outlines a set of purposes that the app can carry out, and maps to those intentions, and the set of conceivable ways a user might request them.

2.6 Perception

Perception in AI is the process of *acquiring, interpreting, selecting, and organizing sensory information*. In AI, the inspection on perception is typically absorbed on the reproduction of human perception, particularly on the perception of *aural and visual signals.* Perception engages interpreting sights, sounds, smells and touch. Accomplishment includes the aptitude to navigate through the world and manipulate objects. If one wants to build robots that live in the world, one must comprehend these processes. Most of all AI is concerned with only cognition, we will frankly add 'sensors and effectors' to them.

However, the problems in perception and action are substantial in their own right and are being confronted by researchers in the field of robotics. In the past, robotics and AI have been principally separate of each other, and they have developed different methods to solve different problems. One major variant between AI programs and robots is that 'AI programs usually operate in computer-stimulated worlds', robots must operate in a 'physical world'. For example, in the case of moves in chess, an AI program can search millions of nodes in a game tree without ever having to sense or touch whatsoever in the real world. A complete chess-playing robot, on the other hand, must be capable of grasping pieces, visually interpreting board positions, and carrying on a range of other activities.

Machine perception is the capability of a computer system to interpret data in a manner that is similar to the way human's use information, their intellects to interact to the world around them. The elementary method that the computers take in and respond to their environment is using 'attached' hardware. Up until lately input was restricted to a keyboard, or a mouse, however advances in technology, both in hardware and software, have permitted computers to take in sensory input in many ways comparable to humans.

Machine perception permits the computer to use this sensory input, as well as conventional computational means of collecting information to gather information with *greater accuracy* and to portray it in a way that is easier for the user. *These include computer vision, machine hearing, and also machine touch.*

The conclusion match of machine perception is to given machines the aptitude to see, feel and perceive the world as humans do, and therefore for machines to be able to elucidate in a human form why they are making those decisions, to warn us when it is failing and more primary, the logic of why it is failing (Tatum,2012). Imagine at point of sale a machine that detects all of your senses and makes suggestions as a solution!

Computer vision is a field that includes methods for acquiring, processing, analysing, and *understanding images* and, in over-all, 'high-dimensional data' from the real world in order to produce numerical or symbolic information, e.g., in the forms of decisions. Computer vision has many uses already in use today such as *facial recognition, geographical modelling, and even aesthetic judgment* (Dahr,2012).

Machine hearing also known as machine listening or computer audition is the ability of a computer or machine to take in and process sound data such as music or speech. This area has a wide range of application including music recording and compression, speech synthesis, and speech recognition (Lyon,2010). Furthermore, this technology permits the machine to duplicate the human brain's ability to selectively concentrate on a particular sound against many other competing sounds and background noise. This specific ability is called the "Auditory Scene Analysis". The technology allows the machine to segment several streams occurring at the same time. Many commonly used devices such as a *smartphones, voice translators, and even cars* make use of some form of machine hearing. Machine touch is a field of machine perception where tactile information is handled by a machine or computer. "Applications include tactile perception of surface properties and dexterity whereby tactile information can enable intelligent reflexes and interaction with the environment" (Turk, 2000).

2.7 Motion and manipulation

Motion and manipulation planning are main competences for a robot, requiring specific illustrations for *geometry, kinematics and dynamics*. "Probabilistic Roadmaps and Rapid Random Trees are thoroughly advanced and mature techniques for motion planners that scale up proficiently and allow for numerous extensions" (La Valle, 2006). The primary concept is to randomly sample the configuration space of the robot (i.e., the vector space of its kinematics parameters) into a graph where each vertex is a 'free configuration' (away from obstacles) and each edge a direct link in the free space between two configurations.

'Initial and goal configurations' are added to this graph, between *which a path is computed*. This path is then changed into a smooth trajectory. "Manipulation planning needs to find *viable sequences* of 'grasping positions', each of which is a limited constraint on the robot configuration that changes its kinematics" (Simeon et al, 2004). "Many other open problems remain in motion and manipulation planning, such as dynamics and stability constraints, e.g. for a humanoid robot" (Kalnoun et al, 2011), or "visibility constraints to allow for visual servicing" (Chamete & Hutchinson, 2011).

Task planning and motion/manipulation planning have been brought together in several works. The Asimov planner (Cambon et al, 2009) syndicates a state-space planner with a search in the motion configuration space. It describes places which are both states, as well as sets of 'free configurations. Places define links between the two search spaces. The state- space search crops a state whose corresponding set of free configurations does not meet existing reachability circumstances. Asimov has been increased to manipulation planning and to multi- robot planning of collaborative tasks, such as two robots assembling a table.

"The integration of motion and task planning" is also explored in (Wolfe etal,2010) with Angelic Hierarchical Planning (AHP). AHP plans over 'sets of states' with the notion of reachable set of states. These sets are not calculated precisely, but bordered, e.g., by a subset and a superset, or by an upper and a lower bound cost function. A high-level action has several likely corrosions into primitives. A plan of high-level actions can be advanced into the product of all possible decompositions of its actions. A plan is usually acceptable if it has at least one feasible disintegration.

With such a plan, the robot chooses ingeniously a feasible disintegrating for each high-level action (AHP refers to the angelic semantics of nondeterminism). The 'bounds' used to characterize reachable sets of states are obtained by simulation of the primitives, including through motion and manipulation planning, for random values of the state variables.

A dissimilar coupling of a hierarchical task planner is to use fast *geometric suggests* developed in (Kaelbling et al, 2011). These suggesters are triggered when the search in the decomposition tree needs geometric information. They do not solve entirely the geometric problem; however, they provide information that consents the search to continue down to leaves of the tree. The system fluctuates between 'planning phases and execution of primitives', including motion and manipulation actions. Online planning allows one to run motion or manipulation planners (not suggesters) in fully known states. The method assumes that the geometric preconditions of the abstract actions can be calculated rapidly, and efficiently by the suggesters, and that the sub-goals resultant from actions disintegration, are performed in sequence (no parallelism). The resulting system is not complete. Failed actions should be reversible at a reasonable cost. For problems where these assumptions are met, the structure is able to quickly produce correct plans.

2.8 Social intelligence (SI)

While there is no one definition for (SI), one can appraise social artificial intelligence as a form of accumulating and checking through customer history, user-generated content and data from social media channels to create more pertinent content and, as an outcome, a more illustrative experience for followers.
Social AI has the aptitude to deliver a better social experience generally. For an example of what social AI can do, we just have to review *social media*. The social networks have previously incorporated artificial intelligence as part of the platform in many innovative context. From automatic face tagging to the accounts that appear in News Feeds, Social Media has shown what AI can do for the vehicle by assimilating a diversity of AI technologies that help continuously advance the user experience. If one enables machines to take upkeep of all of the arduous tasks, everyday tasks that machines can take care of (such as recommendations and customer support), then marketers can have more ability to centre on the constructive sides of their operations.

The technology that seemed so intimidating in the past, currently may actually become our marketing support, strengthening our performance improvement by freeing marketers from the mundane analysis tasks that keep one locked into the routines of the past, and delivering us with the facts we need to make a profit. For brands publishing multiple new stories or posts per day, automating a significant portion of those messages, can free up time for developing more significant content and monitoring replies. The intelligent bot for example verifies and predicts how stories will perform on social media, as well as recommending what stories editors should push and promote. For marketers looking for engagement levels to be active while keeping the numbers of hours spent creating content down, this can be a positive.

Furthermore, there is a number of facial recognition technologies; Facebook for example took its algorithm to the subsequent height using AI. With its immense database of images, Facebook's algorithm is endlessly refining through machine learning. Every time someone tags a photo, it is added to a huge, user-driven wealth of knowledge database that aids and progresses the whole facial recognition algorithm.

According to Facebook, it is able to accurately identify a person 98 per cent of the time. Such facial recognition software on a broader measure could have numerous applications for a brand's 'social strategy'. A platform that uses AI to contribute to social media, reflects the fact that workloads of social media managers have hit an all-time high. Social media teams have been allocated an overpowering number of responsibilities that go beyond basic 'content creation' — they are now obliged to perform a positive level of customer service as well. Ill-advisedly, customer support has become a major time user. There are a number of ways social AI can help social media teams ease the pressures of providing *instant support* in order to spend their time much more effectively, including:

- Identifying which inquiries are coming from real people and which are coming from bot accounts.

- Creating a queue for responses that prioritizes high-profile users first.

- Identifying your happiest followers and the ones who are engaging with your brand the most so focus can be placed on them.

- Uncovering which tools followers to send you a message so that you can avoid dangerous links and spam used.

The historical marketer role of "pushing" content must be addressed to focusing more on two-way conversations and co-creation. AI will guide the conversations in the beginning, but humans must move in at some point for the actual engagements, or will they? Marketers must also accept that they will need to serve customers in real time. Instant responses are now expected on social media, and these expectations will only solidify over the next years.

Making sure the marketing team is set up within to control rapid turnarounds on social media, and applying automated response technology if demanded, will safeguard your brand, and that one is prepared to deal with these customer expectations using AI in both the short and long term.

Four main application areas exist for (SI), One application is the conception of Web 2.0 services and tools (for example, *blogs, wikis, social networks, RSS, collaborative filtering, and bookmarking*) to reinforce effective online communication for social communities. Another application is entertainment software, which stresses on constructing intelligent objects (programs, agents, or robots) that can cooperate with human users. Both applications emphasize the technology side and use social theories as strategies for designing and framing computational systems.

A third application subject is the business and public sector, which includes various e-business, healthcare, economic, political, and digital government systems, as well as artificial engineering systems in provinces of significant community influence. A fourth application area is forecasting, which includes a variety of predictive systems for planning, evaluation, and training in areas ranging from counter- terrorism to market analysis to pandemic and disaster response planning.

To simplify the development of social software, one central issue is the *representation of social information and social knowledge*. Other key issues are the displaying of social behaviour at both the single and collective levels and analysis and prediction techniques for social systems and programs. Social information designates societies' structures, such as social relations, institutional structure, roles, power, influence, and control. From a distinct agent's position, social knowledge defines agents' cognitive and social states (for example, actors' reasons, meanings, and attitudes). Social information and social knowledge deliver a basis for *inferring, planning, and coordinating social activities*. The description of social structure and relations are classically represented via 'nodes and ties' in network representation, such as social networks. For social networks, the important representational issue is the advance of network models whose assets reflect the social realism. Upcoming network models must characterise features of this reality in a social context, including individual agents' attitudes, goals, and meanings.

Since any specific network representation is an idea of the real society, it's correspondingly important to find the right level of abstraction to fit the intended applications. "The Semantic Web is promising, in providing the tools and formalism for such specifications" (Berners –Lee et al, 2006). At the micro level, agent-based social sculpting emphases on the *cognitive modelling of social behaviour and individual agents' interactions*. The important research subjects incorporate computational modelling and social reasoning of agents' beliefs, motivational goals, emotions, intentions, trustworthiness, social responsibility, and commitments. At the macro level, the agent-based method models systems encompassing autonomous and interactive agents, through multi agent social simulation. Simulating complex social processes advances many research questions such as model specification (for example, the basic assumptions, parameters, interrelations, and rules), experimental design, and challenging the simulation model.

Other research challenges comprise representing social context, modelling individual and cultural differences, and how social institutions, norms, and group behaviour arises from micro-level agent connections. *Research gaps exist between individual cognitive modelling and multi- agent social simulation.* "Fresh studies have in progress tried to explore the two fields' junction and synergy for a clearer of individual cognition and sociocultural pro- cesses and how to integrate cognitive and social sciences into computing technologies. Statistical methods have been used to analyse and predict the costs and benefits associated with various strategies, policies, and decision-making methods" (Popp et al, 2006).

These techniques cover structural equations, cellular auto-mata, Bayesian networks and hidden Mark- ov models, system dynamics, and agent- based approaches. Furthermore, advancement made in datamining, machine learning, and visualization techniques help recognize internal relationships, and patterns from empirical data. To examine human social phenomena, further analytic techniques from quantitative and computational social sciences also show a key role. Social computing allows structure of social systems and software and accepts for embedding actionable social knowledge in applications rather than just describing social information.

Inside social network analysis, old-style methods have concentrated on static networks for small groups. "As the technologies move onward, one key task for social network analysis is to design methods and tools for modelling and analysing large-scale and dynamic networks" (Breiger etal,2003; Dai,2006).

2.9 Creativity

Computational creativity (also known as artificial creativity, mechanical creativity, creative computing or creative computation) is a multi-disciplinary initiative that is positioned at the crossover of the arenas of AI, cognitive psychology, philosophy, and the arts.

The objective of computational creativity is to replica, mimic or copy creativity using a computer, to achieve one of several ends:

- To develop a program or computer proficient in human-level creativity.
- To improve understanding of human creativity and to develop an algorithmic perspective on creative behaviour in humans.
- To invent programs that can progress human creativity without inevitably being creative themselves.

The field of computational creativity deliberates theoretical and practical subjects in the investigation of creativity. Theoretical effort on the nature and correct description of creativity is offered in matching with applied work on the application of systems that show creativity, with one element of function informing the other.

Subsequently no single viewpoint or description appears to offer a complete picture of creativity, the AI researchers Newell, Shaw and Simon (1963), developed the mixture of novelty and practicality into the foundation of a multi-pronged view of creativity, one that practices the subsequent four standards to categorize a given answer or solution as creative:

1. The solution is original and beneficial (either for the individual or for society)
2. The solution requests that we castoff ideas we had formerly acknowledged
3. The solution outcomes from powerful inspiration and doggedness
4. The solution comes from refining a problem that was originally unclear

Previous to 1989, artificial neural networks had been used to replica individual aspects of creativity. Peter Todd (1989) first trained a neural network to replicate musical melodies from a training set of musical pieces. Then he used a change algorithm to adapt the network's input parameters.

The network was capable to randomly set fresh music in a favourably uncontrolled manner (Todd,1989; Bharucha &Todd,1989; Todd & Boy,1991) In 1992, Todd expanded this work, using the distal teacher method that had been developed by Paul Munro, (1987) Paul Werbos, (1989) and D. Nguyen and Bernard Widrow, Michael I. Jordan and David Rumelhart (1989).

In the 'novel approach' there are two neural networks, one of which is delivering training patterns to another. In later attempts by Todd, a composer would select a set of melodies that describe the melody space, position them on a 2-d plane with a mouse-based graphic interface, and train a connectionist network to produce those melodies, and listen to the new "interpolated" melodies that the network generates corresponding to intermediate points in the 2-d plane.

Supplementary, a neuro-dynamical model of semantic networks has been proceeded to study how the connectivity structure of these networks connects to the intensity of the semantic constructs, or ideas, they can create. It was recognized that semantic neural networks have a richer semantic dynamics than those with other connectivity structures, and may deliver understanding into the key questions of how the physical structure of the brain controls one of the most metaphysical features of the human mind – *its capacity for creative thought* (Marupaka & Minai, 2011).

Linguistic Creativity uses AI for account divulging and story production such as poems, rhymes and jokes. Certain software even invents news stories and summaries of for example, sport results. Computational creativity in the music field has concentrated both on the production of musical scores for use by human musicians, and on the cohort of music for performance by processors. In 1994, a Creativity Machine architecture was able to 11,000 musical hooks by training a synaptically perturbed neural net on 100 melodies, that had emerged on the top ten list over the last 30 years.

In 1996, a self-bootstrapping Creativity Machine noticed audience facial manifestations through an improved machine vision system and improved its musical abilities to generate an album. Computational creativity in the production of visual art has also had some noticeable achievements in the creation of both *abstract art and representational art*.

A developing subject of computational creativity is that of *video games*. ANGELINA for example is a system for creatively developing video games in Java by Michael Cook. One major aspect is called Mechanic Miner a technique which can create short segments of code which perform as simple *game mechanics*.

Creativity is also advantageous in tolerating for unfamiliar solutions in problem solving. In psychology and cognitive science, this exploration area is called *creative problem solving*. "The Explicit-Implicit Interaction (EII) theory of creativity has lately been applied using a CLARION -based computational model that allows for the simulation of development and insight in problem solving" (Helie & Sun, 2010). The significance of this computational creativity project is not on performance per se (as in artificial intelligence projects) but rather on *the clarification of the psychological processes leading to human creativity and the reproduction of data gathered in psychology experiments*. Several artists are reacting to a world of quickening change and rapid digitization through their composition.

Developing artistic vehicles like 3D printing, virtual reality and artificial intelligence are providing artists with unique forms of self-expression. Various artists are also consenting the increase of intelligent machines and leveraging the man-machine symbiosis to create progressively unique works of art. In detail, advances in robotics and AI are confronting the very definition of what it requires to be an artist: *creating art is no longer exclusive to human beings*.

Some artists are using digital tools to engage their viewers in the artistic two-way experience. The installation uses projections of the participants' own bodies to explore the creative process through digital shapes, hence allowing participants to interact with the work and undergo a captivating experience. Without participants, the work of art is incomplete. Virtual reality could allow artists themselves to create art in a virtual space. Google Tilt Brush is a program that allows users, regardless of artistic background or experience, to create works of art in a three-dimensional virtual space. Described as "a new perspective in painting," the Tilt Brush interface allows endless possibilities of artistic production.

Technology has not only given rise to more accessible tools for the production of art but has also fast-tracked the process by which art is funded, marketed and distributed. In the age of the Internet and a progressively connected world, the impact of an artist is no longer bound by the physical limitations of a gallery. Access to art and the production or distribution tools required to leave your artistic mark are no longer exclusive to the elite or the exceptionally talented. With powerful platforms like social media and crowd-funding campaigns, today's artists can market their innovative work to the world at a low cost. At the end of the day, to produce our imagination is a distinctively human act. All of us have the desire to express ourselves, whether through words, visuals or music. As new mediums of self-expression are made more accessible to all of us, the creative possibilities are infinite in marketing.

2.10 General intelligence

The term "Artificial General Intelligence" (often abbreviated "AGI") has no broadly accepted precise definition, but has multiple closely related meanings, e.g.

The capacity of an engineered system to:

1. Display the same rough sort of general intelligence as humans; or,
2. Display intelligence that is not tied to a highly specific set of tasks; or
3. generalize what it has learned, including generalization to contexts qualitatively very different than those it has seen before; or,
4. Take a broad view, and interpret its tasks at hand in the context of the world at large and its relation thereto an engineered system displaying the property of artificial general intelligence, to a significant degree
5. The theoretical and practical study of artificial general intelligence systems and methods of creating them

AGI is part of the broader fields of Artificial Intelligence (AI) and Cognitive Science. It is also closely related to other areas such as Metalearning and Computational Neuroscience.

The field of artificial intelligence has spawned a vast range of subset fields and terms: machine learning, neural networks, deep learning and cognitive computing, to name but a few. However here we will turn our attention to the specific term 'artificial general intelligence', thanks to the Portland-based AI company Kimera Systems' (momentous) claim to have launched the world's first ever example, called Nigel.

The AGI Society defines artificial general intelligence as "an emerging field" aiming at the building of "thinking machines"; that is general-purpose systems with intelligence comparable to that of the human mind (and perhaps ultimately well beyond human general intelligence). *AGI would, in theory, be able to perform any intellectual feat a human can.* It is also referred to as 'strong AI' or 'full AI'. However, Kimera Systems insists that is precisely what it has done. It says 'Nigel' is a "breakthrough achievement in artificial intelligence coming decades before most experts predict such AI technology could be ready for commercial deployment".

Artificial General Intelligence (AGI) is artificial intelligence that matches or exceeds human intelligence; the intelligence of a machine that can successfully perform any intellectual task that a human being can. It is a primary goal of artificial intelligence research and an important topic for science fiction writers and futurists. AGI is also referred to as *strong AI* and has the ability to perform "general intelligent action." Science fiction associates strong AI with such human traits as consciousness, sentience, sapience and self-awareness. Artificial General Intelligence research aims to create AI that can replicate human-level intelligence completely. Many different definitions of intelligence have been proposed (such as being able to pass the Turing test), but there is to date no definition that satisfies everyone. While mainstream researchers have devoted little attention to AGI, with some claiming that intelligence is too complex to be completely replicated in the near term.

Some small groups of computer scientists are doing AGI research, however. Organizations pursuing AGI include the Adaptive AI, Artificial General Intelligence Research Institute, the Singularity Institute for Artificial Intelligence, and Texai. The term Artificial General Intelligence distinguishes work on AGI from more mainstream, less ambitious, "narrow AI" projects. *Narrow AI* is very good at a specific task, such as playing chess, but is not capable of readily adapting to new tasks and being applied to other uses. Unlike AGI, narrow or "weak AI" is simply the use of software to study or accomplish specific problem solving or reasoning tasks that do not encompass - or in some cases are completely outside of - the full range of human cognitive abilities. Some believe that a simulated human brain model could be one of the quickest means of achieving strong AI, as it would not require complete understanding of how intelligence works. A very powerful computer would simulate a human brain, often in the form of a network of neurons. Another alternative strategy is to begin an AI as a blank slate in a virtual world and allow it to grow and learn in an interactive social simulation such as Second Life and become an increasingly powerful AGI.

Artificial Narrow Intelligence (ANI) refers to a machine's ability to perform a single task extremely well and may be even better than a human.ANI works wonders in cases where a machine is expected to run automated tasks that are generally simple and repetitive in nature such as data collection in marketing. Bots are a perfect example of ANI. Whether you want a restaurant recommendation or a weather update, bots today have numerous uses. *Bots function by pulling data from larger databases and finding just the right answer that you were looking for* whether it is a restaurant recommendation or traffic update for your route. Bots have started to be a part of our everyday lives.

Customer service is one area for which ANI is a benefit. ANI technology has enabled bots to answer customer queries, which are simple and repetitive in nature. Bots being able to deliver consistency, accuracy, and speed in customer service is benefiting organizations in building/maintaining their brand name.

Artificial General Intelligence (AGI) is based on the principle that machines can be made to think. As per AGI, machines have the ability to represent human mind and can function in the similar fashion as human brain.
If this is true, then machines will be able to reason, think and do all functions that a human is capable of doing. However, the technology of AGI is still in its embryonic stage and would need deep research and long years for it to become a fully functional reality.

The Goal:

Both AI areas are developed with different goals to achieve. The focus of Artificial Narrow Intelligence is narrow. It focuses on developing technology that is capable of executing a *single task effectively*, providing excellent service to the customer in that particular area. Whereas, Artificial General Intelligence focuses on a broad aspect. Its goal is to develop a technology that can think and function so similar to humans that it can be capable of taking place of humans where decision-making is required.

Intelligence Level:

Artificial Narrow Intelligence machines focus only on *one area* and hence their intelligence is limited to that. Also, ANI technology does not enable them to do complex tasks like a human brain. On the other hand, machines that will be empowered with AGI will have the brain to reason out like a human. Its intelligence with match or may be even exceed human intelligence.

Areas of Application:

Artificial Narrow Intelligence can be applied in areas where the *work is repetitive* and does not involve any decision-making. It can be applied where the work can be predefined and more of information processing is required. AGI, on the other hand, is expected to be capable of being applied in broader areas, areas where decision-making and analysis is required. Almost all the areas where human brain is required to do the work, AGI can have its application

Revision

- Debate the 10 goals of (AI) as discussed in this chapter
- In 500 words explain how (AI) could be used in marketing, use examples
- Outline the meaning of social intelligence
- Explain how (AI) could be used creatively

3 Approaches

Introduction

The (AI) approaches used by researchers include applications cybernetics and brain stimulation as well as symbolic use covering the fields of cognitive simulation, logic, anti-logic and knowledge. Also, sub-symbolic using embodied intelligence, computation and soft computing. All these areas are of interest to marketing in creating understanding of mind processes.

Chapter Learning Outcomes

⬚ Build a constructive knowledge of symbolic and sub-symbolic (AI).

⬚ Gain an appreciation of their application in marketing.

⬚ Have a greater understanding of cognitive processes.

• Consider how cybernetics and brain simulation could be useful in understanding

• Human actions.

⬚ Having successfully completed the module, you will be able to:

⬚ 1. Critically assess the goals of (AI) basics in marketing.

⬚ 2. Assess the applications of (AI) in today's world.

⬚ Having completed the module, you will be able to:

⬚ 1. Understand the variety of (AI) approaches and their uses.

• 2. Be able to explain the principal goals of each in (AI).

Critical thinking

Having successfully completed this topic, you will be able to: 1. Critically evaluate the variety of approaches of (AI). 2. Understand and debate elements of (AI) to management.

OBJECTIVES

(AI) research has three approaches, which are defined as computational psychology, computational philosophy, and computer science. Computational psychology is used to make computer programs that mimic human behaviour. Computational philosophy is used to develop an adaptive, free-flowing computer mind. Implementing computer science serves the goal of creating computers that can perform tasks that only people could previously accomplish (Shapiro, 1992). Together, the human like behaviour, mind, and actions make up artificial intelligence. In marketing it has taken on many forms from computation to communication stimulation of messages.

3.1 Cybernetics and brain simulation

Talking about marketing today is a great test. It is much more than philosophy, technique, tool or discipline. For decades, marketing scholars and experts have been trying to reach the consumer audience in the best manner possible and to tap into the mind of the consumers. The first co-communication channel for touching customers is advertising, it is considered one of the fundamental parts of marketing. The term "capturing minds" was present even in 1928 and was connected to the advertising practice. The power of advertising is large, and the manipulation of media is happening on a daily basis, an individual is exposed to over three million impacts per day. Therefore, advertising is important because its product interest at the first sight. Today, in some cases advertisers can forecast behaviour and accordingly pay attention to *what should they say and how should they say it*. Manipulating emotions is important constituent of communication and promotion tools used by marketing. Accordingly, the roots of communication can be found in psychology. Even in the 20th century Barneys (1938) indicated that propaganda was not science like chemistry but has got some new frameworks engaging mass psychology (psychology of the human masses). Barney's work was one of the first to use the term "science", it was introduced when talking about propaganda, advertisement and influence on consumers' purchase decisions.

One of the ways to inspect the brain is via EEG- electroencephalogram. This so-called "passive" technology is using sensors to secure *electrical signals* produced by brainwaves (Pradeep 2010). The device was the first used for discovering the brain signals and looked like a swim cap. The first studies were done back in 1979 (Morin 2011). However, it was not very accurate, as Ornstein (1991) described, comparing it to the hearings to understand what was happening in New York by listening the noise from different areas from satellite placed 250 miles above the ground. In other words, it could be said that it is based on assumptions on what is happening between neurons. In addition, research found the outer area of cortex is represented by EEG (Ornstein 1991). This area is of particular interest for marketing researchers, because it plays meaningful role in human creativity, thoughts and action. Ohme et al. (2009) presented the main benefit of the EEG, which is very high temporal resolution, meaning it can monitor brain changes second by second.

It is important to mention that these techniques were used, as it was an easy to gain certain insight and pictures of how brain works. Even so, EEG technology is reinforced by advanced computers with statistical programs such as MATLAB- a high-level specialized computing language and environment for data visualization, analysis and numeric computation (Ohme et al. 2009). It serves as a prodigious contribution to EEG research. As an addition to EEG, there is EMG (electromyography) which as a tool is good for measuring and evaluating the physiological properties of facial muscles and has a long history of research in the context of emotions (Ohme et al. 2009). Therefore, this tool can be perceived as a channel for defining and examining both, existence of emotions and their intensity.

EEG and EMG technology are used by neuromarketing agencies due to its relatively low cost (Morin 2011). However, more prompt results can be obtained by *magnetic resonance technologies*.

Functional Magnetic Resonance Imaging can precisely indicate the *activity of certain brain parts by measuring oxygen levels in blood that flows within the brain* (Pradeep 2010). MRI is used for observing other body parts as well, but in neurological terms, fMRI is used for observing the brain. Advantages of this method are in its speed, which is scanning the whole brain in approximately three seconds and the possibility of repetition without concerning the negative effects of the person (Alčaković and Arežina 2011). Pradeep (2010) mentioned that disadvantage of the fMRI for marketing purposes, it was that the time for added blood supply to reach specific brain area could take up to 5 seconds. Therefore, the reaction of the brain can be late if the subject is shown some advertising during the examination.

Other brain research methods are magnetic resonance imaging (MRI), near infrared spectroscopy (NIRS), positron emission tomography (PET), event related potentials (ERP), magneto encephalography (MEG), transcranial magnetic stimulation (TMS) and eye tracking (Zurawicki 2010). However, aforementioned EEG and fMRI are the most frequent and most well-known. Certainly, every human brain is exclusive, just like fingerprints. However, Wilson et al. (2008) advocated that by involving more subjects in the study, researchers prepared brain images of different persons and this had the ability to make mass comparisons. Subsequently, it is possible to create certain patterns and points of connection and similarities between individuals in the study and with additional information taken out from the different fields included in the matter create a comprehensive image of reactions, both biological and psychological. Wilson et al. (2008) defined, the *"possibility and opportunity to influence consumers without their full awareness might increase, as a result of the research of brain activity"*. However, it is impossible to ignore that the humans are systems consisted not only of biological processes, but also *vertigo of emotions, feelings and reasons*.

One of the most particular characteristic of humans is the possession of *emotions and feelings and moreover, awareness of them*. Emotions and feelings are quite important for marketers because all of them are trying to evoke some emotion or feeling in that person and make them change behaviour.

Emotions are the main human drivers, while subsidiary roles are given to habits and cognitive factors (Ambler et al. 2004). According to Damasio (1994), there are primary and secondary emotions. Primary are *innate emotions* that by the research logic start to develop from the birth and depend on limbic system (Damasio 1994). They are basic human mechanisms and are more unconscious and automatic. Secondary emotions are built upon them and they arise when person becomes aware of connections, sense, experience and consistency. By the definition given by Damasio (1994), secondary emotions occur when person "experience the emotion" and feels the change in the body and the conscious which is at a higher level, although changes within the body are unconscious and cannot be stopped.

Damasio made claim to differences between 'emotions and feelings. He describes it as "all emotions generate feelings, but not all feelings originate in emotions" (Damasio 1994). In addition, there are *varieties of feelings*. Damasio (1994) explains in his work how some are based on universal emotions like happiness, sadness, anger, fear and disgust, and others are based on variations of universal emotions, like euphoria, melancholy, panic, and they happen from *experiences*. Background feelings can be pleasant or unpleasant and people are usually subtly aware of them (Damasio 1994). Affected by these feelings, humans make decisions, behave, act and interact with others for better or worse.

Behind the understanding of the brain, there is always subject of 'reason', meaning that *everything decided by the brain means it is seen as reasonable*. However, the situation in reality differs. Emotions makeshift in mental states, sometimes even changing memories and ideas without the knowledge of a person (Ornstein 1991). When people feel, they think, it is inseparable. Ornstein (1991) explains that a brain gets *emotional information* through separate system of nerve paths, through the limbic system to the cortex, and thus *emotions are out of the conscious control*. This happens when we feel something even though we know we should not. In other words, *we buy something we know we do not really need or can afford*. Recent analysis, as Ornstein (1991) outlined, has shown that there are 'differences' between *left and right hemisphere* of the brain in emotional expression, where the *left responds to the verbal content and the right to the tone and gestures*. As Ornstein (1991) claims, "it is the most primary system, when people ask question if something is good or bad". Feeling comes first because of the two things. The first one is that they appeared first in the *mind's evolution* and secondly they are result *of human' experiences* (Ornstein 1991). Basically, not knowing why we like something, or why we are attracted to it, it can have a basis that is beyond our possibility of human understanding. It is assumed that the emotions evolved during the evolution to satisfy in the optimal way and the needs of organisms (Ornstein 1991).

Sometimes, people have spontaneous actions, which they call "without thinking". The same happens when we move; we do not stop and decide that we will move, it leaves the place for noticing *new things*. Spontaneous actions begin before people decide to act, more precisely, that decision is unconscious and independent (Ornstein 1991). The majority of information our brain receives is processed unconsciously. Pradeep (2010) was more precise about this and concluded that out of 11 million bits of information our senses are taking in a second, the conscious brain can process only 40 bits per a second the rest relies on the subconscious brain, which mathematically equals 99.999 per cent. Ornstein elaborated the struggling with the mind and the reason at the first place in a following sentence:

"Reason is all; our mind, as we have it, is what we are stuck with, and the best we can hope for is some kind of eloquence as we realize we're the pawns of fate. Maybe computers will help us (Ornstein 1991).

The other side of the discussion is *consciousness,* possible to understand more easily. Our picture of the world is based on sense and information we receive, expectations, hopes, fantasy and other cognitive processes, and is built upon consciousness, but we are aware only of a small portion of what our minds are taking in (Ornstein 1991). The information we receive is stored and this becomes knowledge. Advertising is meant to inform and persuade and based on exposure forms opinion. Many of our inner workings work as a team in order to give consistent interpretation of the environment, what I call 'our reality'. Conscious processes are more flexible, take effort, happen at one time and are thus inefficient according to (Ornstein 1991).

Beyond the conscious we can also find the phenomenon called subliminal perception. Subliminal perception is the ability of humans to *perceive things without knowing about their perception*, i.e. without being conscious of them. This is the proof to the claim that the brain worked well before self- awareness (Ornstein 1991). Ornstein (1991) defined the subliminal stimuli as "sensory information below the threshold of conscious perception". It is difficult to defend oneself from these influences, because it is hard to know and recognise them. When we are thirsty, we think of brands of beverages we have been exposed to. However, it is useful to understand the effects for marketing. As Ornstein (1991) mentioned, subliminal messages affect sensitivity, behaviour and perceptual mechanisms. These subliminal messages have been present in media for some time a good example is 'placement in films and TV, the product or name we recognise, the symbol'. It brings up the question in marketing of mind controlling and influence, the ethics issue. Examples of these are pictures in milliseconds, backwards messages, signs and meanings in speech. A good example of how emotion- related transfer turns on the brain is considered totally different than a voluntary act, Damasio (1994). The face can have the same expression, the smile normal, the field for the movement is the same in both cases and face was shaped as it should be.

However, if the smile is 'provoked' by humorous remark, meaning it brings out some emotions, it is triggered in the brain in a totally different area. This is precisely the description of how it is probable to recognize *a fake versus true smile*. Often it is possible to know that eyes tell the truth and know it is correct. There are certain muscles involved in laughing and smiling. The first group are eye muscles, and the other mouth and face muscles, where the first group can be controlled only unconsciously and the others consciously (Damasio 1994).

After the original neuroeconomic papers, marketing scholars have recognized the potential for neuroscientific methods as a new approach instead of quantitative and qualitative research (Javor et al. 2013). Now, it is possible to consider a combination of medical knowledge, technology and marketing in one sentence and have some completely new approach. Thus, neuromarketing was born and it was in 2004 based on work by (Touhami et al 2011).

However, some authors claim that the term was coined in 2002 by Lewis and Briger, while the brain's response to marketing stimuli had dated from 1969 (Kalliny and Gentry 2010).

Moreover, Fisher et al. (2010) claimed that it was June 2002 when a press release by Atlanta advertising firm, Bright House announced there was a business division using fMRI in marketing research process the company opened a neuromarketing division in 2001 (Wilson et al. 2008). The focus was on scanning the brain and understanding the brain language. And the brain expresses constantly. As Lindstrom (2008) stated in his work, this process might be unconscious and instantaneous, but it happens every second, minute, hour and day for the rest of our lives.

There are diversities of definitions of neuromarketing, one of them is that it signifies the application of neuroscientific methods in a process of analysing and understanding human behaviour regarding markets and exchanges in marketing (Lee and Senior, 2008). As Kalliny and Gentry (2010) mentioned, neuroscientific methods have permitted researchers to study the *cortical activity* directly and at the moment when the subject is exposed to marketing stimuli. So far, there has been dozens of studies in the field of neuromarketing, in other words, the application of functional magnetic resonance imaging for market research (Eser et al. 2011).

The core question is: Why? Why do we buy certain product, why do we like some brand or why do we enjoy it? Lindstrom (2008) realized that the answers are in the brain and *the keys for building the future of brands lays exactly there*. Hidden emotions, subconscious feelings, desires and thoughts push purchase decision which consumers make every day. Besides debates and conjectures arising when mentioning neuromarketing, Lindstrom (2008) did not believe that neuromarketing was an instrument of corrupt governments or crooked advertisers, but simply a research tool.

It tries to ascertain what consumers are already thinking about products or brands (Lindstrom 2008). Examining from the researchers' position, neuromarketing was born at the juncture of qualitative and quantitative branches of traditional marketing research (Lindstrom, 2008). *"It actually represents the future of marketing and the path to optimization in understanding the consumers."* It can provide insight in countless procedures within the market exchange. There are certain areas measured in neuromarketing and these are considered to be: *Attention, Emotional Engagement, Memory, Purchase Intent/Persuasion, Novelty, Awareness/Understanding/Comprehension* which all provide a level of effectiveness (Pradeep 2010). These neuro- metrics were developed by NeuroFocus, Inc. founded by Dr. A.K. Pradeep. All neuromarketing research needs to have robust theoretical background, including experimental hypotheses, goals and methods (Lee and Senior 2008). Fisher et al. (2010) defined, "neuromarketing had dual characteristic according to different authors- business activity and academic field".

Javor et al. (2013) mentioned that in 2008 there were 800,000 hits on Google for the term "neuromarketing", while in 2017 that number rose up to 3,4 million hits. It cannot be claimed that the neuromarketing is a key to everything marketing, since it includes study of human brain and scientists have not understood it completely.

But the science has been improving and technology developing, and all this can contribute in creating the chiefly good way for companies to understand and reach their customers.

According to the IXP Marketing Group, approximately 21, 000 new brands are introduced per year around the world, and based on history data, only few reach the next year on the shelves (Lindstrom 2008). This is expensive which makes marketers think about costs, wasted material and unrealized desires. Therefore, it is important for marketers, as well as economists to understand why consumers *behave the way they do.*

George Loewenstein, a behavioural economist said that "a lot of what happens in the brain is emotional, not cognitive" (Lindstrom 2008). The irrefutable fact is that there are unique *imprints in subconscious* that are made if something causes a neurological response. Pradeep (2010) explains they are called *Neurological Iconic Signatures* and they presented what were the most powerful elements about a product from the perspective of the subconscious. Findings from the field of cognitive neuroscience, neurobiology, organizational neuroscience or neuromarketing can contribute to each other, as well as other sciences and practices. For example, recent research on cognitive neuroscience research covering emotions, defines it as the process of decision-making, this is relevant to organizational marketing decision making (Senior et al. 2011).

Human behaviour studies are always context- laden (Javor et al, 2013), the study of consumer behaviour requires inspection in daily, real-world situations. According to the Javor et al (2013), there have been three concepts of neuromarketing that are predominantly relevant for neurologists and the study of the human brain: *(1) relation of reward system with decision- making and brand preference, (2) neurobiological background of trust and (3) the ethical issues attached to the story of neuromarketing.*

One of the fundamental ways to capture the brains precious attention is by *novelty, innovation or unfamiliarity* (Pradeep 2010). The human brain reacts to something that stands out from the crowd and something that has never been seen or tried before. The purpose of good marketing communication is the same. That is, the first contact in marketing. If it is thinkable to make successful first impression, later on, the job of loyalty transfer is. Addressing contact, another concept, according to the Pradeep (2010) is eye contact in communications. This is important for social beings, because it reveals the *empathic emotions, nearness and understanding.* Consider also *pleasure/reward images*, which are enticing for brains, especially if one knows exactly what they are (Pradeep 2010). This shows the simplicity of a brain response, meaning that it desires the reward/pleasure for a given attention, answering the question at the same time: What is the benefit? What advertisers and marketers need to focus on, among everything else, is that *benefit of their products, actions, and campaigns for customers' brains to understand.*

When trying to pursue customers to buy a product, or simply to attract them, there is one interesting concept in research- *to find their discomfort.* Here, it is not the story about the physical or psychological pain as an ailment, but the discomfort for the product. To explain a pizza company found out in a survey that the customers' pain was not the taste of pizza or how hot it was.

The number one issue of pizza customers was *the anxiety of not knowing when the pizza will arrive* (Renvoise and Morin 2007). When they realised this through research, they made a great marketing offer. Renvoise and Morin (2007) cite their very successful slogan: *Thirty minutes or less (or it's free).* The marketing team established the discomfort and find the way to solve it and customers value it. Therefore, a customer story, according to the Renvoise and Morin (2007) is 80 to 100 per cent the *proof for the gain of the product.*

If the company wants to "communicate to the old brain" it should use the power of the word "you". By using this word, any of the message building blocks can become customer- centric (Renvoise and Morin 2007). In creating the message for customers as well as the advertisement, there is also the great power of colours. Renvoise and Morin (2007) explain that colours have influenced the old brain at the subconscious level. It is possible to check the symbol of various colours as well as which companies are using them in the world. It is interesting to think about the marketing strategy of these companies, and if they are accomplishing those aims from colour meanings.

If you think of Coke (red and white); Mc Donald's (red and yellow): USA (red white and blue); AMX (blue). The reaction to things, products, advertisement and external stimuli are based upon memory in most cases. Memory can be positive or negative regarding certain contact from the past. If it is positive, humans accept that memory, and if it is negative, they try to avoid it. The question is where do the memories live in the brain? Pradeep (2010) elaborated that most of the studies concluded that there was *no single centre in the brain in charge for long- term memory*. Therefore, many centres in the brain interrelate in creating storage of memories.

Relations between psychology and marketing are relatively nearby. As Lee and Chamberlain (2007) explain, marketing, strategy, economic behaviour, operation research and similar subjects are based on the development of the behavioural, social psychological or cognitive fields, while on the other side, achievements within psychology can owe much to economic and organizational contexts. Neuromarketing should be used to *confirm, reconfigure, or improve conventional theories of consumer behaviour* (Fugate 2007). That is, *consumer behaviour before, during and after the purchase is very valuable*. Consumer behaviour is a disciplined study, among all behaviour of individuals, groups or organization during the process of selection, usage and disposal of the products and services, including experiences and ideas to satisfy needs and impact of those processes on consumers and society in general (Husić- Mehmedović, Kukić and Čičić 2012) .

Hefer and Cant (2013) put forward that *consumer behaviour is constructed of consumer activities* (buying and using) and consumer responses (expressive, social and psychological). It can be comprehended that they are reliant on each other.

For example, psychological responses one can be obtained in a customer's head space, when s/he envisages a product, how it can be used, observing the characteristics of the product and relating them to own experience, needs and desires. On the other hand, expressive responses, for instance, are related to feelings and emotions, the way product sways a customer's state of mind.

Example of social responses are the actions during the purchase decision making, or activity, including comparing prices, store atmosphere, ads, etc.

Looking at Neuromarketing there are several applications for this science based on my research, they are:

- Consumer behaviour and perception

An understanding of why people behave a particular way, what could be done to change behaviour.

- Needs and wants

Understanding the drivers behind a decision to buy a commodity(real need or imagined want). The influence of communication and peer pressure

- In store behaviour and traffic planning

How do people shop, why do they move in a particular way, what attracts them?

- Planned and impulse purchases

The mind set variations between a considered purchase and impulse

- Consumer response

Response to offers and deals

- Merchandising

Attractive / not attractive

- Pricing

The psychology of pricing, mixed offers, premium, low cost, value equation

- Co-creation

The best way to interact, to give the customer a bespoke item

- Messaging / Communication

Value propositions that resonate

- Packaging

Shape, colour, size, ease, visual impact

- Taste / Texture/ Look / Feel

Personal preferences

- Performance of a product or service

What to measure and how to measure it

- Research

Cognitive insight to improve satisfaction, delight, long term equity

3.2 Symbolic

A symbol is an easily recognizable representation of a deeper meaning. Marketing and small business professionals often use symbols to represent their business or brand, to make advertising materials easier to read and understand, and to convey deeper meanings through writing. However, in recent times symbolic marketing has a wider application. In advertising the technique is useful to communicate complex or abstract ideas. And to communicate any idea quickly and vividly. ... A simile is a figure of speech that uses "like" or "as" to compare two different things in a way that creates a more vivid expression. Symbolic culture is the cultural realm constructed and inhabited uniquely by Homo sapiens and is differentiated from ordinary culture, which many other animals possess. Symbolic culture is studied by archaeologists, social anthropologists and sociologists. A symbol-intensive brand is a brand adopted not only for its functional benefits, but above all, for the strong symbolism and significance that it is able to transmit, allowing a consumer to express his or her identity, to signal status or manifest a sense of belonging to a group.

In sociology and anthropology, symbolic capital can be referred to as the resources available to an individual on the basis of honour, prestige or recognition, and serves as value that one holds within a particular culture. A war hero, for example, may have symbolic capital in the context of running for political office. In sociology, a significant symbol is a gesture (usually a vocal gesture) that calls out in the individual making the gesture the same (i.e., functionally identical) response that is called out in others to whom the gesture is directed (Mind, Self and Society 47) (Ritzer, 2003). In summary, some of the common elements that make up individual cultures are *symbols, language, values, and norms*. A symbol is anything that is used to stand for something else. People who share a culture often attach a specific meaning to an object, gesture, sound, or image.
In a marketing context 'symbolic' has many applications it is mostly used in branding and communication where a symbol is used to reflect a meaning. A great example is the Nike Swoosh, even on its own it stands for all the values of Nike. Symbolic capital in the Nike context could be the sponsorship of runners such as Husain Bolt. The Nike symbolic identity is "Just do it".

Many researchers like to think of AI as having two camps.

One that is termed *'knowledge rich'* which encodes as much knowledge of its domain as possible in the system being built. The idea is that you learn something new only when it is only a little bit more than you already know. This area includes, *Expert Systems, Case based reasoning, some natural language processing etc. etc.* In this branch of AI, the problem and much domain knowledge are openly encoded in the algorithms used. This is the symbolic AI camp.

In contrast the *'knowledge free'* branch of AI sees AI as not needing specialist knowledge, it just needs the ability to learn. This area includes Genetic Algorithms, Neural Networks (ANN) and other biologically stimulated techniques.

Here the main idea is to have a representation in which the answers do not seem to have a clear representation of the problem domain. In ANN for example there are sets of weights that are being sought. These weights do not, at least when we start the learning process, and do not have any relationship to what we are trying to learn or the answers that we are trying to produce. Another good example of how these differ is in natural language translation. In traditional computer linguistics we encode much grimmer and semantics into our systems. In non-symbolic AI systems, we use something like the statistics of co-occurrence in large examples of texts that have been translated.

Symbolic artificial intelligence is the collective name for all methods in artificial intelligence research that are based on *high-level "symbolic" (human-readable) representations of problems, logic and search*. Symbolic AI was the dominant paradigm of AI research from the mid-1950s until the late 1980s. The approach is based on the assumption that many aspects of intelligence can be achieved by the manipulation of symbols, an assumption defined as the "physical symbol systems hypothesis" by Allen Newell and Herbert A. Simon in the middle 1960s.

The most successful form of symbolic AI is 'expert', which use a network of production rules. Production rules connect symbols in a relationship similar to an If-Then statement. The expert system processes the rules to make deductions and to determine what additional information it needs, i.e. what questions to ask, using human-readable symbols. Symbolic AI was intended to produce general, human-like intelligence in a machine, whereas most modern research is directed at specific sub-problems. Research into general intelligence is now studied in the sub-field of artificial general intelligence.

Machines were initially designed to formulate outputs based on the inputs that were represented by symbols.

Symbols are used when the input is definite and falls under certainty. But when there is uncertainty involved, for example in formulating predictions, the representation is done using "fuzzy logic".

3.2.1 Cognitive simulation

Purchasing products that consumers have not used before can be a marketing challenge (e.g., a new car, house, computer). Other products provide consumers with new experiences (e.g., a person's first trip to Europe, a 3-D movie). A widespread characteristic of these products and experiences is that although they are not inevitably new to the market, *many consumers may not have used or experienced them before.* For products for which consumers have constant existing preferences, consumers often do not need to commence a considered evaluation stage before choice and are less receptive to the evaluation context.

However, for other products, such as those mentioned previously, consumers do not yet have well informed preferences and need to go through an *evaluation stage* before forming their preferences (Bettman, Luce, and Payne 1998). In these situations, to increase consumers' product evaluation and purchase intention, marketers often ask consumers to "Imagine yourself..." interrelating with the product or engaging consumers in narrative stories or transformational advertisements during their evaluation stage. How effective are these types of mental imagery strategies? Several studies have suggested that imagining a product experience can have powerful effects on consumers' product attitudes (Escalas 2004; Keller and Block 1997).

Mental simulation is the *copied mental representation of events* (Taylor and Schneider 1989). The role of mental simulation or mental imagery has been widely studied in various areas of psychology (Taylor et al. 1998) and in different marketing contexts (e.g., MacInnis and Price 1987; Shiv and Huber 2000; Zhao, Hoeffler, and Dahl 2009). However, there is robust evidence that not all types of mental simulation are equally effective in changing behaviour. Research in psychology has identified two distinct types of mental simulation: *process simulation*, which focuses on the process of going through the steps of reaching a goal, and *outcome simulation*, which focuses on the desirable outcome of realising the goal (Pham and Taylor 1999). The key question here is whether a cognitive processing approach would lead to more favourable evaluations with 'process or outcome' simulation. Prior research with a cognitive perspective indicates that for products that consumers have not used before, consumers naturally focus more on the product *usage process* (i.e., learning cost) than product benefits (Mukherjee and Hoyer 2001).

Furthermore, this research has indicated a negative impact on evaluations when consumers focus on the usage process and the associated learning cost. Moreover, other studies have shown that it is problematic for consumers to visualize the detailed cognitive process of how they would use the features of an unfamiliar product, leading to less favourable evaluations (Dahl and Hoeffler 2004).

Given consumers' primary focus on the product usage process and the associated costs during the evaluation stage, how could marketers enhance product evaluation? Prior work has indicated that for these products, *switching consumers' cognitive focus from the usage process to the product benefits increases product evaluations* (Mukherjee and Hoyer 2001).

Changing to a simulation environment likely engages *operant conditioning* because participants learn to adjust their decision-making behaviours as a result of positive or negative consequences that are contingent on their *previous* decision-making. Operant conditioning relates to *voluntary responses*, which a structure performs will fully in order to produce a desired outcome. A system operates on its environment in order to produce some desirable result, i.e., the law of effect... reactions that are satisfying are more likely to be repeated, and those that are not satisfying are less likely to be repeated (Thorndike 1932).

Thorndike's early research formed the foundation for the work of B.F. Skinner who furthered the study of *operant conditioning* by illustrating how *behaviour varied as a result of alterations in the environment* (Feldman 1990).

Skinner argues that learning takes place in an attempt to switch the environment, i.e., to obtain favourable outcomes. Control is gained by means of a heuristic process during which one's behaviour results in a more favourable response than other behaviours. The reward (more favourable response) *reinforces the behaviour*. As such, *reinforcement* is contributory in teaching subjects, a specific behaviour that gives them more control over the outcome (Schiffman 1987). Learning theory would suggest that underlying the behavioural decisions made by a simulation participant (e.g., price setting, advertising expenditure level, sales force size, etc.) is a *learning process* that leads to the determination of what types of decisions work and what types of decisions do not work in a simulation competition. For example, if a partaker concludes that low price is important to success, the suitable behavioural response is to 'set a low price.'

This would suggest consistent cognitive-behavioural decision-making. The nature of this association is in a simulation context. Given this expectancy, it would be proper to analyse the cognitive and behavioural choice structures of accomplices in order to determine the nature of the behavioural replies expected based on the identified cognitive structures. Behavioural structures of the decision-making process of participants can determine if they have understood the nature of the environment with which they had to contend. If the results indicate that the correct cognitive thought processes have occurred, then suitable behavioural decisions are expected.

The simulation game entitled LAPTOP: A Marketing Simulation (Faria and Dickinson 1987) can be used to investigate the focus of a study since this game allows the game administrator to determine the importance (i.e., weight) of each parameter of the cooperation. In particular, the parameters can be set such that two theoretically meaningful experimental environments are created.

While a number of studies have focused on the behavioural aspect of the decision-making process in simulation competitions (e.g., see Dickinson, Faria, and Whiteley 1988; Faria, Dickinson, and Whiteley 1991), research examining the cognitive decision-making process from the perspective identified here is relatively new (e.g., see Whiteley, Dickinson, and Faria 1992). Furthermore, in those studies examining the behavioural domain, the results indicate that game players do not seem to have made behavioural decisions that indicate that they had drawn *correct cognitive conclusions* about the nature of the simulation environment that they faced.

A key precursor of predicted preference reversal is a shift in the natural focus from usage process toward *product benefits*. In the current research, two factors that could serve the function of shifting consumers' focus away from the usage process, and toward product benefits.

According to previous research, the dependable prediction is that under a *cognitive-focused mode*, simulating the naturally ignored product aspect leads to more favourable product evaluation, and under an *affective-focused mode*, simulating the naturally prominent product aspect leads to more positive product evaluation. Prior work that has ascertained consumers' natural focus on the *usage process is based on utilitarian products* (e.g., a refrigerator in Mukherjee and Hoyer 2001). When consumers expect *functional utility* from utilitarian products, it is important for them to get the use out of the product with a minimum amount of time and effort (Babin, Darden, and Griffen, 1994). As such, it is not surprising that purchasers mostly focus on the usage process and the anticipated learning costs. In contrast, *hedonic products offer experiential benefits* (i.e., fun, pleasure, and excitement; Dhar and Werten- broch 2000). In the long run, with hedonic products (phones, games, cosmetics) consumers are primarily seeking enjoyment.

3.2.2 Logic-based

During its relatively short history, AI has been slowly influenced by logical ideas. AI has drawn on many research methodologies: the value and relative significance of logical formalisms is cross-examined by some leading researchers and has been debated in the literature. It is difficult to find a major philosophical theme that does not become intertwined with issues having to do with *reasoning*. *Implicatures*, for illustration, have to parallel to *inferences* that can be carried out by a rational interpreter of dialogue. Whatever causality is, causal relations should be inferable in ordinary common-sense marketing settings. Whatever credence is, it should be possible for rational agents to make plausible inferences about the beliefs of other agents. The goals and standing constraints that inform a rational agent's behaviour must permit the formation of reasonable plans.

In particular, logical theories in AI are separate from implementations. They can be used to provide insights into the 'reasoning problem' without directly informing the implementation. Direct implementations of philosophies from logic—theorem-proving and model-construction techniques—are used in AI, however, the AI theorists who rely on logic to model their problem areas are free to use other implementation techniques as well.

Thus, in Moore 1995b (Chapter 1), Robert C. Moore distinguishes three uses of logic in AI; *as a tool of analysis, as a basis for knowledge representation, and as a programming language*. In response to the need to design this declarative section, a subfield of AI known as *knowledge representation* emerged during the 1980s. Knowledge representation deals primarily with the *representational and reasoning challenges* of this separate component. The distinction between *mathematical* and *philosophical* logic may well be incidental in relation to the overall goals of the subject, since technical rigor and the use of mathematical methods seem to be essential in all areas of logical research.

However, the distinction between the two subfields has been enlarged by differences in the sorts of professional training that are available to logicians, and by the views of individuals on what is considered 'significant for the field'.

The importance of applications in logical AI, and the scale of these applications, *represents a new methodology for logic—one that would have been impossible without mechanized reasoning.* This practice forces theoreticians to think through problems on a new scale and at a new level of detail, and this in turn has a philosophical effect on the resulting theories.

McCarthy's methodological position has not changed substantially since it was first expressed in McCarthy (1959) and expounded and edited in McCarthy & Hayes 1969. The motivation for using 'logic' is that even if the ultimate implementations do not directly and simply use logical reasoning techniques like theorem, proving a logical formalization helps us to understand *the reasoning problem itself.*

The claim is that without an understanding of what the *reasoning problems are, it will not be possible to implement their solutions correctly.* Reasonable as this spiritual argument may seem, it is in fact contentious in the context of AI; a substitute methodology would seek to study or develop the desired behaviours. The representations and reasoning that this methodology would produce might well be too complex to characterize or to understand at a conceptual level.

McCarthy's long-term objective with logic was to formalize *common sense reasoning,* the prescientific reasoning that is used in dealing with *everyday problems.* An early example of such a problem, mentioned in McCarthy 1959, is getting from home to the airport. Other examples include:

1. *Narrative understanding.* The reasoning involved in reconstructing implicit information from narratives, such as sequencing of eventualities, and inferred causal connections.

2. *Diagnosis.* For instance, detecting faults in physical devices.

3. *Spatial Reasoning.* For instance, reasoning about the parts of rigid bodies and their shapes, and their relation to the shape of the whole.

4. *Reasoning about the attitudes of other agents.* For instance, making informed guesses about the beliefs and desires of other agents, not from "keyhole observation" but from conversational clues of the sort that could be obtained in a brief, interactive interview.

Nonmonotonic logic is the first sustained effort within logical theory to resolve this discrepancy. As such, it represents a potential for a sweeping expansion of the scope of logic, as well as a meaningful quantity of technical data. The consequence relations of *classical logics* are monotonic. That is, if a set Γ of formulas implies a consequence C then a larger set $\Gamma \cup A$ will also imply C. A logic is *nonmonotonic* if its consequence relation lacks this property. *Preferred models* provide a general way to induce a nonmonotonic consequence relation.

In the early stages of its emergence in logical AI, many researchers seem to have thought of nonmonotonic reasoning as a general method for reasoning about 'uncertainty'.

However, by the end of the 1980s, treatments of entirely quantitative probabilistic reasoning were not only possible in principle but were visibly preferable in many sorts of applications to methods involving nonmonotonic logic.

Priorian tense logic shares with modal logic a specialized concentration on issues that arise from using the *first-order theory of relations* to explain the logical phenomena, a belief that the important temporal operators will be quantifiers over world-states, and a rather distant and foundational approach to actual specimens of temporal reasoning. Of development, these temporal logics do harvest some rationalities. Planning difficulties in marketing provide one of the most abundant platforms for merging logical analysis with AI applications. On the one hand there are many practically important applications of *automated planning*, and on the other *logical formalizations* of planning are sincerely helpful in understanding the problems, and in designing algorithms.

The reinforcement of temporal reasoning, and in particular of reasoning about actions and plans, is the best-developed fruitful extension of modern formalization techniques to domains other than mathematical theories.

This difference has required the creation of new methodologies. One methodological innovation is the development of a *library of scenarios for testing the adequacy of various styles*, and the creation of *specialized domains like the blocks-world domain*.

To convey whether a plan achieves its objective, you need to see whether the objective holds in the plan's absolute condition. Doing this requires *predictive* reasoning a type of reasoning that was completely neglected in the *tense-logical literature*. As in mechanics, projection involves the inference of *later states from earlier ones*. But (in the case of simple planning problems at least) the forces at work are controlled by actions rather than by differential equations. The investigation of this *qualitative forms of temporal reasoning*, and has related sorts of reasoning (e.g., plan recognition, which seeks to infer goals from observed actions, and narrative explanation, which seeks to fill in implicit information in a temporal narrative) are one of the most impressive chapters in the brief history of *common sense theory*.

While for many AI logicists, the objective of *action formalisms* is to clarify an important aspect of common-sense reasoning, most of their research is unacquainted by an important source of insights into the commonsense view of time—namely, *natural language*. Multilingual persons concerned with the semantics of temporal constructions in natural language, like the AI community, have begun with ideas *from philosophical logic* but have found that these ideas need to be customized in order to deal with the phenomena. A principal discovery of the AI researchers has been the importance of *actions and their relation to change*. Similarly, a valuable discovery of the "natural language logicists" has been the importance of *different kinds of events* (including structured composite events) in explaining natural language. From work such as this, the idea of "natural language metaphysics" (see, for instance, Bach 1989) has appeared. John McCarthy's precise long-term goal was the formalization of common-sense knowledge, which has been accepted and pursued by a relatively small, but active, sub community of AI researchers.

This collective formalization effort (1) pursues to explain many areas of knowledge, and (2) tries to see how this *formalized knowledge* can be transported onto moderately complex common-sense reasoning problems. The first book-length treatment of this topic, **Davis 1991**, divides the general problem into the following subtopics.

1. Quantities and Measurements
2. Time
3. Space
4. Physics
5. Minds
6. Plans and Goals
7. Society

Several of these topics overlay with concerns of qualitative physics and qualitative reasoning community. There is sense in the hope that the mixture of logical methods with planning applications in AI can empower the development of a far more comprehensive and suitable theory of *practical reasoning* so important for marketers to understand.

As with many complications having to do with common sense reasoning, the level and complexity of the validations that are required are beyond the customary practices of philosophical logic. However, with computational methods of applying and analysis, the formalizations with areas such as cognitive robotics, are to help as laboratories for developing and testing ideas.

3.2.3 Anti-logic or scruffy

Imagine objects from the point of view of a consumer. It's not hard after all, as each of us, when we take off our marketing and hats for a moment, is also a consumer. We are bombarded by advertising and promotional messages all day. Aside from the sheer volume of marketing messages, they are also increasingly pervasive: popping up in windows on our computers, on park benches, on television screens in lifts or even in public spaces. And a lot of advertising, particularly in certain categories, has certain sameness to it. The overall outcome for many consumers is fatigue or, even worse, cynicism or confusion. Many consumers have trained themselves to ignore advertising and marketing messages, to tune them out, or at least to distrust them. Is it possible then that we have reached the peak of advertising? In the race to out-compete each other and to claim a small share of consumers' fleeting attention, are we as marketers just trying too intensely and creating too much sound?
Those questions are at the heart of a slate of new marketing approaches that some have grouped under the umbrella term "antilogic-marketing." There are different ideas afoot as to what it really means but if you boil them down you get a new framework for marketing that influences everything from how you try to reach prospective consumers, to how often you try, and how you engage with them once you do.

At its center, antilogic marketing is built around a couple of simple ideas:

⬚ Consumers are clever and inspired. They want honest and useful information, and they want marketers to respect their intelligence.
⬚ Everybody is selling something; be unusual. Be innovative and creative in order to draw the market to you.

Here are some ideas:

1. "Be short, be dazzling, and be vanished." Think: less noise, more shock. In the age of information overload, you can anti-market by being more succinct and by keeping things simple.

2. Be honest, even glaringly honest. In the best case, this builds integrity and trust in your brand. At the least, it manages consumer expectations and can even have the effect of turning a disadvantage into an advantage.
Perhaps one of the most famous examples of painful honesty in marketing comes from Amsterdam's Hans Brinker Budget Hotel. For a decade now, the hotel has made a virtue of its limited choice, limited service, and the very few amenities on offer.
The result of its praised marketing efforts? Hans Brinker has seen a dramatic increase in occupancy rates and profitability, and an equally spectacular decline in customer complaints (because everybody knows exactly what to expect from a night at the hotel).

3. Be unpredictable. Try something different and, at all costs, avoid cliché and the same selling points that everyone else in your space is using.

Reverse psychology is a tactic that is sometimes advanced in anti-marketing. In this case, the marketer is not so subtly appealing to a female demographic in its packaging.

4. Do not endorse, attract. Avoid shouting at customers with large, pervasive marketing campaigns. Instead, attract them with engaging, honest creative.

For example :Marmite trades on the strong positive or negative reactions it tends to trigger with customers in this simple, engaging creative.

And, where possible, create a sense of individuality or rarity. In an age of abundance and information overload, these qualities in themselves can be distinct selling positions.
To some, antilogic-marketing is a significant, next evolution of marketing practice and perhaps the logical result of "overload marketing" where the efforts of brands and advertisers to out-spend and out-compete each other have reached past the limits of their effectiveness.

3.2.4 Knowledge-based

Knowledge discovery and learning is an iterative process that extends the collection of marketing data mining techniques into a knowledge management framework, though data mining techniques are usually applied to the complete database, it is possible to mine a statistically representative sample of the data. To mine the data set, the marketer may use one or more of several data mining techniques such as *neural networks, tree-based methods, rule induction methods, or other statistical models*. The outcome of the data mining efforts is evaluated to identify the *usefulness of the resulting patterns* to the solution of the marketing problem and the accuracy of prediction of future customer behavior from a known set of data. This assessment gives further insights into the data set and helps the marketer to refine the data-mining model. The iterative learning process continues until the model is acceptable.

One of the important issues in knowledge management is the *organization, distribution and refinement of knowledge*. Knowledge can be generated by data mining tools, can be acquired from third parties, or can be refined or refreshed knowledge. The collected knowledge can then be organized by *indexing the knowledge elements, filtering based on content and establishing linkages and relationships among the elements.*

This knowledge is then integrated into a knowledge base and distributed to the decision support applications.

Marketing decisions, such as promotions, distribution channels and advertising media, based on *traditional segmentation* approaches result in poor response rate and increased cost. Today's customers have such diverse tastes and preferences that it is not possible to group them into large homogenous populations to develop marketing strategies anymore. Due to lack of appropriate tools and techniques to analyze these huge databases, a wealth of customer information and buying patterns is permanently hidden in marketing and unutilized in such databases. Knowledge-based marketing, which uses appropriate data mining tools and the knowledge management framework, tackles this need and helps leverage knowledge hidden in databases. There are three major areas of application of data mining for knowledge-based marketing — 1. customer profiling, 2. deviation analysis, and 3. trend analysis.

Machine learning (ML), an artificial intelligence (AI) discipline are geared toward the technological development of human knowledge, it has impacted the marketing big data ecosystem big time. So, what areas of the marketing big data ecosystem do we see being impacted by machine learning?

I believe we will see a focus in four major areas:

1. Automated data visualization (including ML results) will become richer, and user-friendly.

2. Content analysis (textual, lexical, multimedia/rich) will be used to drive better marketing conversations.

3. Incremental ML techniques will become more prevalent, leading to real-time, not just on-going and automated, changes in marketing execution.

4. Learning from ML results will accelerate the growth and skills of marketing professionals.

Being able to visualize relationships in data drives confidence. Confidence drives good decision-making, which in turn drives execution. Current tools, such as Tableau and QlikView, give a rich palette of data visualization widgets that can be applied to structured and unstructured data. The challenge here is not one of structure, but *one of understanding*. Visualization tools are most effectual when you understand the underlying data. ML techniques find boundaries in data, which often belie our initial understanding; so, finding the best visual representation is usually through trial and error. Without the visual representation, confidence in the ML findings isn't as strong as it should be. In marketing the growth of the analyst / interpreter of data has become a key member of the marketing team and good ones are highly prized.

3.3 Sub-symbolic

Symbols are objects that refer to other entities and have the ability to be combined in rule-governed methods, so that an unlimited collection of meaningful units can be generated from a finite set of elements. *Symbols may be images or words.* Deliberating the classical symbolic approach within cognitive psychology, intelligent beings are *symbol systems* operating on representations that have the format of symbolic codes. Until recently, symbolic architectures of the mind have been accepted as the leading approach in cognitive science and artificial intelligence. This conventional symbolic architecture follows the general design of the von Neuman computer and includes some alteration of processing units such as *cushion memories, short-term memory, long-term memory and switch structures* which oversee the operation and integration of these processing units (Bucci, 1997).

More recently, models based on differing constructions have been suggested which have been termed sub-symbolic, connectionist, or parallel distributed processing (PDP) models. These models highlight representations and processes in which the elements are *not isolated*, where organization is not clear-cut, and processing occurs simultaneously in multiple parallel channels.

Sub-symbolic architectures tackle the in essence the *infinite array of rapid and complex computations*, often carried on outside of awareness, frequently without explicit metrics, dimensions, or units, in most of the common acts of everyday life, for example in entering a queue of people, taking down an object from a high shelf, or picking up an object that has fallen.

In sub-symbolic (connectionist) theory information is parallel processed by simple calculations realized by neurons. In this approach a *simple sequence pulses represent information*. Sub-symbolic models are based on a comparison human brain, where cognitive activities of brain are interpreted by theoretical concepts that have their origin in neuroscience:

(1) Neuron received information from its neighbourhood of other neurons,

(2) Neuron processes (integrated) received information,

(3) Neuron sends processed information other neurons from its neighbourhood.

3.3.1 Embodied intelligence

Resource-based theory views heterogeneity among organisations and those assets secured semi permanently to the organisation that allow its managers to create and execute value-creating marketing strategies as fundamental in explaining an organisations market performance (Barney, 1991).

Academics have made a number of recent developments, collectively labelled 'dynamic capabilities' theory, addressing these limitations in traditional resource-based theory (Newbert, 2007; Zott, 2003).

Dynamic Discourse (DC) theory for example proposes that since marketplaces are dynamic, rather than simple diversity in a organisations' means and talents, it is the skills by which firms' properties are acquired and deployed in ways that match the firm's market environment that explains inter firm performance variance over time (e.g., Eisenhardt and Martin, 2000; Makadok, 2001; Teece, Pisano, and Shuen, 1997). These capabilities engage complex coordinated patterns of skills and knowledge that, over time, become entrenched as organizational routines (Grant, 1996). They are distinguished from other organizational processes by being *performed properly* relative to rivals (Bingham, Eisenhardt, and Furr, 2007; Ethi- raj *et al.*, 2005). Capabilities are energetic when they enable the organisation to implement new strategies to reflect changing market conditions by combining and transforming available marketing resources in new and different ways (e.g., Teece *et al.*, 1997).

Hult, Ketchen, and Slater (2005) demonstrated the value of a market information processing perspective on marketing operations (MO). This delineates MO as the extent to which an organisation engages in the generation, dissemination, and response to market intelligence pertaining to current and future customer needs, competitor strategies and actions, channel requirements and abilities, and the broader business environment (e.g., Kohli and Jaworski, 1990).

Drawing on traditional resource-based theory, the literature theorises that organisations with superior MO achieve superior business performance because they have *a greater understanding of customers' expressed wants and latent needs, competitor capabilities and strategies, channel requirements and developments, and the broader market environment than their rivals* (e.g., Hult and Ketchen, 2001; Jaworski and Kohli, 1993).

Knowledge may be categorized as *explicit--knowledge* that is clearly spelt out and relatively easy to transfer--and *tacit knowledge*--which cannot be easily transmitted via books, blue-prints, or lectures. The knowledge hypothetically is realizable by the combination of individual team members' stocks of tacit knowledge and is conceived of as *embedded knowledge*. Since embedded knowledge is difficult to manage, organisations that are effective at managing it can potentially possess distinctive competitive advantage in developing new and better products. Organizational knowledge can be viewed from a "routines" perspective, which has had a long and enduring tradition in the organizational literature (Stene, 1940; Simon, 1947; March and Simon, 1958; Cyert and March, 1963; Neison and Winter, 1982). The notion of routine refers to the regular and predictable patterns of organizational behaviour (Nelson and Winter, 1982).

Giving to this view, organisations are *repositories of productive knowledge* (Winter, 1991), and this knowledge exist in in the routines that inspire the behaviour of organizational participants in working together.

Apple for example is a repository of technical knowledge and innovation. Nelson and Winter (1982) suggest that routines are the *organizational counterpart of individual skills*. While a routine-based conception of organizational knowledge focuses on how organizations do things (Winter, 1991), other researchers have concentrated on how organizations *store and retrieve information from its history when making current decision*s (Walsh and Ungson, 1991).

According to this perspective of organizational knowledge, organizational memory is viewed as the *stored information from an organization's history that can be brought to bear on present decisions.*

3.3.2 Computational intelligence and soft computing

The expression computational intelligence (CI) usually refers to the ability of a computer to learn a specific task from data or experimental observation. Even though it is commonly considered a synonym of soft computing, there is still no commonly accepted definition of computational intelligence.

Generally, computational intelligence is a set of nature-inspired computational methodologies and approaches to address complex real-world problems to which mathematical or traditional modelling can be useless for a few reasons: the processes might be too complex for mathematical reasoning; it might contain some uncertainties during the process; or the process might simply be stochastic in nature. Undeniably, *many real-life problems cannot be translated into binary language (unique values of 0 and 1) for computers to process it. Computational Intelligence therefore provides solutions for such problems* (Siddique etal,2013).

The methods used are close to the human's way of reasoning, i.e. it uses inexact and incomplete knowledge, and it is able to produce control actions in an adaptive way. CI therefore uses a combination of five main complementary techniques. The *fuzzy logic* which enables the computer to understand natural language, *artificial neural networks* which permits the system to learn experiential data by operating like the biological one, *evolutionary computing*, which is based on the process of natural selection, *learning theory*, and probabilistic methods which helps dealing with uncertainty imprecision. Excepting those main principles, currently popular approaches include biologically inspired algorithms such as swarm intelligence and artificial immune systems, which can be seen as a part of *evolutionary computation, image processing, data mining, natural language processing, and artificial intelligence*, which tends to be confused with Computational Intelligence.

But although both Computational Intelligence (CI) and Artificial Intelligence (AI) seek similar goals, there's a clear distinction between them.

Computational Intelligence is thus a way of *performing like human beings*. Indeed, the characteristic of "intelligence" is usually attributed to humans. More recently, many products and items also claim to be "intelligent", an attribute which is directly linked to the reasoning and decision making.

Although Artificial Intelligence and Computational Intelligence seek a similar long-term goal: reach general intelligence, which is the intelligence of a machine that could perform any intellectual task that a human being can; there's a clear difference between them. According to Bezdek (1994), Computational Intelligence is a subset of Artificial Intelligence. There are two types of machine intelligence: the artificial one based on hard computing techniques and the computational one based on soft computing methods, which enable adaptation to many situations.

The main applications of Computational Intelligence include computer science, engineering, data analysis and bio-medicine.

Fuzzy logic

As explained before, fuzzy logic, one of CI's main principles, consists in *measurements and process modelling made for real life's complex processes* (Rouse, 2006). It can confront incompleteness, and most importantly ignorance of data in a process model, contrarily to Artificial Intelligence, which requires exact knowledge.

This technique tends to apply to a wide range of domains such as control, image processing and marketing based decision making. But it is also well introduced in the field of household appliances with washing machines, microwave ovens, etc. For example, the auto floor cleaner robot.

Fuzzy logic is mainly useful for approximate reasoning, and does not have learning abilities (Siddique,2013) a qualification much needed that human beings have. It enables them to improve themselves by *learning from their previous mistakes*.

Neural networks

This is why CI experts work on the development of artificial neural networks based on the biological ones, which can be defined by 3 main components: the *cell-body* which processes the information, *the axon*, which is a device enabling the signal conducting, and the *synapse,* which controls signals. Therefore, artificial neural networks are doted of distributed information processing systems enabling the process and the learning from experiential data. Working like human beings, fault tolerance is also one of the main assets of this principle (Stergiou et al 2015).

Concerning its applications, neural networks can be classified into five groups: data analysis and classification, associative memory, clustering generation of patterns and control all critical in modern marketing operations. Generally, this method aims to analyse and classify data, proceed to face and fraud detection, and most importantly deal with nonlinearities of a system in order to control it (Somers et al, 2009). Furthermore, neural networks techniques share with the fuzzy logic ones the advantage of enabling data clustering.

Evolutionary computation

Based on the process of natural selection firstly introduced by Charles Robert Darwin, the evolutionary computation consists in capitalizing on the strength of natural evolution to bring up new artificial evolutionary methodologies (De Jong, 2006) It also includes other areas such as evolution strategy, and evolutionary algorithms which are seen as problem solvers. Much of marketing effort is problem solving (who, what, why and where).

This principle's main applications cover areas such as optimization and multi-objective optimization, to which traditional mathematical one techniques aren't enough anymore to apply to a wide range of problems such as DNA Analysis, scheduling problems.

Learning theory

Still looking for a way of "reasoning" close to the humans' one, learning theory is one of the main approaches of CI. In psychology, learning is the process of bringing together cognitive, emotional and environmental effects and experiences to acquire, enhance or change knowledge, skills, values and world views (Ormrod, 1995; Illeris, 2004). Learning theories then helps understanding how these effects and experiences are processed, and then helps making predictions based on previous experience (Worrell, 2015). In customer insight reasoning is a key factor in understanding human behaviour, by analysis one can then model reasoning to make products and communication more relevant.

Probabilistic methods

Being one of the main elements of fuzzy logic, probabilistic methods firstly introduced by Paul Erdos and Joel Spencer (1974), aim to evaluate the outcomes of a Computation Intelligent system, mostly defined by randomness (Palit et al, 2006) Therefore, probabilistic methods bring out the possible solutions to a reasoning problem, based on prior knowledge.

3.4 Statistical

Marketers, specifically, are tapping into the power of automation, freeing themselves from the more mundane tasks so they can be more impactful. Automation solutions, such as artificial intelligence and machine learning, are inventing new efficiencies and helping marketers enhance their marketing efforts to focus on their most profitable customers as well as understand their business environments external and internal better. This delivers informed decision making and thus reduces risk and maximises marketing return on investment. Artificial Intelligence deals with building *systems that can learn from data*, instead of explicitly programmed instructions. Statistical Modelling is a subfield of mathematics which deals with finding *relationship between variables* to predict an outcome.

Statistical Relational Artificial Intelligence (StarAI) syndicates logical (or relational) AI and probabilistic (or statistical) AI are much in use by marketing tems. Relational AI contracts very successfully with *complex domains* involving many and even a varying number of objects connected by complex relationships, for example numerous customer touch points, while statistical AI manages thoroughly the uncertainty that originates from imperfect and strident descriptions of the domains.

Both fields achieved significant successes over the last thirty years. Relational AI positioned the basis of *knowledge representation* and has significantly widened the application domain of data mining especially in bio- and chemo-informatics. It now signifies some of the best examples of scientific discovery by AI systems in research literature. Statistical AI, in particular the use of *probabilistic graphical models*, has revolutionized AI in marketing, by manipulating probabilistic independencies.

The independencies stipulated in such models are natural, and provide arrangement that enables competent reasoning and learning, and allow one to model complex domains.

Many AI glitches arising in a wide variety of fields such as machine learning, diagnosis, network communication, computational biology, computer vision, and robotics have been sophisticatedly encoded and cracked using probabilistic graphical models.

However, both fields evolved essentially independently until about fifteen years ago, when the potential originating from their mixture started to emerge in research. Statistical Relational Learning (SRL) was proposed for *exploiting relational descriptions in statistical machine learning methods* from the field of graphical models. Languages, such as Markov Logic Networks, Relational Dependency Networks, PRISM, Probabilistic Relational Models were created. ProbLog permit the *user to reason and learn with models* that explain complex and uncertain relationships among domain entities.

Meanwhile, the scope of SRL was meaningfully advanced in StarAI to cover all forms of reasoning and models of AI. StarAI is at the present time an ample area including many and varied methods. One major example is given by neural-symbolic paradigms, that address the long-standing problem of combining symbolic and connectionist approaches for knowledge representation, learning and reasoning, with new impulse coming from the area of deep learning.

3.5 Integrating the approaches

Marketing strategy is the means by which the marketing objectives will be achieved. In recent years, the use of computer-based information systems in the field of strategic marketing has been increasingly highlighted. Researchers have attempted to develop Decision Support Systems (DSS) to support strategic marketing decisions. Recently, artificial neural networks (ANNs) have also been harnessed to aid the process of strategic marketing decisions. More recently, efforts have been made to build hybrid systems to assist marketing strategy formulation. A framework for a hybrid intelligent system in support of marketing strategy development has been proposed by (Li et al, 2009) with five objectives: to help strategic analysis; to couple strategic analysis with managers input; to integrate the strengths of diverse support techniques and technologies; to combine the benefits of different strategic analysis models; and to help strategic thinking. Most systems fail to provide even *moderate* help for the following five types of requirements: help couple strategic analysis with managerial judgement; provide strategic analysis assistance; help strategic thinking; cope with uncertainty and fuzziness; and help understand the factors that affect marketing strategy development.

Each organization needs are typically different, and therefore the application of AI to a marketing system needs to appreciate 1. Structure 2. Depth of knowledge 3. Availability of data. The *decision environment* must consider 1.Time constraints 2. Market dynamics and 3.Organization culture.

In many marketing led organizations the integration of AI systems requires an umbrella view of the enterprise to ensure that there is integration of tasks from raw materials, production, warehousing, distribution, sales, finance, retail (on and off line), and the customer needs and wants including after sales service.

Revision

- Outline in 100 words your understanding of cybernetics and brain simulation
- Debate the differences between Symbolic and Sub Symbolic approaches in AI
- Review the role of statistics in marketing today
- In approaches what is the definition of the term 'scruffy'

4 Tools

Introduction

In the course of 6 decades of research, AI has developed a large number of tools to solve the most difficult problems in computer science. A few of the most general of these methods are discussed in this chapter.

Chapter Learning Outcomes

⬚ AI capability in search and optimization.

⬚ Understanding of terminology such as logic, probabilistic methods, classifiers.

⬚ An appreciation of neural networks.

⬚ Concepts of control theory and evaluation.

⬚ Having successfully completed the module, you will be able to:

⬚ 1. Critically assess the tools of (AI) basics in marketing.

⬚ 2. Assess the applications of tools of (AI) in today's world.

⬚ Having completed the module, you will be able to:

⬚ 1. Understand the variety of (AI) tools and their uses.

• 2. Be able to explain the principal goals of each in (AI).

Critical thinking

Having successfully completed this topic, you will be able to:1. Critically evaluate the variety of tools used in (AI) .2. Understand and debate the tool elements of (AI) to management.

OBJECTIVES

Many problems in AI can be solved in theory by intelligently searching through many possible solutions, the tools we use assist us in this process, building insight and understanding that forms better marketing decisions.

4.1 Search and optimization

Fifteen years ago, if you "searched" an e Commerce store to find a product, you'd be unlikely to find the result you had in mind unless you knew its name or title exactly. Today's "search" is after much smarter, and the improved capacity not only help you find information on Google, but it helps you find the right products on Amazon or Target.com, the right movies on Netflix, and more. Fifteen years ago, typing "men's flip flops" at Nike.com may not have yielded the results you were looking for. Today, it very much does.

Search improvement for e-Commerce and marketing has improved due to the same underlying factors that have improved "search" at large, including:

- Technologies like Elasticsearch are now comparatively mainstream, allowing any small e Commerce stores to have search that goes past simply matching keywords.

- Data-as-a-Service companies (like Indix, among others) make it easier than ever to draw from search data from other larger sources, informing your own online product search without having to train your own search models from scratch.

- Other improvements, such as: Software to detect common misspellings is now more commonplace and can calibrate for misspellings by context (IE: "Season cikets" can be understood to mean "season tickets", while "cikets" alone might be more difficult to discern without context).

Google has done good work of simplifying and explaining some of their own search improvements and developments in their "Inside Search" writings. In the future, consumers can expect more and more e Commerce sites to follow in the footsteps of Google and others in implementing *autosuggest, suggested corrections, "advanced" search options, and other such improvements*. Web sites invest significant resources in trying to *influence their visibility* among online search results. In addition to paying for sponsored links, they invest in methods known as search engine optimization (SEO) that improve the ranking of a site among the search results without improving its quality. A search engine is a website that provides searching results as a service to its visitors: they enter queries (search phrases) into a search form and the SE returns a k number of results for this query displaying them in an ordered list. This list - often referred to as the organic list - contains a number of links to other websites in the order of the relevance of their content for the given search phrase.

In addition to the organic results, the search engine displays sponsored links to generate revenue. Sponsored links are characteristically displayed above and rightward of the organic results for a search query and look similar to the search results but are clearly marked as advertisement. These links are sold to advertisers through an auction in which they submit bids and are awarded different positions on the page.

The outcome of the auction is usually determined by the order of the bids - corrected for the differences in the likelihood that consumers click on a particular link - and each advertiser pays the next highest (corrected) bid. We assume that there is a second price auction to determine the allocation of the sponsored link and the highest bidder receives the link.

4.2 Logic

A Knowledge Based Agent are Agents That Reason Logically
The central component of a knowledge-based agent is its knowledge base; a knowledge base is a set of representations of facts about the world. The knowledge level or epistemological level is the most abstract. If TELL and ASK work correctly, then most of the time we can work at the knowledge level and not worry about lower levels. The logical level is the level at which the *knowledge is encoded into sentences.* The implementation level is the level that runs on the mediator architecture. By a complex set of pointers connecting machine addresses corresponding to the individual symbols.
What is Inference in computers?
- Logics : consists of syntax, Symantec's and proof theory.
- Propositional logic, symbols represent whole propositions (facts).
- Ontological commitments have to do with the nature of reality and Temporal logic assumes that the world is ordered by a set of time points or intervals and includes built-in mechanisms for reasoning about time.
- Fuzzy logic can have degrees of belief in a sentence, and also allow degrees of truth: a fact need not be true or false in the world but can be true to a certain degree.
- First-order logic makes a stronger set of ontological commitments, the main one is that the world consists of objects, that is, things with individual identities and properties that distinguish them from other objects.
Among these objects, various relations hold. Some of these relations are functions, relations in which there is only one "value" for a given "input. "Examples of objects, properties, relations, and functions are
- *Objects*: people, houses, numbers, theories, Ronald McDonald, colours, baseball games, wars, centuries . . .
- *Relations*: brother of, bigger than, inside, part of, has colour, occurred after, owns .
- *Properties*: red, round, bogus, prime, multi-storied.
- *Functions*: father of, best friend, third inning of, one more than .

Higher-order logic allows us to calculate over relations and functions as well as over objects. For example, in higher-order logic we, can say that two objects are equal if and only if all properties applied to them are equivalent: Vx, y (x = y) & (Vp p(x) O p(y)) .(V stands "for every").The simplest possible kind of agent has rules directly connecting perceptions to actions. These rules resemble reflexes or instincts.

For example, if the agent sees a glitter, it should do a grab in order to pick up the gold.

There are limitations of simple reflex agents for example consider climb problem: A pure reflex agent cannot know for sure when to climb, because neither having the goal nor being in the start is part of the percept; they are things the agent knows by forming a representation of the world.
Reflex agents are also unable to avoid infinite loops. The presence of an explicit goal allows the agent to work out a sequence of actions that will achieve the goal.
There are at least three ways to find such a sequence
1.*Inference*: It is not hard to write axioms that will allow us to ASK the KB for a sequence of actions that is guaranteed to achieve the goal safely.
2. *Search*: We can use a best-first search procedure to find a path to the goal.
3. *Planning*: This involves the use of special-purpose reasoning systems designed to reason about actions.
The knowledge engineer must understand enough about the domain in question to represent the important objects and relationships, representation language, implementation of the inference procedure.
Let us consider Knowledge engineering versus programming. Steps in development of a knowledge base to support marketing are:
1) Decide what to talk about.
2) Decide on a vocabulary of predicates, functions, and constants.
3) Encode general knowledge about the domain.
4) Encode a description of the specific problem instance.
5) Pose queries to the inference procedure and get answers.

A general-purpose ontology should be applicable in more or less any special-purpose domain (with the addition of domain-specific axioms).) In any sufficiently demanding domain, different areas of knowledge must be unified because reasoning and problem solving may involve several areas simultaneously.
There are Different Logical Reasoning Systems the four main categories of logic systems are:
1.*Theorem provers* and logic programming languages
2. *Production systems*
3. Frame systems and semantic networks
4. *Description* logic systems.

With Table-based indexing the keys to the table will be predicate symbols, and the value stored under each key will have four components:
1. A list of positive literals, for that predicate symbol.
2. A list of negative literals.
3. A list of sentences in which the predicate is in the conclusion.
4. A list of sentences in which the predicate is in the premise.

Tree-based indexing is one form of combined indexing, in that it essentially makes a combined key out of the sequence of predicate and argument symbols in the query.

The cross-indexing strategy indexes entries in several places, and when faced with a query *chooses the most promising place for retrieval*. Logic programming tries to extend these advantages to all programming tasks.

Any computation can be viewed as a process of making explicit the consequences of choosing a particular program for a particular machine and providing particular inputs Algorithm = Logic + Control.

In Description Logics the principal inference tasks are:

1. *Sub Sumption* : checking if one category is a subset of another based on their definitions.
2. *classification* : checking if an object belongs to a category.

4.3 Probabilistic methods for uncertain reasoning

The history of probabilistic models of thought is, in a sense, as old as probability theory itself. Probability theory has forever had a *dual aspect*, serving both as a *normative* theory for 'correct' reasoning about chance events, but also as a *descriptive* theory of how individuals' reason about uncertainty – as providing an analysis.

The cognitive sciences belief is the brain as a data processor; and information processing typically involves implying new information from information that has been originated from the senses, from linguistic input, or from memory.

This progression of inference from old to new is seen as separate to pure mathematics, typically uncertain. Probability theory is, in principle, is a *calculus for uncertain inference*, at least rendering to the *subjective interpretation of probability*. Thus, probabilistic methods have theoretically broad application to unclear inferences from sensory input to environmental layout; from speech signal to semantic interpretation; from goals to motor output; or from observations and experiments to symmetries in nature.

Probability has, nevertheless, only lately become a major emphasis of consideration in the cognitive sciences. One reason is that the field has often focussed on *computational architecture* (e.g. symbolic rule-based processing vs. connectionist networks), rather than the *character of the inferences, probabilistic* or otherwise, executed in that architecture.

A second reason is that recognised approaches to uncertain reasoning in psychology and artificial intelligence have frequently been studied using *non-probabilistic methods*, such as default logics, non-monotonic logics, or different heuristic techniques.

A third reason is that probabilistic methods have classically been viewed as too constrained in scope to be relevant to cognitive processes described over linguistic structural similes, logical representations, and networks of interconnected processing units.

Complicated probabilistic models can be connected to cognitive processes in a variety of ways.

This diversity can advantageously understood in terms of Marr's (1982) celebrated distinction between three levels of computational explanation:
the *computational* level, which specifies the nature of the cognitive puzzle being solved, the information involved in solving it, and the logic by which it can be solved; the *algorithmic* level, which stipulates the representations and processes by which solutions to the problem are computed; and the *implementational* level, which specifies how these *depictions and processes are realized in neural terms.*
Sophisticated probabilistic models are obtaining ever more wide application across the cognitive and brain sciences. A great deal of cognition is concerned with dealing, highly effectively, with spectacularly complex problems of probabilistic inference. I suggest that probabilistic methods are expected to be increasingly important theoretical tools for understanding cognition in marketing processes involving markets and consumers.

4.4 Classifiers and statistical learning methods

Statistical learning refers to a set of tools for *modelling and understanding complex datasets.* It is a recently developed area in statistics, and blends with parallel developments in computer science, and in particular machine learning. The field encompasses many methods such as the *lasso and sparse regression, classification and regression trees, and boosting and support vector machines.* With the explosion of "Big Data" problems statistical learning has become a very hot field in many scientific areas as well as marketing, finance and other business disciplines.

Classification problems occur often, perhaps even more so than regression problems. Some examples include:

1. A person arrives at the emergency room with a set of symptoms that could possibly be attributed to one of three medical conditions. Which of the three conditions does the individual have?
2. An online banking service must be able to determine whether or not a transaction being performed on the site is fraudulent, on the basis of the user's IP address, past transaction history, and so forth.
3. On the basis of DNA sequence data for a number of patients with and without a given disease, a biologist would like to figure out which DNA mutations are deleterious (disease-causing) and which are not.

Just as in the regression setting, in the classification setting we have a set of training observations that we can use to build a *classifier.* We want our classifier to perform well not only on the training data, but also on test observations that were not used to train the classifier.

The concept of classification using the simulated Default data set is interested in example in predicting whether an individual will default on his or her credit card payment, on the basis of annual income and monthly credit card balance. We can plot annual income and monthly credit card balance for a subset of 10, 000 individuals.

The left-hand panel can display individuals who defaulted in a given month in orange, and those who did not in blue. (The overall default rate is about 3%, so one could plot only a fraction of the individuals who did not default.) It appears that individuals who defaulted tended to have higher credit card balances than those who did not. In the right panel two pairs of boxplots could be used. The first to show the distribution of balance split by the binary default variable; the second is a similar plot for income.

In classification we learn how to build a model to predict default (Y) for any given value of balance (X and income (X). Since Y is not quantitative, the simple linear regression model is not appropriate.

Classification is the problem of identifying to which of a set of categories (sub-populations) a new observation belongs, on the basis of a training set of data containing observations (or instances) whose category membership is known. An example would be assigning a given email into "spam" or "non-spam" classes or assigning a diagnosis to a given patient as described by observed characteristics of the patient (gender, blood pressure, presence or absence of certain symptoms, etc.). Classification is an example of *pattern recognition.*

In the terminology of machine learning Alpaydin (2010) classification is considered an instance of supervised learning, i.e. learning where a training set of correctly identified observations is available. The corresponding unsupervised procedure is known as clustering, and involves grouping data into categories based on some measure of inherent similarity or distance.

Often, the individual observations are analysed into a set of quantifiable properties, known variously as explanatory variables or *features.* These properties may variously be categorical (e.g. "A", "B", "AB" or "O", for blood type), ordinal (e.g. "large", "medium" or "small"), integer-valued (e.g. the number of occurrences of a particular word in an email) or real-valued (e.g. a measurement).

Other classifiers work by comparing observations to previous observations by means of a similarity or distance function. Classification and clustering are examples of the more general problem of pattern recognition, which is the assignment of some sort of *output value to a given input value.* Other examples are regression, which assigns a real-valued output to each input; sequence labelling, which assigns a class to each member of a sequence of values (for example, part of speech tagging, which assigns a part of speech to each word in an input sentence); parsing, which assigns a parse tree to an input sentence, describing the structure of the sentence; etc.

A common subclass of classification is probabilistic classification. Algorithms of this nature use *statistical inference* to find the best class for a given instance. Unlike other algorithms, which simply output a "best" class, probabilistic algorithms output a probability of the instance being a member of each of the possible classes. The best class is normally then selected as the one with the highest probability. However, such an algorithm has numerous advantages over non-probabilistic classifiers:

- It can output a confidence value associated with its choice (in general, a classifier that can do this is known as a *confidence-weighted classifier*).
- Correspondingly, it can *abstain* when its confidence of choosing any particular output is too low.
- Because of the probabilities which are generated, probabilistic classifiers can be more effectively incorporated into larger machine-learning tasks, in a way that partially or completely avoids the problem of *error propagation*.

Statistical models are used by data technologists for *prediction and inference*. With the rapid developments in internet technology, genomics, financial risk modelling, and other high-tech industries, rely increasingly more on data analysis and statistical models to exploit the vast amounts of data at their fingertips. The tools useful for tackling modern-day data analysis problems are varied. Many of these are essential building blocks, but we also include techniques at the cutting-edge of technology for handling big-data problems. From the vast array of tools available, I have selected what I consider are the most relevant and exciting. The list of topics includes (Friedman, Springer-Verlag, 2009).

- Linear methods: regression, logistic regression (binary and multiclass), Cox model.
- Bootstrap, cross-validation, and permutation methods.
- Regularized linear models: ridge, lasso, elastic net. Post-selection inference. Glmnet package in R, and other software.
- Trees, random forests, and boosting.
- Unsupervised methods: clustering (prototype, hierarchical, spectral), principal components and other low-rank methods, sparse decompositions.
- Support-vector machines and kernel methods.
- Deep learning and neural networks.

The goals of learning are *understanding and prediction*. Learning falls into many categories, including supervised learning, unsupervised learning, online learning, and reinforcement learning. From the perspective of statistical learning theory, supervised learning is best understood. Supervised learning involves learning from a training set of data. Every point in the training is an input-output pair, where the input maps to an output. The learning problem consists of inferring the function that maps between the input and the output, such that the learned function can be used to predict output from future input.

Depending on the type of output, supervised learning problems are either problems of *regression or problems of classification*.

If the output takes a continuous range of values, it is a regression problem. Classification problems are those for which the output will be an element from a discrete set of labels. Classification is very common for machine learning applications. In facial recognition, for instance, *a picture of a person's face would be the input, and the output label would be that person's name*. The input would be represented by a large multidimensional vector whose elements represent pixels in the picture.

After learning a function based on the training set data, that function is validated on a test set of data, data that did not appear in the training set.

4.5 Neural networks

Little (1979) emphasized the importance of supporting marketing managers with high-quality information. In order to compete, information is a fundamental instrument. With the provision of good information, the MDSS seeks to help make improved, informed, timelier and more effective marketing decisions.

The advantages of effective and timely decisions are not always perceptible, but these are the main reasons for the existence of an MDSS. Sales are influenced by many stimuli, such as price, product, promotion and place (also well known as the 4-Ps); hence, they are extremely problematic to forecast. Neural Network technology can be applied in many areas especially when the problem domain encompasses *classification, recognition and prediction*. A neural network is an assortment of *organised modest processing elements*. Every connection in a neural network has a weight ascribed to it. The back-propagation algorithm has advanced as one of the most widely used learning processes for multi-layer networks. It is selected for use because of its suitability for applications, which *involve predictions*. The typical back propagation neural network generally has an *enter layer, some hidden layers and an output layer*. The nodes in the network are attached in a feed forward behaviour, from the input layer to the output layer. The influences of connections are given original values. The error between the projected output value and the actual value is back proliferated through the network to update weights. This is an administered learning procedure that tries to minimize the error between the *desired and the predicted yields*. The relationship can be found through a cluster of mappings with constant time interval. The key feature of this kind of network is that it *is able to map an extracted pattern from the input stimuli to the output; hence, it is for classification*. In marketing planning the ability to see patterns in data although historical in nature allow an ability to predict the future and run scenarios with different variables. The speed and accuracy of such data analysis are major benefits.

This is because the nodes in the hidden layers are able to *learn to react to exclusivity* in the input layer. This uniqueness is actually the *correlation activities of the input layer nodes* (Marren etal, 1990). These joins can affect each other; e.g., the first node can affect or be correlated to the last node. Such relationships between the input nodes provide a foundation for more abstract representation of the input information in the next higher layer. As the network are *exercised* under supervision with different examples provided, it acquires the aptitude to *generalize*.

This ability is aimed into the hidden layer nodes during the training so that when earlier unseen patterns are presented, the network is indisputably able to identify and classify that pattern accordingly. In order for a feed forward network to function productively, its ability to diagnose features amongst the input nodes must be guaranteed. This is where the hidden nodes must be proficient to diagnose the general features of the input pattern. Such features must be suitably general so that the network is not led into over fitting. Considering the multi-faceted demands of the marketing domain and the myriad sets of available marketing data, it can be very problematic to draw anything relevant from the available data because of the unconnected and non-linearity of much of marketing data as it is usually stored in silos.

A study was carried out by Proctor (1992) on the role of neural networks in marketing. The strength of a neural network is its aptitude to obtain the *relationships of non-linearly dependent variables*. This was further emphasized by Dutta *et al.* (1997), who incorporated neural networks into a Decision Support System (DSS). In a separate work, Venugopal and Baets (1994) also proposed using neural networks in *retail sales forecasting, direct marketing and target marketing*. Compared with other traditional statistical methods, neural networks necessitate only minimum knowledge to the problem's assembly (Hill & Ramus,1994). No prior knowledge of the statistical distribution of the data is required because the network acquires an internal relationship between the variables. All these make neural networks particularly suitable to complex classification problems in which the mapping justification is either fuzzy, inconsistent, or completely unknown. Most business and marketing applications can be considered to be categorized under fuzzy classifications (Schocken & Arivav,1994), and this is the area that neural networks can be of sound service. When used for fuzzy classification, neural networks can be said to be able to see through " clutter and noise".

As stated by T. Hill (1994), there are three intrinsic limitations for regression MDSS models. First, they are based on linear combinations of decision variables only; second, human understanding is fundamental to specify the model or data trans-formations; third, there are no learning facilities although new situations arise, and the results need to be appraised frequently. Neural Networks do not suffer from the limitations of regression models and have been proven to be able to learn functional relationships from input variables to predict results (Yao etal, 1997).

4.6 Deep feedforward neural networks

A feedforward neural network is an artificial neural network wherein connections between the 'units' *do not form a cycle*. As such, it is dissimilar from recurrent neural networks.

The feedforward neural network was the first and simplest type of artificial neural network devised. In this network, *the information moves in only one direction, forward, from the input nodes, through the hidden nodes (if any) and to the output nodes*. There are no cycles or loops in the network (Zell,1994).

The simplest kind of neural network is a *single-layer perceptron* network, which contains of a single layer of output nodes; the inputs are supported directly to the outputs via a series of weights. In this way it can be assumed the easiest kind of feed-forward network. Multi-layer networks use a diversity of learning techniques, the most general being back-propagation. At this point, the output values are contrasted with the correct answer to compute the value of some predefined error-function. By different practices, the error is then fed back during the network. Employing this information, the algorithm regulates the weights of each connection in order to reduce the value of the error function by some minor amount. After repeating this process for a sufficiently large number of training cycles, the network will generally unite to some state where the error of the calculations is small (Roman etal, 2007).

Suppose we have a network of perceptron's that we'd like to use to learn to solve some problem.

For example, the inputs to the network might be the raw pixel data from a scanned, handwritten image of a digit. And we would like the system to learn weights and biases so that the harvest from the network appropriately classifies the digit. To see how learning might work, suppose we make a small change in some weight (or bias) in the network. What we would like for this small change in weight, to cause only a small corresponding change in the output from the network.

This property will make learning possible. But as it occurs, a slight change in weights guides to a large change in output. So, using a neuron model like *sigmoid* can solve this issue. Given this description of neural networks and how they work, what real world applications are they suited for? Neural networks have comprehensive application to real world business problems. In fact, they have already been successfully applied in many industries.

Since neural networks are unrivaled at recognizing patterns or trends in data, they are well suited for prediction or forecasting needs in marketing including:

- sales forecasting
- industrial process control
- customer research
- data validation
- risk management
- target marketing

But to give you some more precise examples; ANN are also used in the following specific templates: recognition of speakers in communications; diagnosis; recovery of telecommunications from faulty software; interpretation of multi meaning Chinese words; undersea mine detection; texture analysis; three-dimensional object recognition; hand-written word recognition; and facial recognition.

4.7 Deep recurrent neural networks

Recurrent Neural Networks (RNNs), and specifically a variant with Long Short- Term Memory (LSTM), are enjoying renewed interest as a result of successful applications in a wide range of machine learning problems that involve *sequential data*. However, while LSTMs provide results in practice.

Recurrent Neural Networks, and specifically a variant with Long Short-Term Memory (LSTM) Hochreiter & Schmidhuber (1997), have recently emerged as an effective model in a wide variety of applications that involve sequential data. These include language modelling Mikolov et al. (2010), handwriting recognition and generation Graves (2013), machine translation Sutskever et al. (2014); Bahdanau et al. (2014), speech recognition Graves et al. (2013), video analysis Donahue et al. (2015) and image captioning Vinyals et al. (2015); Karpathy & Fei-Fei (2015).

Recurrent Neural Networks (RNNs) have a long history of applications in various *sequence learning tasks* Werbos (1988); Schmidhuber (2015); Rumelhart et al. (1985). Despite their early successes, the difficulty of training simple recurrent networks Bengio et al. (1994); Pascanu et al. (2012) has encouraged various proposals for improvements to their basic architecture.

Among the most successful variants are the Long Short-Term Memory networks Hochreiter & Schmidhuber (1997), which can in principle store and retrieve information over long time periods with explicit gating mechanisms and a built-in constant error carousel.

An artificial neural network (ANN), often just called a "neural network" (NN), is a mathematical model or computational model based on biological neural networks, in other words, is an *emulation of biological neural system.* It consists of an interconnected group of artificial neurons and processes information using a connectionist approach to computation. In the majority cases an ANN is an adaptive system that changes its structure based on external or internal information that flows through the network during the learning phase. The feedforward neural network was the first and perhaps simplest type of artificial neural network devised. In this network, the information moves in only one direction, forward, from the input nodes, through the hidden nodes (if any) and to the output nodes. There are no cycles or loops in the network. A neural network has to be configured such that the application of a set of inputs produces (either 'direct' or via a relaxation process) the desired set of outputs (Fausett,1994). Various methods to set the strengths of the connections exist. One way is to set the *weights explicitly*, using a priori knowledge. Another way is to 'train' the neural network by feeding it teaching patterns and letting it change its weights according to some learning rule. In more practical marketing terms neural networks are non-linear statistical data modelling tools. They can be used to *model complex relationships* between inputs and outputs or to *find patterns in data.* Using neural networks as a tool, data warehousing firms are harvesting information from datasets in the process known as data mining. The difference between these data warehouses and ordinary databases is that there is actual anipulation and cross-fertilization of the data helping users makes more informed decisions. *Neural networks essentially comprise three pieces: the architecture or model; the learning algorithm; and the activation functions* (Haykin,1999).

Neural networks are programmed or "trained" to store, recognize, and associatively retrieve patterns or database entries; to solve combinatorial optimization problems; to filter noise from measurement data; to control ill-defined problems. In summary, to estimate sampled functions when we do not know the form of the functions. It is precisely these two abilities (pattern recognition and function estimation) which make artificial neural networks (ANN) so prevalent a utility in data mining.

ADVANTAGES OF NEURAL NETWORKS:

- High Accuracy: Neural networks are able to approximate complex non-linear mappings.
- Noise Tolerance: Neural networks are very flexible with respect to incomplete, missing and noisy data.
- Independence from prior assumptions: Neural networks do not make a priori assumptions about the distribution of the data, or the form of interactions between factors.
- Ease of maintenance: Neural networks can be updated with fresh data, making them useful for dynamic environments.
- Neural networks can be implemented in parallel hardware.
- When an element of the neural network fails, it can continue without any problem by their parallel nature.

In my marketing experience (NN) are excellent in:

- Classification of consumer spending patterns
- New product analysis
- Identification of customer characteristics
- Sales forecasting

4.8 Control theory

In looking to comprehend individual behaviour, believers of Perceptual Control Theory (PCT) change the emphasis from an actor's obvious events—for example, the visible results of decision-making—to the actor's insights. The theory begins with the supposition that actors seek to *control their perceptions*, in other words, to keep them quite constant within the range of their opportunities.

Positioning it more correctly, PCT theorists theorise that 'control' is a procedure by which individuals maintain a controlled variable stable relative to an internally held orientation state through actions that oppose the effects of disturbances that might affect their perceptions of that variable (Powers 2004; Powers 2005; Powers 2008; McClelland 2004; McClelland and Fararo 2006).

Monitoring performance provides one informational means to help "planned marketing activities produce desired results", as stated by Jaworski (1988) in his definition of marketing control. Control theory supposes that management has a strategy and a recognized set of intermediary stages (plans) with which actual performance can be contrasted.

Metrics selection for example is a fundamentally rational process by which "marketing managers can learn to improve performance by altering the utility levels associated with marketing control variables" (Fraser and Hite 1988, p.97).

Merchant (1998) describes control as being both *reactive* (like a cybernetic feedback loop) and *proactive* in expecting problems before they can harm market performance: "Controls, then, include all the devices managers use to ensure that the behaviours and decisions of people in the organization are consistent with the organization's objectives and strategies." This enlarges the concept in a stimulating method and implies that the costs of control, including the behavioural effects, need to be *balanced against the advantages*. At the equivalent period, it does not essentially change the theory on control. Kotler (2003) lists four types of marketing controls (*annual-plan, profitability, efficiency and strategic*). These characterize whether the enterprise is selecting the right goals (strategic), whether they are being achieved (effectiveness or annual plan), where the company is making or losing money (profitability) and the return on each marketing expenditure (efficiency). Therefore, *control theory* adopts that management creates goals of whatever type. Having completed the metrics needed to compare goals with performance is defined.

4.9 Languages

Artificial intelligence researchers have developed several specialized programming languages for artificial intelligence.

- AIML (meaning "Artificial Intelligence Mark-up Language") is an XML dialect for use with A.L.I.C.E.-type chatterbots.
- IPL was the first language advanced for artificial intelligence. It includes features intended to support programs that could perform general problem solving, such as lists, associations, schemas (frames), dynamic memory allocation, data types, recursion, associative retrieval, functions as arguments, generators (streams), and cooperative multitasking.
- Lisp is a practical mathematical notation for computer programs based on lambda calculus. Linked lists are one of the Lisp language's major data structures, and Lisp source code is itself made up of lists. As a result, Lisp programs can manipulate source code as a data structure, giving rise to the macro systems that allow programmers to create new syntax or even new domain-specific programming languages embedded in Lisp.

- There are many dialects of Lisp in use today, among which are Common Lisp, Scheme, and Clojure.
- Smalltalk has been used extensively for simulations, neural networks, machine learning and genetic algorithms. It implements the clearest and most well-designed form of object-oriented programming using message passing.
- Prolog is a declarative language where programs are expressed in terms of relations, and execution occurs by running *queries* over these relations.
- Prolog is particularly useful for symbolic reasoning, database and language parsing applications. Prolog is widely used in AI today.
- STRIPS is a language for expressing automated planning problem instances. It expresses an initial state, the goal states, and a set of actions. For each action preconditions (what must be established before the action is performed) and post conditions (what is established after the action is performed) are specified.
- Planner is a hybrid between procedural and logical languages. It gives a procedural interpretation to logical sentences where implications are interpreted with pattern-directed inference.
- POP-11 is a reflective, incrementally compiled programming language with many of the features of an interpreted language. It is the core language of the Poplog programming environment developed originally by the University of Sussex, and recently in the School of Computer Science at the University of Birmingham which hosts the Poplog website, It is often used to introduce symbolic programming techniques to programmers of more conventional languages like Pascal, who find POP syntax more familiar than that of Lisp. One of POP-11's features is that it supports first-class functions.
- Python is widely used for artificial intelligence, with packages for a number of applications including General AI, Machine Learning, Natural Language Processing and Neural Networks. Companies like Narrative Science use Python to create an artificial intelligence for Narrative Language Processing.
- Haskell is also a very good programming language for AI. Lazy evaluation and the list and LogicT monads make it easy to express non-deterministic algorithms, which is often the case. Infinite data structures are great for search trees. The language's features enable a compositional way of expressing the algorithms. The only drawback is that working with graphs is a bit harder at first because of purity.
- Wolfram Language includes a wide range of integrated machine learning capabilities, from highly automated functions like Predict and Classify to functions based on specific methods and diagnostics. The functions work on many types of data, including numerical, categorical, time series, textual, and image.
- C++ (2011 onwards)
- MATLAB
- Perl

4.10 Evaluating progress

Artificial intelligence and machine learning are already transforming the technological landscape. From digital assistants to image-recognition software to self-driving cars, what was once the material of science fiction is now developing a reality. But what exactly does it mean for marketing and advertising executives? It could get us closer to one of advertising's most-sought goals: *relevance at scale and also faster and more effective marketing action.*

Beforehand, we are going to see changes to the way marketers do business. Technological developments have always created new opportunities for storytelling and marketing.

Just as the arrival of TV brought a period of truly mass advertising and reach, and the internet and mobile brought a new level of aiming and framework. AI will change *how people interact with information, technology, brands, and services.*

AI and machine learning could get us closer to of one of advertising's most-sought goals: relevance at scale.

 What does this mean for marketers? The further integration of technology into the physical world creates new consumer interactions that are even more simple and instantaneous. Put another way, high consumer expectations will be higher than ever. This will pose a challenge for brands—and countless prospects. A big part of the opportunity for marketers is how AI will help us fully realize personalization—and relevance—at scale. With platforms like Search and YouTube reaching billions of people every day, digital ad platforms finally can attain communication at inordinate scale.

This scale, combined with customization possible through AI, means marketers soon be able to tailor campaigns to consumer intent 'in the moment'. It will be like having a million planners in your pocket.

We are moving closer to a point where campaigns and customer interactions can be made more relevant end-to-end—from planning to creative messaging to media targeting to the retail experience. Marketers will be able to consider all the indicators we have at the customer level, so we can consider not only things like a consumer's colour and tone preferences, but also purchase history and contextual relevance. And all of this will be optimized *on the fly in real time.*

So how can AI help improve what you're doing today in your marketing efforts? The launch of the Pixel phone last year is a good example of how Google is starting. A big part of their strategy for launch, was *experimenting with machine learning* to help us reach and engage our target audience.

Google turned to a new DoubleClick tool called <u>Custom Algorithm</u> that uses machine learning to enlarge the number of viewable impressions bought on premium placements. By making intelligence of historical data, it increases the likelihood that ads are supplied to the most relevant audience. The results for Pixel were impressive. When compared to other campaigns that did not use the tool, impressions on premium inventory more than tripled and viewable CPM fell 34%.

Optimization driven by machine learning presents opportunities well beyond media targeting, of course. Instacart has used TensorFlow open-source machine-learning platform, to build a machine-learning model to define its shoppers and could follow them to select items at a store. In a different example, brands like Coca-Cola are using AI to reinvent how consumers engage with their products through their smartphones.

The Walt Disney Co. is using language processing to trigger an audio soundtrack when you're reading a story aloud to your child. We also have to ask how AI and machine learning will spark new ideas and push the boundaries of creativity and data usage. With new tools, what will makers, artists, and musicians design? And how will that affect the marketing world we work in? New forms of creativity will provide new ways of telling brand stories, and new media platforms as well.

Let us now list some other AI marketing applications:

- Behavioural targeting
- Collect – Reason and Act
- Machine learning
- Data mining
- CRM and CEM applications
- Automated planning and Scheduling
- Computer Vision software
- Face and Voice Recognition
- Concept mining
- Document capture and analysis
- Pattern classification
- Forecasting and scenario modelling
- Expert System
- Distribution automation
- Social computing

AI and machine learning are already helping to solve problems marketers face. Undoubtedly, there will be marketing and advertising solutions—and many new opportunities—we haven't even thought of yet.

Revision

- Discuss the concepts of search and optimisation, use examples
- In AI, what is meant by 'Neural Networks', 50 words please
- In 100 words explain in your own words ' control theory
- In 50 words explain 'Logic" in AI.

5 Applications

Introduction

Modern artificial intelligence techniques are pervasive and are too numerous to list, however high-profile examples of AI include autonomous vehicles (such as drones and self-driving cars), medical diagnosis, creating art (such as poetry), proving mathematical theorems, playing games (such as Chess or Go), search engines (such as Google search), online assistants (such as Siri), image recognition in photographs, spam filtering, prediction of judicial decision (Aletras, 2016) and targeting online advertisements, data collection and analysis.

Chapter Learning Outcomes

⬚ An appreciation of the range of AI applications.

⬚ An understanding of AI use in various industries.

⬚ Review of how AI has become an enabler.

⬚ The flexibility of AI.

⬚ Having successfully completed the module, you will be able to:

⬚ 1. Critically assess the applications of (AI) basics in marketing.

⬚ 2. Assess the applications of tools of (AI) in today's world.

⬚ Having completed the module, you will be able to:

⬚ 1. Understand the variety of (AI) applications and their uses.

• 2. Be able to explain the principal goals of each in (AI).

Critical thinking

Having successfully completed this topic, you will be able to:1. Critically evaluate the variety of applications used in (AI) .2. Understand and debate the elements of (AI) to management.

OBJECTIVES

To provide a picture of AI uses in industry and show the benefits of AI in solving problems, completing tasks with speed and accuracy. AI is flexible and malleable making its use limitless.

5.1 Competitions and prizes

There are a number of competitions and prizes to promote research in artificial intelligence. The main areas promoted are: general machine intelligence, conversational behaviour, data-mining, robotic cars, robot soccer and games. Most competitions provide awards including cash for the winners, some in the games world only offer the merit of winning. Here are some examples:

- The World Computer Chess Championship
- The Ing Prize was a substantial money prize attached to the World Computer Go Congress.
- The AAAI General Game Playing
- The General Video Game AI (GVG-AI) Competition
- The 2007 Ultimate Computer Chess Challenge
- The annual Arimaa Challenge
- 2K Australia
- The Google AI Challenge
- Cloudball

In a marketing context AI can be used for competitions online and via social networks making the relationship between the customer and the seller closer and more valuable as it can improve loyalty and equity.

5.2 Healthcare

Artificial intelligence is moving into the healthcare industry by supporting doctors and nurses. According to Bloomberg Technology, Microsoft has developed AI to help doctors find the right treatments for cancer. There is an inordinate amount of research and drugs developed relating to cancer. In part, there are more than 800 medicines and vaccines to treat cancer. This choice can undesirably affect the doctors, because there are too many possibilities to choose from, making it more problematic to choose the right drugs for the patients.

Microsoft is working on a project to develop a machine called "Hanover". Its objective is to commit to memory all the papers necessary for cancer and help forecast which combinations of drugs will be most effective for each patient. One project that is being operated on is fighting myeloid leukaemia, a fatal cancer where the treatment has not improved in decades. Another study was reported to have found that artificial intelligence was as good as trained doctors in identifying skin cancers.

Another study is using artificial intelligence to try and screen multiple high-risk patients, and this is done by asking each patient several questions based on data acquired from live doctor to patient interactions.

There was a recent study by surgeons at the Children's National Medical Centre in Washington which productively demonstrated surgery with an autonomous robot. The team supervised the robot while it performed soft-tissue surgery, stitching together a bowel during open surgery, and doing so sounder than a human surgeon, the team claimed. IBM has created its own artificial intelligence computer, the IBM Watson which has beaten human intelligence in many levels. Watson was taken to a game show 'jeopardy' to try-out its intelligence and was able to win the game show against the jeopardy champions. Watson did not just won Jeopardy against the champions but, Watson was also declared a hero when it was able to successfully diagnosed a women who was suffering from leukaemia.

5.3 Automotive

Developments in AI have added to the growth of the automotive industry through the creation and evolution of self-driving vehicles. As of 2016, there are over 30 companies utilizing AI into the creation of driverless cars for example. A few companies involved with AI include Tesla, Google, and Apple. Many mechanisms contribute to the working of self-driving cars. These vehicles incorporate systems such as braking, lane changing, collision prevention, navigation and mapping. Together, these systems, as well as high performance computers are integrated into one multifaceted vehicle. Recent developments in autonomous automobiles have made the innovation of self-driving trucks even achievable, though they are still in the testing phase. The UK government has passed legislation to begin testing of self-driving truck platoons in 2018, self-driving truck platoons are a fleet of self-driving trucks following the lead of one non-self-driving truck. Meanwhile, the Daimler, a German automobile corporation, is testing the Freightliner Inspiration which is a semi-autonomous truck that will only be used on the highway.

One main factor that influences the ability for a driver-less automobiles to function is *mapping*. In general, the vehicle would be pre-programmed with a map of the area being driven. This map would incorporate data on the approximations of streetlight and curb heights in order for the vehicle to be aware of its environs. However, Google has been working on an algorithm with the purpose of eliminating the need for pre-programmed maps and instead, creating a device that would be able to *adjust to a variety of new surroundings*.

Some self-driving cars are not equipped with steering wheels or brakes, so there has also been research focused on creating an algorithm that is capable of maintaining a safe environment for the passengers in the vehicle through awareness of speed and driving conditions.

5.4 Finance

Financial institutions have long used artificial neural network systems to detect charges or claims outside of the norm, highlighting these for human investigation. The use of AI in banking can be traced back to 1987 when Security Pacific National Bank in USA set-up a Fraud Prevention Task force to counteract the unauthorised use of debit cards. Apps like Kasisito and Moneystream are using AI in financial services.

Banks use artificial intelligence systems today to systematize operations, maintain book-keeping, invest in stocks, and manage properties. AI in a bank is an everyday occurrence with cash machines and also bank teller terminals that can provide account data, complete transactions with a tap of a keyboard. AI can react to changes overnight or when business is not taking place for example in Retail it can review sales and complete refills for low stock items, while analysing customer purchases and profiles. In August 2001, robots beat humans in a simulated financial trading competition where stocks were bought and sold. AI has also reduced fraud and financial crimes by monitoring behavioural patterns of users for any abnormal changes or anomalies, this has saved millions of man hours and reduced losses .

5.5 Video games

Artificial intelligence is operated to generate intelligent behaviours principally in non-player characters (NPCs), often replicating human-like intelligence. Rather than learn how best to defeat human players, AI in video games is invented to augment human players' gaming experience. The most common role for AI in video games is *controlling non-player characters* (NPCs). Originators often use behaviours to make these NPCs look intelligent. One of the most widely used tricks, called the Finite State Machine (FSM) algorithm, was initiated to video game design in the 1990s. In an FSM, a designer generalizes all likely circumstances that an AI could encounter, and then programs a particular response for each situation. Essentially, an FSM AI would promptly react to the human player's feat with its pre-programmed behaviour. For example, in a shooting game, AI would assault when human player shows up and then retreat when its own wellbeing level is low. A more advanced method used to enhance the personalized gaming experience is the Monte Carlo Search Tree (MCST) algorithm. MCST exemplifies the strategy of using random trials to solve a problem. This is the AI strategy used in Deep Blue, the first computer program to defeat a human chess champion in 1997. For each point in the game, Deep Blue would use the MCST to first reflect all the possible moves it could make, then consider all the possible human player moves in reply, then consider all its possible responding moves. You can imagine all of the possible moves expanding like the branches grow from a stem–that is why it is called a "search tree".

After repeating this process multiple times, the AI would analyse the payback and then decide the best branch to follow. After taking a real move, the AI would repeat the search tree again based on the results that are still possible. In video games, an AI with MCST design can calculate thousands of possible moves and choose the ones with the best payback (such as more gold) in real time.

Revision

- Debate in 100 words the marketing applications of AI
- Review the core benefits of AI applications in industry
- Explain how Video Games use AI

6 Platforms

Introduction

A platform (or "computing platform") is described as " hardware architecture or software framework (including application frameworks), that permits software to run". As Rodney Brooks pointed out many years ago Brookes (1991), it is not just the artificial intelligence software that delineates the AI features of the platform, but rather the actual platform itself that affects the AI results, i.e., there needs to be work in AI problems on real-world platforms rather than in isolation.

Chapter Learning Outcomes

▢ To obtain an understanding of what is a 'platform'.

▢ To appreciate hardware architecture.

▢ A basic knowledge of platforms to build intelligent applications.

▢ Have an appreciation of the AI Partnership and its goals.

▢ Having successfully completed the module, you will be able to:

▢ 1. Critically assess the platforms of (AI) basics in marketing.

▢ 2. Assess the platform of tools of (AI) in today's world.

▢ Having completed the module, you will be able to:

▢ 1. Understand the variety of (AI) platforms and their uses.

• 2. Be able to explain the principal goals of each in (AI).

Critical thinking

Having successfully completed this topic, you will be able to:1. Critically evaluate the variety of platforms used in (AI) .2. Understand and debate the platforms of (AI) to management.

OBJECTIVES

Platforms are a key component of AI as they provide the hardware architecture or software framework that permits the platform to run. Platforms need to be understood in marketing due to their numerous uses and capabilities.

6.1 Partnership on AI

Artificial intelligence (AI) platforms deliver operators a tool kit to build intelligent applications. These platforms combine intelligent, decision-making algorithms with data, which empowers developers to create a business solution. Some platforms present pre-built algorithms and simplistic workflows with such features as drag-and-drop modelling and visual interfaces that effortlessly connect necessary data to the end solution, while others require a greater knowledge of development and coding. These algorithms can include functionality for image recognition, natural language processing, voice recognition, recommendation systems, and predictive analytics, in addition to other machine learning capabilities.

AI platforms are commonly used by developers to create both the learning algorithm and intelligent application. However, users without rigorous development skills will benefit from the platforms' pre-built algorithms and other topographies that curb the learning curve. AI platforms are very comparable to Platforms as a Service (PaaS), which permit for basic application development, moreover, these products vary by offering machine learning options. As intelligent applications become the norm, it may become commonplace for all PaaS products to begin to provide the same machine learning options as AI Platforms.

To qualify for inclusion in the AI Platforms category, a product must:

- Provide a platform for building intelligent, AI-capable applications.
- Allow operators to create machine learning algorithms and/or offer pre-built machine learning algorithms for more novice users to build applications.
- Present a way for developers to attach data to the algorithms for them to learn and adapt.

When considering a platform look at the following:

- Viability of the vendor and the platform itself. This is always a consideration to avoid costly dead ends.
- Desired target state: Can the platform support all/most of the requirements that I have now? If not, how does the roadmap look like? When do services that I want to offer at a later point in time become available? The more the platform can offer right now the more flexibility I have in adapting my own priorities that are partly dictated by the customers'.

- Intermediate states: Which experiences do have priority for me? These services need to be covered right now.
- Integration-ability of the platform. If it is hard to connect the AI platform to my current technology platform then I need to reconsider, probably also my current technology stack.
- Lock in! Lock in is even more interesting than for normal applications. Not only can the data structures be proprietary, but also e.g. the used artificial neural network (ANN).
- Additionally, any other ANN needs to get trained and validated against the one that is to be replaced, to make sure it delivers better results than the old one. This is a project in itself.

Partnership on AI (full name Partnership on Artificial Intelligence to Benefit People and Society) is a technology industry consortium focused on establishing best practices for artificial intelligence systems and to educate the public about AI. The upswing in AI competencies, fuelled by data, computation, and advances in algorithms for machine learning, perception, planning, and natural language, promise great value to people and society. Efforts of the Partnership on AI will be organized around a set of thematic pillars. These areas of focus may evolve over time as we pursue activities and gather input and feedback.

1. SAFETY-CRITICAL AI

Where AI tools are used to supplement or replace human decision-making, we must be sure that they are safe, trustworthy, and aligned with the ethics and preferences of people who are influenced by their actions.

2. FAIR, TRANSPARENT, AND ACCOUNTABLE AI

Researchers, officials, and the public should be sensitive to these possibilities and we should seek to develop methods that detect and correct those errors and biases, not replicate them. We also need to work to develop systems that can explain the rationale for inferences.

3. COLLABORATIONS BETWEEN PEOPLE AND AI SYSTEMS

Opportunities for R&D and for the development of best practices on AI-human collaboration include methods that provide people with clarity about the understandings and confidence that AI systems have about situations, means for coordinating human and AI contributions to problem solving, and enabling AI systems to work with people to resolve uncertainties about human goals.

4. AI, LABOR, AND THE ECONOMY

While advances promise to inject great value into the economy, they can also be the source of disruptions as new kinds of work are created and other types of work become less needed due to automation. Discussions are rising on the best approaches to minimizing potential disruptions, making sure that the fruits of AI advances are widely shared, and competition and innovation is encouraged and not stifled.

5. SOCIAL AND SOCIETAL INFLUENCES OF AI

AI advances will touch people and society in numerous ways, including potential influences on privacy, democracy, criminal justice, and human rights. For example, while technologies that personalize information and that assist people with recommendations can provide people with valuable assistance, they could also inadvertently or deliberately manipulate people and influence opinions.

6. AI AND SOCIAL GOOD

Value in collaborating with public and private organizations, including academia, scientific societies, NGOs, social entrepreneurs, and interested private citizens to promote discussions and catalyse efforts to address society's most pressing challenges.

7. SPECIAL INITIATIVES

Seek to convene and support projects that resonate with the tenets of our organization.

Revision
- In 100 words describe ' what is a platform'
- Debate the three elements of a platform
- In 100 words explain what to look for when considering a choice of platform
- Debate the purpose if the AI Partnership

7 Philosophy and ethics

Introduction

The philosophy of artificial intelligence attempts to answer such questions as follows, Can a machine act intelligently? Can it solve *any* problem that a person would solve by thinking? Are human intelligence and machine intelligence the same? Is the human brain essentially a computer? Can a machine have a mind, mental states, and consciousness in the same way that a human being can? Can it *feel how things are?*

The ethics of artificial intelligence is the part of the ethics of technology specific to robots and other artificially intelligent beings. It is typically divided into robo-ethics, a concern with the moral behaviour of humans as they design, construct, use and treat artificially intelligent beings, and machine ethics, which is concerned with the moral behaviour of artificial moral agents (AMAs).

Chapter Learning Outcomes

▢ What is the philosophy behind AI?

▢ Consideration of the question emerging due to AI .

▢ The understanding of AI capabilities and risks.

▢ A basic knowledge if AI ethics.

▢ Having successfully completed the module, you will be able to:

▢ 1. Critically assess the philosophy and ethics of (AI) in marketing.

▢ 2. Assess the philosophy and ethics tools of (AI) in today's world.

▢ Having completed the module, you will be able to:

▢ 1. Understand the variety of (AI) philosophies and ethics and their uses.

• 2. Be able to explain the principal goals of each in (AI).

Critical thinking

Having successfully completed this topic, you will be able to:1. Critically evaluate the variety of philosophies and ethics used in (AI) .2. Understand and debate the two areas of (AI) to management.

OBJECTIVES

A chapter that explains the philosophy and ethics related to AI and why this understanding is important. AI application is growing in marketing thus understanding the issues and ethics of AI by marketers will in part ensure the validity of AI in this area.

7.1 The limits of artificial general intelligence

In an exact sense, machine or artificial intelligence can only partially amplify human thinking but cannot replace it. Human thinking exists in various forms:

Logical thinking, intuitive thinking, thinking in images and dialectical thinking.

They have formed a network in human brains and have been developing constantly. While artificial intelligence can only magnify deductive methods used in human activities of understanding and it is not limitless. It cannot function all on its own, surpass human rational thought and reach the ideal state of being limitless. Man has always had nature and environment as models for his numerous attainments and using those models he has succeeded in making machines, tools, and robots with impressive performances (Bergeron,2002). It's been speculated that in the next 40 - 45 years computers could reach the performance of the human brain, and that achievements in the field of artificial intelligence, even to the degree of making synthetic workers (humanoid robots) with feats very much like a humans. We see on various Internet sites posted discussions, courses and opinions on the future performance of artificial intelligence application fields.

However, the specialists in the field are tested to create equipment and software able to cope with the performance of the human brain. There *are valuations of time and memory requirements, operation speed, ethics* concerning how such an artificial intelligence system should seem and operate. There are even anxieties that humankind will have to face an additional risk if some intelligent informatic objects are not restricted in running processes and in making major decisions, if they can program themselves (re-writing codes, re-compiling), etc.

Nevertheless, at this point we should consider certain restrictions and limitations pertaining to artificial intelligence, that researchers will not succeed in overcoming. These are some of these limits (Denning & Metcalf, 1997).

1. *Artificial intelligence must consider the law of entropy.* At this point, the relevant achievements do not take them into account and do not succeed in simulating them. In nature, **the law of entropy** leads to the stabilization of any type of system. The passage from a high level of entropy to a low one and vice-versa consumes energy. Most common movements in nature are the result of applying the law of entropy to a given system. We think that by the symbiosis between the living cell (living organism) and the technical systems, the intelligent control of matter could be achieved.

2. *The entire foundation of artificial intelligence is based on informatic procedures* that mean to circumscribe the intelligent behaviour of a human being, although experts never succeeded in simulating the behaviour of an ape with an ABAC. As we saw previously, the human being has the quality of complicating things very much when he knows what he must do but mostly when he does not know where he is heading.

Therefore, we consider that when the goal is not known very well, the human brain both functionally and structurally will complicate even further the solution procedures, which consumes time and considerable information resources. We strongly believe that bio-techno-systems can be a solution to this problem;

3. *The two pillars of computer science, "0" and "1" together with the truth values "True" and "False" are major borders in artificial intelligence.* Any intelligent information procedure is decomposed eventually in strings of "0" and "1", which leads us to the fundamental objection that intelligent machines will never be like humans. We have to consider that bio-systems also work with intermediary values;

4. *Artificial intelligence is based very much on symbolic logic and has not succeeded in involving so-called affective logic.* In affective logic, combinations of truth values may lead to different evaluations. A possible solution could be obtained by using affective computing (Bergeron,2002), which undertakes to model affective behaviour in various situations.

In a marketing contextualisation the next decades will expose new ways of using AI that speed up processes and knowledge, that support informed decision making. The critical values to marketing are speed and accuracy, both commodities of real value. New applications of AI will appear in marketing that can be used to communicate, analyse data, modelling and scenarios, research in real time, and so much more. Whilst mankind is in control of machines it will control AI development and will become an aid to how, what and why we do things.

7.2 Potential risks and moral reasoning

Widespread use of artificial intelligence could have unintended consequences that are dangerous or undesirable. Scientists from the Future of Life Institute, among others, described some short-term research goals to be how AI influences the economy, the laws and ethics that are involved with AI and how to minimize AI security risks.

In the long-term, the researchers have proposed to *continue optimizing function while minimizing possible security risks* that come along with new technologies. Machines with intelligence have the potential to use their intelligence to make ethical decisions.

Research in this area includes "machine ethics", "artificial moral agents", and the study of "malevolent vs. friendly".

In marketing we have already encountered consumer back lash over the use of technology in the volume of communication thrown at the public, and also issues with 'tracking data' that is used to profile consumers and make them buy more with attractive offers, upgrades, cross selling.

There is no doubt consumer data is being 'sold on' and electronic information is vulnerable to virus, attacks, identity stealing, financial data abuse/ stealing. No AI system is 100% safe, undesirable agents can try and steal, corrupt data for their own end game. The moral marketing compass needs to balance benefits against the risks of the use of AI and related machines and protect consumers.

7.2.1 Existential risk

Expansions in artificial intelligence (AI) have the prospective to enable people around the world to succeed in up till now not thought of ways. Such progresses might also give *humanity tools* a question to address other sources of risk. Despite this, AI also poses its own dangers. AI systems perform in ways that sometimes surprise researchers. At the moment, such AI systems are usually quite narrow in their competences - for example being excellent at Go, or at minimizing power consumption in a server facility. If researchers invented a machine intelligence which was a sufficiently good general logic thinker, or even better at general reasoning than people are, it might become problematic for human agents to affect its functioning. If AI behaved in a way, which did *not reflect human values*, it might pose a real danger to humanity. Such a machine intelligence (as seen in science fiction), might use its intellectual dominance to develop a decisive strategic advantage over humans. If its behaviour was for some reason mismatched with human wellbeing, it could then pose a (risk to mankind). Note that this does not depend on the machine intelligence gaining consciousness or having any ill will towards humanity.

It is sensible to think that on-going research in AI, machine learning, and computing infrastructure will eventually make it possible to build AI systems that not only equal, but far exceed human competences in most spheres. Current research on AI and machine learning is at least a few decades from this grade of capability and generality, but it would not be surprising if it were not achieved. Causes of risk from super intelligent systems could be for example, oppressive governments could use these systems to do aggression on a large scale, the evolution to a super intelligent economy could be difficult to navigate, and some advanced AI systems themselves could turn out to be moral patients (Bostrom,2015).

7.2.2 Devaluation of humanity

In the long term, a significant question is what will happen if the mission for strong AI succeeds and an AI system becomes superior than humans at all cognitive tasks. As pointed out by I.J. Good in 1965, planning smarter AI systems is itself a cognitive task. Such a system could hypothetically undergo recursive self-improvement, triggering an intelligence explosion leaving human intellect further behind.

By inventing ground-breaking new technologies, super intelligence might help us eradicate war, disease, and poverty, and so the creation of strong AI might be the biggest positive event in human history. Some researchers however have expressed concern, that AI it might also create a disaster, unless humans learn to align the goals of the AI with ours before it becomes 'super intelligent'.

There are some who question whether AI superiority will ever be achieved, and others who insist that the creation of super intelligent AI, is guaranteed to be beneficial. Both of these are possibilities, but also researchers must recognize the potential for an artificial intelligence system to deliberately or accidentally cause great human harm.

It is my believe research today will help us better formulate for, and avoid such potentially negative consequences in the future, thus enjoying the benefits of AI while avoiding pitfalls, two scenarios however are most likely (Russell, 2017):

1. That some AI is programmed to do something *devastating*: Autonomous weapons are artificial intelligence systems that are programmed to kill. In the hands of the wrong person, these weapons could easily cause mass casualties. Moreover, an AI arms race could unintentionally lead to an AI war that also results in bulk human and robotic casualties. To avoid being turned off by the enemy, these weapons would be designed to be exceptionally difficult to "turn off," so humans could credibly lose control of such a situation. This risk is one that's present even with narrow AI but grows as levels of AI intelligence and independence intensify.

2. The AI is programmed to do something *beneficial*, but it develops a destructive method for achieving its goal: This can happen whenever we fail to fully align the AI's goals with ours, which is noticeably difficult. If you ask an obedient intelligent car to take you to the airport as fast as possible, it might get you there however, doing not what you wanted, but exactly what you asked for. If a super intelligent system is tasked with an aspiring geo engineering project, it might wreak havoc with our ecosystem as a side effect, and view human attempts to stop it, as a threat.

From a marketing perspective imagine you are running a promotion using AI systems that gave prizes after customers purchased x amount. Someone hacks your system and the awarding of prizes is accelerated a thousand-fold, the financial impact and negative publicity could be huge. None the less this a doomsday scenario for marketers, the upsides of AI must be controlled and consistent with the boundaries set by humans who control machines.

7.2.3 Decrease in demand for human labour

It is reasonable to assume artificial intelligence and robotics will be used in the production of goods and services, in fact we have examples of this phenomena already with automation of production lines for cars and also the use of automated handling systems for the picking and delivery of goods. Amazon for example is utilising Technology in its warehouses to deliver goods and services and is contemplating using drones to deliver parcels. There is no doubt some jobs completed by humans will become obsolete and taken over by machines who will be programmed to complete tasks. In a marketing context AI could be seen as an enabler that reduces mundane tasks and speeds up delivery of information, goods and services thus saving money.

Marketing is also saving on human capital in the context of automated systems for Customer experience management and also customer relationship management. Marketing is also using AI and metrics to manage complex data and provide Dashboard output in an automated context for the organization saving time and human resources. As AI development increases it is reasonable to assume and Marketing Will take on these new technologies and through adaption improve performance and also the organizations profits.

The various roles in marketing will change, with more demand for strategists and individuals with the technical and analytical skills. I can also see in marketing the use and application of AI in the communications process through the development of creative and the delivery of messages in dynamic formats such as 3-D and virtual reality. Beyond this it could well be possible for marketers to use artificial intelligence and robotics at point of sale to demonstrate a product or service reducing the cost of human intervention. While automation will eliminate very few occupations entirely in the next decade, it will affect portions of almost all jobs to a greater or lesser degree, depending on the type of work they involve. Automation is now going beyond routine manufacturing activities, it has the potential, at least with regard to its technical feasibility, to transform sectors such as healthcare and finance, which involve a substantial share of knowledge work. Technologies could automate 45 percent of the activities people are paid to perform and that about 60 percent of all occupations could see 30 percent or more of their constituent activities automated, again with technologies available today (McKinsey, 2017).

7.2.4 artificial moral agents (AMA)

An agent is a software that knows how to do things that you could probably do yourself if you had the time" (Borking/Van Eck/Siepel 1999). Also, agents may delegate task to other human or artificial agents or collaborate with other agents. They are designed to perceive the context in which they operate and react to it. Also, agents are proactive, therefore one does not need to start an agent (in contrast to a program), but they are designed to decide for themselves when and how to perform a task. Therefore, they may be perceived as autonomous artefacts. Agents may serve as an interface for human- machine-interaction by acting as an artificial personality, or they might be designed to observe and report on computer systems.

An AMA is an Artificial Agents (AA) guided by norms, which we as human beings consider to have a moral content. To stay with the example of a web bot: One might think of certain content (propaganda, communications) as conflicting with moral norms. Thus, an AMA might respect this norms while searching the internet and will not present this kind of content as result unless explicitly being told to do so.

Moral agency is an individual's ability to make moral judgments based on some notion of right and wrong and to be held answerable for these actions (Taylor,2003). A moral agent is "a being who is capable of acting with reference to right and wrong." (Webster, 2017) The tenure *artificial moral agent* has taken on two usages in research.
The first is in the debate on whether it is conceivable for an artificial system to be a moral agent such as artificial systems and moral responsibility. The second usage branches from efforts to build machines with ethically significant behaviours as in machine ethics. The proper distinction between these two usages has itself been a key point of debate (Bandura, 2002).
In marketing humans make most of the moral judgements based on what is right and wrong, what the laws governing marketing allow: in communication, on packaging, creative, we are the 'the moral compass.' Moral agency is embedded in a broader socio-cognitive self-theory encompassing affective self-regulatory mechanisms rooted in personal standards linked to self-sanctions to provide a level of decency.

Moral functioning either human or machine is thus governed by self-reactive selfhood and regulations in marketing rather than by dispassionate abstract reasoning. The self-regulatory mechanisms governing moral conduct do not come into play unless, they are activated by the marketer and there are many psychosocial mechanisms by which moral self-sanctions are selectively disengaged from inhumane conduct. The moral disengagement may center on the cognitive restructuring of *inhumane conduct* into a benign or worthy one by moral justification, sanitizing language and exonerative social comparison; disavowal of personal agency in the harm one causes by diffusion or displacement of responsibility; disregarding or minimizing the injurious effects of one's actions; and attribution of blame to, and de-humanization of, those who are victimized.

Social cognitive theory adopts an inter actionist perspective to morality in which moral actions are the products of the reciprocal interplay of personal and social influences. Given the many mechanisms for disengaging moral control at both the individual and collective level, civilized life requires, in addition to humane personal standards, safeguards built into social systems that uphold compassionate behavior, and renounce cruelty.

7.2.5 Machine ethics

Operational systems (for example, self-driving cars) need to obey both the law of the land and our values. AI oversight systems ("AI Guardians") is a method to tackling this challenge, and to react to the potential risks associated with increasingly autonomous AI systems. These AI oversight systems help to verify that operational systems did not drift unduly from the guidelines of their programmers, and to bring them back in submission if they do drift. AI systems not only demand some kind of oversight, but this oversight must be provided—at least in part—not by humans exclusively, but by a new kind of AI system, *the oversight ones*. AI needs therefore to be guided by AI. One reason is that AI operational systems are *learning systems*. These systems do not stop collecting data once they are introduced; instead, they continue to data mine, and 'experience' is used by the system to improve their performance. These AI systems may hence wander considerably from the procedures their program writer originally gave them. But no mortal can monitor these changes, let alone in real time, and regulate whether they are legal and ethical. Second, AI systems are becoming highly *opaque*, "black boxes" to human beings.

There are three ways that algorithms become opaque: *Intentional opacity*, for example with proprietary algorithms that a government or corporation wants to keep secret; *Technical illiteracy*, where the complexity and function of algorithms is beyond the public's knowledge; and *Scale of application*, where either "machine learning" and/ or the number of different program writer involved renders an algorithm opaque even to the systems analyst.

In marketing many issues come to mind with Machine Ethics for example consider:

- Privacy issues for emotion data retrieval, storage and dissemination. This is a general issue that is not specific to emotional interaction with machines. The impact of incorrect evaluation and its consequences. The complexity of evaluating the human emotional state remains a significant challenge.

- Would we accept a machine employing the power of human-like emotional reactions to a particular stimulus? A clear analogy of this issue is apparent in commercial marketing, which monitors and targets the emotions of consumers through presenting fabricated opinions and emotions. This opens a range of new dangers concerning *personal integrity*. The domain of advertising already has ethical (and legal) restrictions on how to manipulate audience intentions.

Affective machines may draw directly on similar restrictions when looking to modify a *user's affective state* through private social engagement.

- The predictability of technological progress reflects our dependency on it. There are two aspects to this: our dependency on machines, and the feeling we have when they are dependent on us. The second is related to emotional manipulation by machines.

- A machine's *inability to lie* would be seen as a core feature in the design of the system. While people do not have full control over their emotions, a machine, by having complete control over its expressive capabilities, *could lie with a straight face.*

7.2.6 Malevolent and friendly AI

The literature on AI risk (Sotala & Yampolskiy, 2015) suggests a number of safety measures which should be implemented in any advanced AI project to minimize potential negative impact. Simply reversing the advice would in many cases lead to a decisively unsafe system.
In fact, the number of specific ways in which a malevolent designer may implement hazardous intelligent software is limited only by one's imagination, and it would be unfeasible to exhaustively research review.

In "AGI Failures Modes and Levels", (Turchin,2015) describes a number of ways in which an intelligent system may be *dangerous* at different stages in its development.

Among his examples, AI:
- Hacks as many computers as possible to gain more calculating power
- Creates its own robotic infrastructure by the means of bio engineering
- Prevents other AI projects from finishing by hacking or diversions
- Has goals which include causing suffering
- Interprets commands literally
- Overvalues marginal probability events

It is no astonishment then that this inquisitiveness about AI is spreading through marketing departments as friendly AI in marketing has its uses. Artificial intelligence can even now be found undertaking routine marketing tasks to almost perfect criterions, and with non-exhaustive levels of enthusiasm. Many of us in marketing will encounter a marketing virtual agent on a daily basis for example, when being asked qualifying questions, or delivering automated answers to standard questions. However, their potential goes far beyond these areas, and presents exciting opportunities at every stage of the customer journey. For example:

Big data.

Making meaning of data is one of the keystone of Artificial Intelligence marketing. The 'collect, reason & act' cycle is put into high performance with AI adding superior scale, automation and targeting to marketing efforts. People are still extremely tranquil about granting brands access to their data, allowing it to be collected and integrated from multiple sources to predict what you need before you even realised you needed it. This takes the form of product recommendations, proactive customer service, dynamic pricing and triggered offers.

Assisted search.

AI is gently reinventing Search. Google's RankBrain is the deep learning system powering the autosuggest and related searches topographies that we've become accustomed to. It is also following the semantic analysis of *voice search* — determining whether somebody is searching in distress, frustration or curiosity and respond accordingly. Augmenting for an *AI-first world* will become a key requirement for marketing departments and it will be brands, not search engines, that customers will criticize if the answers to their search are not relevant or up to date.

Conversational commerce.

Voice assistants create a break to interpose compelling content into everyday situations, such as recipes in the kitchen, linked to an ecommerce platform. It's this unique integration of web sites that is tending marketing competitors on their toes.

Personalisation.

The Banking sector is one industry accepting AI as a means to getting close to customers again.

We stay loyal with our banks out of convenience not loyalty. Banks have become too self-satisfied with the complexities and barriers to entry providing a lack of incentive to get the basics right. That is until now. Challenger banks are forcing them to up their game and AI can ironically make them appear more human.

For example, Swedbank's Nina new web assistant is engaging in 40,000 conversations per month and able to handle more than 350 different customer questions. Of course, banking is far from the only industry in which customer service is lacking.

Visual commerce.

Due to AI and machine learning, a customer is now able to take a picture of a jacket they see in the street, match it to a pin on Pinterest and be directed to a retailer who has it in stock. AI is closing the gap between online and offline experience-led commerce.

Media buying.

With online advertising's truthfulness issues out in the open, AI media agency Blackwood Seven is making the big networks look closely. Their AI alternative is giving brands the capability to plan, purchase and heighten their media buying in-house without the usual agency percentage, saving money.

Design.

Creativity is innocently seen as resistant from AI, however algorithm-driven design and creative direction is already demonstrating to be a cost-effective solution for a lot of industries. AI-powered logo maker LogoJoy uses machine learning to make it feel like you are functioning with a real designer and is already claiming strong revenues only one year after launching. While not suitable for all occasions or clients, the AI designer is proving to be a capable, cheap and immediate solution for over 1,000 bootstrapped businesses a month.

Customer service.

Left under human supervision, it is extraordinary how important regions of customer experience have been taken for granted. Research would indicate that repetitious, repetitive everyday jobs activates automatic decision making and makes employees more likely to behave unprofessionally.AI is increasingly stepping up to reduce waiting times, cut costs, close sales, personalise messages and provide the results customers are looking for. Human intervention is still necessary in a lot of those instances — as checks for the algorithms and to make final decisions — meaning our marketing jobs are safe for the time being at least.

7.3 Machine consciousness, sentience and mind

Researchers offer assumed definitions of "consciousness", for instance defining it as "self- awareness", "what it is like to be something", "experience", "being the subject of seeming" or "having somebody home", notwithstanding the fact that nothing is achieved by describing one unclear expression in terms of another. It is extensively accepted that biological organisms use evidence about the environment in choosing actions.

Often evidence, about their own state both physical and mental is also used: deciding whether to move towards visible food or visible water on the basis of current needs. So, when we converse about information-processing virtual machines, this is no stranger than our everyday thinking about social, economic, and political states and processes and causal interactions between them.

Like many deep concepts in science, "information" is *implicitly* defined by its role in our theories and our designs for working systems. To illustrate this point, we offer some examples of processes involving information in organisms or machines:

- External or internal actions triggered by information,
- Segmenting, clustering labelling components within a structure (i.e. parsing),
- Trying to derive new information from old (e.g. what caused this? what else is there? what might happen next? can I benefit from this?),
- Storing information for future use (and possibly modifying it later),
- Considering and comparing alternative plans, descriptions or explanations,
- Interpreting information as instructions and obeying them, e.g. carrying out a plan,
- Observing the above processes and deriving new information thereby (self-monitoring, self- evaluation, meta-management),
- Communicating information to others (or to oneself later),
- Checking information for consistency.

Only a *conscious machine* can demonstrate a subjective understanding of whether a scene depicted in some ordinary photograph is "right" or "wrong." This ability to assemble a set of details into a picture of reality that makes eminent sense—or know, say, that a plane is flying backwards—defines an indispensable property of the conscious mind. A roomful of IBM supercomputers, in contrast, still cannot fathom *what makes sense* in a scene. The advent of the computer has radically changed the relationship between human beings and machines. Decades ago, the human asked the machine to represent their physical labour. Currently the computer does the intellectual labour also on our behalf when we stroke a key. A personal computer can process the enormous amount of data management and analysis, which the human cannot without time and effort. It is understandable that the contemporary society and marketing does not survive today without the computer network, not to mention the banking system, the flight reservation system, and the e-commerce on the Internet. Or from the viewpoint of culture, new computer tools such as the computer graphics and synthesizer, expand the likelihood and enjoyment of entertainment. Research on artificial intelligence and sensitivity control technology progresses in recent years, and the technology of imitating human thinking, feeling, and sensitivity have now been recognized.

However, research on Sentience as the way of idea generation and intuition that are the origin of human being's intellectual production activity seems to have just started. Sentient robots (those capable of not only perception but also feelings) are useful only when they work in near closeness with humans.

Humans understand each other more completely by using communications channels beyond language—such as speech prosody, facial expressions, and body language. In time it would seem sensible to endow robots with more than just the *ability to interact through menus or simple spoken commands*. Because of the emotional model and its successive output accurately reflect the robot's state and its understanding of the world, human–robot team efforts should prove more efficient.

For space application as an example, examples of such robots might be the control computers on the space station (the present-day incarnation of the HAL 9000) or human–rover teams exploring and mapping planetary surfaces (the year 2015 version of *Star Wars*' C3PO).

However, the practicality of a robot's emotional aspects decreases as a function of the increasing cycle time of communications response. This point is obvious for deep-space probes, whose communications with humans are more akin to sending surface-mail letters than to having a conversation. When the robot works autonomously for long periods of time—such as an intelligent satellite monitoring sunspot activity—there is little need for sentience or anything more than a graphical display and a command menu.

Building 2D metric maps indoors, using sonars or laser scanners is now, as is collision avoidance and corridor following based on sonar or vision technology. Said systems provide the foundation for commercial remote- presence robots, built on top of the Internet infrastructures. Such a remote robot with local perception and intelligence can perform useful work in a harsh or hard-to- reach location if a person can provide long- latency supervisory commands. In research many systems are available for tracking moving objects visually from a (temporarily) static camera, as are commercial systems for *real-time* stereo depth maps.

 Active vision systems with eye movement, smooth pursuit, and vestibular ocular reflexes now proliferate. Finding people on the basis of skin colour or face detection is common, Facial recognition has received intense research attention, and there is a real payoff with practical recognition now a reality in many applications such as credit cards, passports, cosmetics. Recent work combining voice structure understanding, facial detection, and gesture and expression understanding has led to the first few robots that can engage in genuine social interactions with robot-naive people. And finally, the first steps have been made toward robots developing a practical understanding of human intent, attention, and knowledge, a set of capabilities that autistics humans never develop.

7.3.1 Consciousness

"Consciousness" is a vague term, referring to many different phenomena. Each of these phenomena needs to be explained, but some are easier to explain than others. At the start, it is useful to divide the associated problems of consciousness into "hard" and "easy" problems.

The easy problems of consciousness are those that seem directly susceptible to the standard methods of cognitive science, whereby a phenomenon is explained in terms of computational or neural mechanisms. The hard problems are those that seem to *resist* those methods.

The easy problems of consciousness include those of explaining the following phenomena:

▢ The ability to discriminate, categorize, and react to environmental stimuli
▢ The integration of information by a cognitive system
▢ The reportability of mental states
▢ The ability of a system to access its own internal states
▢ The focus of attention
▢ The deliberate control of behaviour
▢ The difference between wakefulness and sleep

All of these phenomena are associated with the notion of consciousness. The really hard problem of consciousness is the problem of *experience*. When we think and perceive, there is a whir of information-processing in our brains, but there is also a subjective aspect. As Nagel (1974) has put it, there is *something it is like* to be a conscious organism. This subjective aspect is experience.

In marketing brand consciousness concerns the mental orientation to select products that are well-known and highly advertised brand name (Sproles and Kendall, 1986). Consumers often state personal characteristics and preferences through brand (Manrai et al., 2001). Those consumers with high levels of brand consciousness have a habit of buying more expensive and well-known brands (Liao and Wang, 2009; Sproles and Kendall, 1986). They use the brands as *symbols* of status and prestige (Escalas and Bettman, 2005; Jamal and Goode, 2001). They gain self-assurance in constructing their own self-identity and present such an identity to others (Phau and Teah, 2009; Wang et al., 2009). Therefore, they are willing to pay a price premium for a well-known brand's product (Liao and Wang, 2009; Sproles and Kendall, 1986).

7.3.2 Computationalism and functionalism

Computationalism is the hypothesis that the functional relations between mental inputs, outputs, and internal states are *computational*. Computationalism per se is neutral on whether those computational relations constitute the nature of mental states. Modern computationalism was framed by Warren McCulloch in the 1930s and published for the first time by him and his collaborator Walter Pitts in the 1940s (McCulloch & Pitts, 1943).

McCulloch and Pitts held that the conclusive relations between mental inputs, outputs, and internal states were *computational*. According to McCulloch and Pitts, the computations assumed by their theory of mind were performed by *specific neural mechanisms*.

McCulloch and Pitts both presented demanding mathematical techniques for designing neural circuits that functioned those computations. Finally, they held that by explaining mental phenomena in terms of *neural mechanisms*, their theory solved the mind–body problem, but they did not formulate an explicit solution to the mind–body problem. The logician Alan Turing suggested (and solved) the problem of giving a char- acterization of computing machines in the widest logic—mechanisms for solving problems by operational series of logical operations. This suggests the idea of seeing whether a 'Turing machine' could contain of the elements used in neurological theories of the brain; that is, whether it could *consist of a network of neurons*. Such a nerve network could then serve as a 'hypothetical model' for the brain and its function. (Oppenheim & Putnam, 1958).

Fodor (1965) initiated in the philosophical literature both the notion that psychological theories were *functional analyses* and the notion *that psycho- logical theories were like TM tables* in that they were metaphors of transitions between state types. Both themes would be very successful in philosophy of psychology. Fodor's (1965) description of *phase one* psychological theories as having the same form as TM tables paved the way for the later identification of psychological functional analyses and computer programs. In a paper published a few years later (Fodor, 1968b), Fodor repeated his view, already present in Fodor (1965), that psychological theories *provided descriptions of psychological functions*.

But this time, he added that psychological theories were law like expression as lists of instructions: 'the paradigmatic psychological theory is a list of instructions for producing behaviour' (Fodor, 1968b, p. 630).

7.3.3 Strong AI hypothesis

Strong artificial intelligence or, True AI, may refer to:

- a hypothetical machine that exhibits behaviour at least as skill full and flexible as humans do, and the research program of building such an artificial general intelligence.
- Computational theory of mind, the philosophical position that human minds are, in essence, computer programs. This positioning, was named "strong AI" by John Searle (1992) in his Chinese room argument.
- Artificial consciousness, a hypothetical machine that possesses awareness of external objects, ideas and/or self-awareness.

Searle identified a philosophical position he calls "strong AI":

The appropriately programmed computer with the right inputs and outputs would thereby have a mind in exactly the same sense human beings have minds.

The definition hinges on the distinction between *simulating* a mind and *actually having* a mind. Searle writes that, "according to Strong AI, the correct simulation really is a mind. According to Weak AI, the correct simulation is a model of the mind" (Searle, 2009).

The position is implicit in some of the statements of early AI researchers and analysts. For example, in 1955, AI founder Herbert A. Simon declared that "there are now in the world machines that think, that learn and create" (Hanard, 2001), and claimed that they had "solved the venerable mind–body problem, explaining how a system composed of matter can have the properties of mind." "AI wants only the genuine article: *machines with minds,* in the full and literal sense. This is not science fiction, but real science, based on a theoretical conception as deep as it is daring: namely, we are, at root, *computers ourselves*" (Haugeland,1985).

Searle also ascribes the following positions to advocates of strong AI:

- AI systems can be used to explain the mind;
- The study of the brain is irrelevant to the study of the mind; and
- The Turing test is adequate for establishing the existence of mental states.

7.3.4 Robot rights

Robot rights are the moral obligations of society towards its machines, similar to human rights or animal rights (Evans, 2002). Robot rights, such as right to exist and perform its own mission, may be linked to robot duty to serve human, by analogy with linking human rights, to human duties before society (Sheliazhenko, 2017).

These may include the right to life and liberty, freedom of thought and expression and equality before the law. The issue has been under consideration by the Institute for the Future and by the U.K. Department of Trade and Industry.

Experts disagree whether specific and detailed laws will be required soon or safely in the distant future (Henderson, 2007). A recommendation of the European Parliament to the EU Commission has suggested in the future sentient AI robots could need their own rights and responsibilities, and strict laws banning them from taking over too many jobs across the Continent may become necessary.

7.4 Super intelligence

The traditional approach to determining whether a machine is intelligent is the Turing test (Turing, 1950), which has been extensively debated over the last 50 years (Saygin et al., 2000). Turing realised how problematic it would be to directly define intelligence and thus attempted to sidestep the issue by setting up his now famous imitation game: if human judges cannot effectively discriminate between a computer and a human through tele-typed conversation then we must conclude that the computer is intelligent. Artificial intelligence algorithms frequently find solutions to problems using heuristics and forms of reasoning that are not strictly logical. They discover powerful new designs for difficulties that the system's programmers had never thought of (Koza et al., 2003). They also learn to play games such as chess [Hsu et al., 1995] and backgammon (Tesauro, 1995) at levels superior to that of any human, let alone the researchers who designed and created the system.

Indeed, in the case of checkers, computers are now literally unbeatable as they can play a provably perfect game (Schaeffer et al., 2007).

This leads to what I. J. Good referred to as an intelligence explosion:

"Let an ultrain-telligent machine be defined as a machine that can far surpass all the intellectual activities of any man however clever. Since the design of machines is one of these intellectual activities, an ultrain-telligent machine could design even better machines; there would then unquestionably be an 'intelligence explosion,' and the intelligence of man would be left far behind. Thus, the first ultrain- telligent machine is the last invention that man need ever make" (Good, 1965).

The delineating distinguishing of our human species is intelligence. It is not by superior size, strength or speed that we dominate life on earth, but by our intelligence. If our intelligence were to be knowingly surpassed, it is difficult to imagine what the consequences of this might be. It would certainly be a source of vast ability, and with enormous power comes enormous accountability.

7.4.1 Technological singularity

Moore's Law has been around for some 46 years. It is a descriptor for the movement we have established in the expansion of computer hardware for decades, with no sign of it decelerating, the number of transistors that can be placed on an integrated circuit doubles every two years. The law is named after Gordon Moore, who pronounced this technological pattern in 1965. He co-founded Intel in 1968. Technological singularity, however, was a word invented by Vernor Vinge, the science fiction author, in 1983.

"We will soon create intelligences greater than our own," he wrote. "When this happens, human history will have reached a kind of singularity, an intellectual transition as impenetrable as the knotted space-time at the centre of a black hole, and the world will pass far beyond our understanding."

The belief is that when humans become proficient of creating beings more intelligent than us, its viewpoints that the machines — or their near-descendants — will be able to create intelligences more intelligent than us and critically themselves. This exponential growth of intelligences would work much like Moore's Law — perhaps we can call it Kurzweil's Law — but will have more philosophical importance. When there are intelligences proficient in creating more intelligent beings in swift succession, we enter an age where *technological advances move at a rate, we cannot even dream of right now.*

One can venture as to the changes that Singularity would cause that would enable that exponential growth to persist. Once humans build computers with processing power superior than the human brain and with *self-aware software* that is more intelligent than a human, we will see major enhancements to the speed with which these artificial minds can run. Consider, that with faster processing speeds, these AIs could do the reasoning of a human in *shorter amounts of time*: a year's worth of human processing would become eight months or less, then eventually weeks, days, minutes and at the far end of the range, even down to seconds.

Singularity developments to machine speed and intelligence will empower crossover to human minds. Researchers wonder that such advanced technology would enable us to improve the machine processing power, and the intelligence and accessible memory limits of our own minds would expand through the changing structure of the brain, or 'porting' our minds on to the same tools that these intelligences will run on. Imagine being able to complete a market overview, a strategic marketing plan in a matter of seconds. Imaging being able to create a new product or service that was 100% accurate in its construction and ability, the result would be spectacular.

The thought that human history is approaching a "singularity"—that ordinary humans will someday be surpassed by artificially intelligent machines or cognitively enhanced biological intelligence, or both—has moved from the dominion of science fiction to serious academic debate.

Some singularity theorists predict that if the field of artificial intelligence (AI) continues to develop at its current extreme rate, the singularity could come about in the middle of the present century.

7.4.2 Trans humanism

Transhumanism is a cultural and intellectual crusade that believes we can, and should, improve the human condition through the use of progressive technologies. One of the core concepts in transhumanist thinking is life extension: Through genetic engineering, nanotech, cloning, and other emerging technologies, eternal life may soon be achievable. Equally, transhumanists are interested in the ever-increasing number of technologies that can boost our physical, intellectual, and psychological capabilities beyond what humans are naturally capable of (thus the term *trans*human).

Transcranial direct current stimulation (tDCS), for example, which speeds up reaction times and learning speed by running a very weak electric current through your brain, has already been used by the US military to train snipers. On the more extreme side, transhumanism deals with the concepts of mind uploading (to a computer), and what happens when we finally craft a computer with greater-than-human intelligence (the technological singularity).

The nervousness that surround new, paradigm-shifting technologies is not new, and it has only been amplified by the exponential acceleration of technology that has happened during our lifetime. If you were born say 500 years ago, odds are that you wouldn't experience a single societal-shifting technology in your lifetime — today, a 40 year old will have lived through the creation of the PC, the internet, the smartphone, and brain implants, to name just a few life-changing technologies.

In marketing a chatbot can read the user's profile and respond to general-knowledge questions. In the future it is likely, the chatbot will become increasingly knowledgeable about the user's profiles and mind files, and infer information from tagged multimedia files.. Lifenaut.com is also designed to test the hypothesis that conscious analogues of people can be brought to life based on sufficiently detailed mind file data.

In this AI section we have covered a lot of ground from the history of AI to its goals, approaches and tools, application, platforms, philosophy and ethics, machine consciousness and super intelligence. There is a lot to absorb.

What is clear however is that marketing has embraced AI in many ways to help with reasoning and problems solving, communication and each organizations needs are different.

As I see it the future of AI and marketing is only going to grow, its future applications fall into the following areas-based AI decision support and intelligence systems:

Decision making and data support

Marketing is about decision-making, we are responsible for the money we spent on communications, product development, research, customer relationship management, service and support. The marketing teams' goal is to obtain value for money in other words return on investment and to ensure the business has customers through the building of value propositions. In the past decades marketing lacked the Technology tools to provide the external and internal insight to knowledge-based decision-making. With the artificial intelligence now available this task has become much easier and we now have computerised decision support programs related technologies that reduce risk and provide framework for decision-making. The concept of decision support systems is not new however the technology is, and it is only being in recent decades that marketing teams have gathered the knowledge and experience to use them effectively.

The enterprise information systems in my experience are the backbone of any successful organization and include a highly sophisticated marketing information system the cuts across whole organization delivering up-to-date information and providing the flexibility to make changes to market conditions using the click of a mouse. No longer does an organization have departments that work in silos to be successful each department has to work as a cohesive unit.

Expert systems allow us access to technology that provides Data across all the external channels distribution and retailing, plus, the insight into product and service performance.

I strongly believe without customers you cannot have a business we need to use artificial neural networks as a tool of marketing to understand and gain insight into the minds of the consumer so that we can better match our products and services to their needs and wants.

Research into consumer behaviour that considers mind patterns in Marketing is a positive, as if we can duplicate how humans think and react to certain offers using artificial intelligence, we can then build models that will improve performance. On the other side of this calling is that we would be better informed and in advance be able to predict the performance of marketing action, thus reducing wastage and providing efficiency through hybrid support assistants.

Decision making, modelling and support

The basic principles of marketing management are analysis, planning, implementation and control. Planning is the most important part of marketing management and marketing managers need to make the right plan for a durable success. Good plans denote decision making. Here I am discussing the major marketing decisions what requires for a successful campaign and what marketing managers need to know for making the decision.

Marketing objectives: Setting up the objective is the first task done by the marketing managers. For running a successful marketing campaign, it is very essential that what the team is going to do. Here making the right decision is the key to achieve the goal. Managers should do SWOT analysis and then what requires to develop the present market or how to increase the present value of the company.

Then everything should go through in a proper way by the analysis and make the objectives from the requirements or opportunities from the above analysis.

Marketing strategies: Strategies is the means of the process that objectives are achieved. Objectives mean what is to be done and strategies mean how is to be done. Marketing strategies of the company are the important thing by which the operational decisions are made, and the marketing and corporate objectives achieved within the time periods specified in the plan.

Product & market scope, segments, targets etc.: The Actual condition of the company's marketing program comes from the actual research of marketing mix including product, price, place and promotion. The product and the market scope come from the incisive SWOT analysis. An incisive SWOT analysis is very much important for a successful marketing campaign. Finding out the scope of the products and the market is such a way by which the marketing manager makes the decision. Segmenting the market helps for decision-making because it shows what is needed and what is not needed. Target market helps to find out the existing and potential customers who are more specific and more dynamic.

Company targets: Every company have some target that what things they are going to do and what things they are not going to do. There have specific goals for every country that they must need something for that planning year. In these cases, setting up the target in every sector of the company is very essential like sales target, market target, organizational target, corporate target etc. This will help to make the right decision.

Marketing mix decisions- 4Ps (product, price, place and promotion): Marketing mix decisions are considered as the most important decision-making for marketing managers. It is an important part of planning. The marketing manager should have vast knowledge about the product because marketing manager needs to represent it to the customers through in many ways.

Pricing is a very crucial element as it is the only element in the marketing mix that produces revenue. Implementing products in the right place is very important because targeted customers come from this element of marketing mix. It has been said that the more you promote the product, the more you produce revenue.

Most of the above decisions in marketing can be supported through AI systems and predictive models, however understanding with phrases of the decision-making process is vital and where the marketing team's knowledge and experience in developing strategy become the key. Decision-making is the process of considering four elements, the first element is what is called the intelligence phrase this is where the marketing team looks closely at the external and internal environment to gauge what is possible and what is not. The intelligence phase covers the development of data providing insight many people call this research. The second stage of the decision-making process is called the design phase, where the outcomes and the approach are designed to achieve the agreed outcomes for example revenue, units to be sold, margin, selling price, return on investment. The third phase is called the choice phase this is where your strategic options are developed and considered against the established objectives. In marketing this is a critical stage as it defines what you're going do with clear rationalisation. The fourth phase is called the implementation phase, by implication this is where the project goes live and is implemented in the marketplace. Many products and services fail because the execution of the plan was poor during the rollout stage.

Many people ask me how do you do support decisions in Marketing, the answer it's quite simple, the purpose any commercial enterprise is to make money and to achieve a positive return on investment for the shareholders thus the benchmark in my experience for any marketing action has to be tied back to the financial performance. In the non-profit sector, performance can be measured by customer service satisfaction and loyalty.

Every organization has a hierarchy and the decision-makers usually consist of management and the Board of Directors it is vital the marketing team keep these individuals involved and up to date with progress. Always consider how each member of the management team and board will consider your marketing proposal, for example finance director will only be interested in numbers, the operations director in the processes and timelines.

Decision support systems

MKDSS is a decision support system for marketing activity. The system is used to help businesses explore different scenarios by manipulating already collected data from the past events. It consists of information technology, marketing data, systems tools, and modelling capabilities that enable the it to provide predicted outcomes from different scenarios and marketing strategies.

MKDSS assists decision makers in different scenarios and can be a very helpful tool for a business to take over their competitors. The concepts involved in DSS were first expressed in the early 1970s by Scott Morton.

These systems are used to help solve complex problems by using computer technology and can help businesses with decision making. DSS has progressed since it was first developed in the 70's. The main areas of research that DDS has developed from are theoretical and technological.

There are three types of DSS available; 1. available as a software application, 2. bespoke and 3. user developed.

DSS have many tools Shim (2014), that contain different functions such as; sophisticated database management capabilities with access to internal and external data. Information, and knowledge; powerful modelling functions accessed by a model management system; powerful, yet simple user interface designs that enable interactive queries, reporting, and graphing functions. DSS are used mainly used before a company invests their money into something. One of DSS biggest benefit is it can help to predict the outcome of different scenarios, it can help businesses to save money by preventing failures and put them towards a better cause (Cassie,1997). Decision support systems can help businesses to save time as well. They would not have to waste even a minute in planning and trying to create something which is not going to succeed.

Although DSS has many different functions, they are very user friendly and easy to use, flexible and have strong graphic capabilities.

Modelling and analysis

(MMM) is statistical analysis such as multivariate regressions on sales and marketing time series data to estimate the impact of various marketing tactics (marketing mix) on sales and then forecast the impact of future sets of tactics. It is often used to optimize advertising mix and promotional tactics with respect to sales revenue or profit.

The techniques were developed by econometricians and were first applied to consumer packaged goods, since manufacturers of those goods had access to good data on sales and marketing support. The first companies dedicated to the commercial development of MMM were MMA (then Media Marketing Assessment) started in 1990 and the Hudson River Group founded in 1989. Other early pioneer-users of econometric modelling were the ATG group at the advertising agency JWT in the 1990s and later incorporated into MindShare ATG, Brand Science at Omnicom, and the specialist modelling agency OHAL since the late 1980s.

These agencies took MMM from being a little-used and academic discipline to being a widespread and common marketing tool. Improved availability of data, massively greater computing power, and the pressure to measure and optimize marketing spend has driven the explosion in popularity as a marketing tool.

In the recent times MMM has found acceptance as a trustworthy marketing tool among the major consumer marketing companies. Often in the digital media context, MMM is referred to as attribution modelling.

Business Intelligence

Business intelligence tools analyse massive amounts of information to provide important insights into patterns that indicate the desires and attitudes of clients. Marketing teams can capitalize on this information, organizing campaigns that more precisely target the right audience, and gain a better understanding of which initiatives generate the greatest revenue.
Like the dashboard of a car gives the driver a visual of the most important information he needs to keep driving safely and successfully, a business intelligence dashboard provides a marketer with an overview of the progress of the company. The great benefit of a good dashboard for marketers is that it is easy to use and understand, and cuts through much of the junk data or unnecessary information by highlighting important measurements. It is also simple to turn data into these visuals, which in turn can be easily shared. One major advantage of a dashboard for marketers is the ability to compare several KPI's side by side in one viewing. This may foster insights that would have been obscured without visualization. If using a web analytics tool, a dashboard can portray the conversion rate in one chart, and then the source of the clicks for successful conversions in a chart to the side. Now, the marketer knows exactly where his best online leads are coming from. Dashboards are also a good way for marketers to compare the success of social channels.

It is simple to view how many sales come from each channel, side by side with how many visitors each channel brings in. The most popular medium may not be the most profitable one, in this example. Ultimately, dashboards are a way to make visual sense of the massive amounts of data that other BI tools are sure to provide. Just like the dashboard of the car, a BI dashboard offers a simple summation of important metrics and information that should offer insights on customers, performance, and more.

Collaboration, computing technologies in marketing

Marketing professionals use computer technology to plan, manage and monitor campaigns. By analysing and manipulating data on computers, they can increase the precision of marketing campaigns, personalize customer and prospect communications, and improve customer relationship management. Computer technology also makes it easier for marketing professionals to collaborate with colleagues, agencies and suppliers. With computers, marketing teams store, analyse and manage large volumes of data on prospects and customers. Understanding the demographics, purchasing histories and product preferences of different groups and individuals enables marketers to target products and campaigns with greater precision and to personalize communications.

With cloud resources, marketers can quickly increase computing capacity when they need it. By purchasing additional computing capacity from a cloud service provider, rather than investing in fixed systems, marketers can handle peaks in demand. Increasing website capacity to handle large numbers of campaign responses, for example, ensures that customers do not experience long waiting times. Marketers also use cloud computing to provide the additional capacity for test marketing and to manage large-scale email campaigns.

Marketing automation is now an essential element in lead management, the process of converting sales leads to customers. Marketing automation identifies a prospect's level of interest or intent to buy based on the response to a series of emails. The team can then follow up with detailed information or a sales call, depending on the response. Computer technology gives marketers the opportunity to build dialog and strengthen relationships with customers and prospects.

Marketers must respond to consumers' growing use of the Internet and social media. By monitoring discussions on social networks and product review sites, marketers can gain insight into consumer attitudes and take the opportunity to respond and build dialog.

Field sales teams and distributors require access to marketing support material, such as brochures, presentations, product data sheets, and advertising or email templates. By storing digital versions of campaign material in a secure Web portal and providing access to authorized users, marketers can simplify distribution of support material and increase control over its use. Using desktop video or Web-conferencing tools, marketers can collaborate with colleagues in sales and product development or account teams in advertising agencies and public relations consultancies.

Collaboration tools can speed product development by making it easy for teams to meet and take decisions, rather than trying to arrange face-to-face meetings. Agency teams can discuss or review campaign proposals and changes to ensure they meet deadlines.

Knowledge base systems

The aim of research into Knowledge-Based and Intelligent Engineering is to develop systems that replicate the *analytical, problem solving and learning capabilities of the brain*. These systems bring the benefits of knowledge and intelligence to the solution of complex problems. Listed below are three core areas and sub elements, as one considers these it is quite clear marketing uses and will introduce this technology into marketing processes to save money, time, and improve performance.

Generic Intelligent Tools, Techniques and Algorithms:
Knowledge-Based Systems, Expert Systems, Neural Networks, Fuzzy Techniques and Systems, Genetic Algorithms and Evolutionary Computing, Hybrid Intelligent Systems, Intelligent Agents and Multi-Agent Systems, Knowledge Discovery and Data Mining, Machine Learning, Cognitive Modelling, Knowledge Representation and Management, Planning, Spatial & Temporal Reasoning, Knowledge Acquisition.

Applications using Intelligent Techniques:
Industrial Control and Monitoring, Fault Diagnosis, Robotics, Image Processing, Machine & Computer Vision, Medical & Diagnostic Systems, Financial & Stock Market Monitoring and Prediction, Speech Processing and Synthesis, Natural Language Processing, Environmental Monitoring, Power Electronics & Drives, High Voltage Systems, Engine Control and Vehicle Applications, Intelligent Signal Processing and Wavelets, Intelligent Customer Support systems.

Emerging Intelligent Technologies:
Artificial Intelligence and the Internet, Information Agents on the Internet, Intelligent E-commerce/E-business and E-learning, Intelligent Information Retrieval, Intelligent Web Mining & Applications, Intelligent User Interfaces, Bioinformatics using Intelligent & Machine Learning Techniques, Intelligent Tutoring Systems, Virtual Reality & Multi-Media Intelligent Information Systems, Artificial Life, Biologically Inspired Computation.

The knowledge-based economy places great importance on the diffusion and use of information and knowledge as well as its creation. The determinants of marketing success of enterprises, and of national economies as a whole, is ever more reliant upon their effectiveness in gathering and utilising knowledge. Strategic know-how and competence are being developed interactively and shared within sub-groups and networks, where know-who is significant. The economy becomes a hierarchy of networks, driven by the acceleration in the rate of change and the rate of learning. What is created is a network society, where the opportunity and capability to get access to and join knowledge- and learning-intensive relations determines the socio-economic position of individuals and firms (David and Foray, 1995).

Revision
- Using 100 words outline the core philosophical areas of AI.
- Debate the pro and cons of AI on humanity.
- Provide a description of transhumanism.
- Using 100 words outline " robot rights".

8 References (as they appear in the text)

AI textbooks
Hutter, Marcus (2005). *Universal Artificial Intelligence*. Berlin: Springer. ISBN 978-3-540-22139-5.

Luger, George; Stubblefield, William (2004). *Artificial Intelligence: Structures and Strategies for Complex Problem Solving* (5th ed.). Benjamin/Cummings. ISBN 0-8053-4780-1.

Neapolitan, Richard; Jiang, Xia (2012). *Contemporary Artificial Intelligence*. Chapman & Hall/CRC. ISBN 978-1-4398-4469-4.

Nilsson, Nils (1998). *Artificial Intelligence: A New Synthesis*. Morgan Kaufmann. ISBN 978-1-55860-467-4.

Russell, Stuart J.; Norvig, Peter (2003), *Artificial Intelligence: A Modern Approach* (2nd ed.), Upper Saddle River, New Jersey: Prentice Hall, ISBN 0-13-790395-2.

Russell, Stuart J.; Norvig, Peter (2009). *Artificial Intelligence: A Modern Approach* (3rd ed.). Upper Saddle River, New Jersey: Prentice Hall. ISBN 0-13-604259-7.

Poole, David; Mackworth, Alan; Goebel, Randy (1998). *Computational Intelligence: A Logical Approach*. New York: Oxford University Press. ISBN 0-19-510270-3.

Winston, Patrick Henry (1984). *Artificial Intelligence*. Reading, MA: Addison-Wesley. ISBN 0-201-08259-4.

Rich, Elaine (1983). *Artificial Intelligence*. McGraw-Hill. ISBN 0-07-052261-8.

Bundy, Alan (1980). *Artificial Intelligence: An Introductory Course* (2nd ed.). Edinburgh University Press. ISBN 0-85224-410-X.
History of AI[edit]

Crevier, Daniel (1993), *AI: The Tumultuous Search for Artificial Intelligence*, New York, NY: BasicBooks, ISBN 0-465-02997-3.

McCorduck, Pamela (2004), *Machines Who Think* (2nd ed.), Natick, MA: A. K. Peters, Ltd., ISBN 1-56881-205-1.

Newquist, HP (1994). *The Brain Makers: Genius, Ego, And Greed In The Quest For Machines That Think*. New York: Macmillan/SAMS. ISBN 0-672-30412-0.

Nilsson, Nils (2009). *The Quest for Artificial Intelligence: A History of Ideas and Achievements*. New York: Cambridge University Press. ISBN 978-0-521-12293-1. Other sources[edit]
Asada, M.; Hosoda, K.; Kuniyoshi, Y.; Ishiguro, H.; Inui, T.; Yoshikawa, Y.; Ogino, M.; Yoshida, C. (2009). "Cognitive developmental robotics: a survey". *IEEE Transactions on Autonomous Mental Development*. 1 (1): 12–34. doi:10.1109/tamd.2009.2021702. Archived from the original on 4 October 2013. "ACM Computing Classification System: Artificial intelligence". ACM. 1998. Retrieved 30 August 2017.

Goodman, Joanna (2016). *Robots in Law: How Artificial Intelligence is Transforming Legal Services* (1st ed.). Ark Group. ISBN 978-1-78358-264-8.

Albus, J. S. (2002). "4-D/RCS: A Reference Model Architecture for Intelligent Unmanned Ground Vehicles" (PDF). In Gerhart, G.; Gunderson, R.; Shoemaker, C. *Proceedings of the SPIE AeroSense Session on Unmanned Ground Vehicle Technology*. 3693. pp. 11–20. Archived from the original (PDF) on 25 July 2004.

Aleksander, Igor (1995). *Artificial Neuroconsciousness: An Update*. IWANN. Archived from the original on 2 March 1997. BibTex Archived 2 March 1997 at the Wayback Machine.

Bach, Joscha (2008). "Seven Principles of Synthetic Intelligence". In Wang, Pei; Goertzel, Ben; Franklin, Stan. *Artificial General Intelligence, 2008: Proceedings of the First AGI Conference*. IOS Press. pp. 63–74. ISBN 978-1-58603-833-5. "Robots could demand legal rights". *BBC News*. 21 December 2006. Retrieved 3 February 2017.

Brooks, Rodney (1990). "Elephants Don't Play Chess" (PDF). *Robotics and Autonomous Systems*. 6: 3–15. doi:10.1016/S0921-8890(05)80025-9. Archived (PDF) from the original on 9 August 2007.

Brooks, R. A. (1991). "How to build complete creatures rather than isolated cognitive simulators". In VanLehn, K. *Architectures for Intelligence*. Hillsdale, NJ: Lawrence Erlbaum Associates. pp. 225–239. CiteSeerX 10.1.1.52.9510 .

Buchanan, Bruce G. (2005). "A (Very) Brief History of Artificial Intelligence" (PDF). *AI Magazine*: 53–60. Archived from the original (PDF) on 26 September 2007.

Butler, Samuel (13 June 1863). "Darwin among the Machines". Letters to the Editor. *The Press*. Christchurch, New Zealand. Retrieved 16 October 2017 – via Victoria University of Wellington.

"AI set to exceed human brain power". *CNN*. 26 July 2006. Archived from the original on 19 February 2008.

Dennett, Daniel (1991). *Consciousness Explained*. The Penguin Press. ISBN 0-7139-9037-6.

Diamond, David (December 2003). "The Love Machine; Building computers that care". *Wired*. Archived from the original on 18 May 2008.

Dowe, D. L.; Hajek, A. R. (1997). "A computational extension to the Turing Test". *Proceedings of the 4th Conference of the Australasian Cognitive Science Society*. Archived from the original on 28 June 2011.

Dreyfus, Hubert (1972). *What Computers Can't Do*. New York: MIT Press. ISBN 0-06-011082-1.

Dreyfus, Hubert; Dreyfus, Stuart (1986). *Mind over Machine: The Power of Human Intuition and Expertise in the Era of the Computer*. Oxford, UK: Blackwell. ISBN 0-02-908060-6.

Dreyfus, Hubert (1992). *What Computers Still Can't Do*. New York: MIT Press. ISBN 0-262-54067-3.

Dyson, George (1998). *Darwin among the Machines*. Allan Lane Science. ISBN 0-7382-0030-1.

Edelman, Gerald (23 November 2007). "Gerald Edelman – Neural Darwinism and Brain-based Devices". Talking Robots. Archived from the original on 8 October 2009.

Edelson, Edward (1991). *The Nervous System*. New York: Chelsea House. ISBN 978-0-7910-0464-7.

Fearn, Nicholas (2007). *The Latest Answers to the Oldest Questions: A Philosophical Adventure with the World's Greatest Thinkers*. New York: Grove Press. ISBN 0-8021-1839-9.

Gladwell, Malcolm (2005). *Blink*. New York: Little, Brown and Co. ISBN 0-316-17232-4.

Gödel, Kurt (1951). *Some basic theorems on the foundations of mathematics and their implications*. Gibbs Lecture. In Feferman, Solomon, ed. (1995). *Kurt Gödel: Collected Works, Vol. III: Unpublished Essays and Lectures*. Oxford University Press. pp. 304–23. ISBN 978-0-19-514722-3.

Haugeland, John (1985). *Artificial Intelligence: The Very Idea*. Cambridge, Mass.: MIT Press. ISBN 0-262-08153-9.

Hawkins, Jeff; Blakeslee, Sandra (2005). *On Intelligence*. New York, NY: Owl Books. ISBN 0-8050-7853-3.

Henderson, Mark (24 April 2007). "Human rights for robots? We're getting carried away". *The Times Online*. London.

Hernandez-Orallo, Jose (2000). "Beyond the Turing Test". *Journal of Logic, Language and Information*. 9 (4): 447–466. doi:10.1023/A:1008367325700.

Hernandez-Orallo, J.; Dowe, D. L. (2010). "Measuring Universal Intelligence: Towards an Anytime Intelligence Test". *Artificial Intelligence Journal*. 174 (18): 1508–1539. CiteSeerX 10.1.1.295.9079. doi:10.1016/j.artint.2010.09.006.

Hinton, G. E. (2007). "Learning multiple layers of representation". *Trends in Cognitive Sciences*. 11: 428–434. doi:10.1016/j.tics.2007.09.004.

Hofstadter, Douglas (1979). *Gödel, Escher, Bach: an Eternal Golden Braid*. New York, NY: Vintage Books. ISBN 0-394-74502-7.

Holland, John H. (1975). *Adaptation in Natural and Artificial Systems*. University of Michigan Press. ISBN 0-262-58111-6.

Howe, J. (November 1994). "Artificial Intelligence at Edinburgh University: a Perspective". Retrieved 30 August 2017.

Hutter, M. (2012). "One Decade of Universal Artificial Intelligence". *Theoretical Foundations of Artificial General Intelligence*. Atlantis Thinking Machines. 4. doi:10.2991/978-94-91216-62-6_5. ISBN 978-94-91216-61-9.

James, William (1884). "What is Emotion". *Mind*. 9: 188–205. doi:10.1093/mind/os-IX.34.188. Cited by Tao & Tan 2005.

Kahneman, Daniel; Slovic, D.; Tversky, Amos (1982). *Judgment under uncertainty: Heuristics and biases*. New York: Cambridge University Press. ISBN 0-521-28414-7.

Katz, Yarden (1 November 2012). "Noam Chomsky on Where Artificial Intelligence Went Wrong". *The Atlantic*. Retrieved 26 October 2014.

"Kismet". MIT Artificial Intelligence Laboratory, Humanoid Robotics Group. Retrieved 25 October 2017.

Koza, John R. (1992). *Genetic Programming (On the Programming of Computers by Means of Natural Selection)*. MIT Press. ISBN 0-262-11170-5.

Kleine-Cosack, Christian (October 2006). "Recognition and Simulation of Emotions" (PDF). Archived from the original (PDF) on 28 May 2008.

Kolata, G. (1982). "How can computers get common sense?". *Science*. 217 (4566): 1237–1238. doi:10.1126/science.217.4566.1237. PMID 17837639.

Kumar, Gulshan; Kumar, Krishan (2012). "The Use of Artificial-Intelligence-Based Ensembles for Intrusion Detection: A Review". *Applied Computational Intelligence and Soft Computing*. 2012: 1–20. doi:10.1155/2012/850160.

Kurzweil, Ray (1999). *The Age of Spiritual Machines*. Penguin Books. ISBN 0-670-88217-8.

Kurzweil, Ray (2005). *The Singularity is Near*. Penguin Books. ISBN 0-670-03384-7.

Lakoff, George; Núñez, Rafael E. (2000). *Where Mathematics Comes From: How the Embodied Mind Brings Mathematics into Being*. Basic Books. ISBN 0-465-03771-2.

Langley, Pat (2011). "The changing science of machine learning". *Machine Learning*. 82 (3): 275–279. doi:10.1007/s10994-011-5242-y.

Law, Diane (June 1994). *Searle, Subsymbolic Functionalism and Synthetic Intelligence* (Technical report). University of Texas at Austin. p. AI94-222. CiteSeerX 10.1.1.38.8384 .

Legg, Shane; Hutter, Marcus (15 June 2007). *A Collection of Definitions of Intelligence* (Technical report). IDSIA. arXiv:0706.3639 . 07-07.

Lenat, Douglas; Guha, R. V. (1989). *Building Large Knowledge-Based Systems*. Addison-Wesley. ISBN 0-201-51752-3.

Lighthill, James (1973). "Artificial Intelligence: A General Survey". *Artificial Intelligence: a paper symposium*. Science Research Council.

Lucas, John (1961). "Minds, Machines and Gödel". In Anderson, A.R. *Minds and Machines*. Archived from the original on 19 August 2007. Retrieved 30 August 2007.

Lungarella, M.; Metta, G.; Pfeifer, R.; Sandini, G. (2003). "Developmental robotics: a survey". *Connection Science*. 15: 151–190. CiteSeerX 10.1.1.83.7615 . doi:10.1080/09540090310001655110.

Maker, Meg Houston (2006). "AI@50: AI Past, Present, Future". Dartmouth College. Archived from the original on 3 January 2007. Retrieved 16 October 2017.

Markoff, John (16 February 2011). "Computer Wins on 'Jeopardy!': Trivial, It's Not". *The New York Times*. Retrieved 25 October 2017.

McCarthy, John; Minsky, Marvin; Rochester, Nathan; Shannon, Claude (1955). "A Proposal for the Dartmouth Summer Research Project on Artificial Intelligence". Archived from the original on 26 August 2007. Retrieved 30 August 2017.

McCarthy, John; Hayes, P. J. (1969). "Some philosophical problems from the standpoint of artificial intelligence". *Machine Intelligence*. 4: 463–502. CiteSeerX 10.1.1.85.5082 . Archived from the original on 10 August 2007. Retrieved 30 August 2017.

McCarthy, John (12 November 2007). "What Is Artificial Intelligence?".

Minsky, Marvin (1967). *Computation: Finite and Infinite Machines*. Englewood Cliffs, N.J.: Prentice-Hall. ISBN 0-13-165449-7.

Minsky, Marvin (2006). *The Emotion Machine*. New York, NY: Simon & SchusterI. ISBN 0-7432-7663-9.

Moravec, Hans (1988). *Mind Children*. Harvard University Press. ISBN 0-674-57616-0.

Norvig, Peter (25 June 2012). "On Chomsky and the Two Cultures of Statistical Learning". Peter Norvig. Archived from the original on 19 October 2014.

NRC (United States National Research Council) (1999). "Developments in Artificial Intelligence". *Funding a Revolution: Government Support for Computing Research*. National Academy Press.

Needham, Joseph (1986). *Science and Civilization in China: Volume 2*. Caves Books Ltd.

Newell, Allen; Simon, H. A. (1976). "Computer Science as Empirical Inquiry: Symbols and Search". *Communications of the ACM*. 19 (3): 113–126. doi:10.1145/360018.360022. Archived from the original on 7 October 2008.

Nilsson, Nils (1983). "Artificial Intelligence Prepares for 2001" (PDF). *AI Magazine*. 1 (1). Presidential Address to the Association for the Advancement of Artificial Intelligence.

O'Brien, James; Marakas, George (2011). *Management Information Systems* (10th ed.). McGraw-Hill/Irwin. ISBN 978-0-07-337681-3.

O'Connor, Kathleen Malone (1994). "The alchemical creation of life (takwin) and other concepts of Genesis in medieval Islam". University of Pennsylvania.

Oudeyer, P-Y. (2010). "On the impact of robotics in behavioral and cognitive sciences: from insect navigation to human cognitive development" (PDF). *IEEE Transactions on Autonomous Mental Development*. 2 (1): 2–16. doi:10.1109/tamd.2009.2039057.

Penrose, Roger (1989). *The Emperor's New Mind: Concerning Computer, Minds and The Laws of Physics*. Oxford University Press. ISBN 0-19-851973-7.
Picard, Rosalind (1995). *Affective Computing* (PDF) (Technical report). MIT. 321. Lay summary – *Abstract*.

Poli, R.; Langdon, W. B.; McPhee, N. F. (2008). *A Field Guide to Genetic Programming*. Lulu.com. ISBN 978-1-4092-0073-4 – via gp-field-guide.org.uk.
Rajani, Sandeep (2011). "Artificial Intelligence – Man or Machine" (PDF). *International Journal of Information Technology and Knowledge Management*. 4 (1): 173–176. Archived from the original (PDF) on 18 January 2013.

Searle, John (1980). "Minds, Brains and Programs". *Behavioral and Brain Sciences*. 3 (3): 417–457. doi:10.1017/S0140525X00005756. Archived from the original on 18 January 2010.

Searle, John (1999). *Mind, language and society*. New York, NY: Basic Books. ISBN 0-465-04521-9. OCLC 231867665.

Shapiro, Stuart C. (1992). "Artificial Intelligence". In Shapiro, Stuart C. *Encyclopedia of Artificial Intelligence* (PDF) (2nd ed.). New York: John Wiley. pp. 54–57. ISBN 0-471-50306-1.

Simon, H. A. (1965). *The Shape of Automation for Men and Management*. New York: Harper & Row.

Skillings, Jonathan (3 July 2006). "Getting Machines to Think Like Us". *cnet*. Retrieved 3 February 2011.

Solomonoff, Ray (1956). *An Inductive Inference Machine* (PDF). Dartmouth Summer Research Conference on Artificial Intelligence – via std.com, pdf scanned copy of the original. Later published as Solomonoff, Ray (1957). "An Inductive Inference Machine". *IRE Convention Record*. Section on Information Theory, part 2. pp. 56–62.

Tao, Jianhua; Tan, Tieniu (2005). *Affective Computing and Intelligent Interaction*. Affective Computing: A Review. LNCS 3784. Springer. pp. 981–995. doi:10.1007/11573548.

Tecuci, Gheorghe (March–April 2012). "Artificial Intelligence". *Wiley Interdisciplinary Reviews: Computational Statistics*. Wiley. 4 (2): 168–180. doi:10.1002/wics.200.

Thro, Ellen (1993). *Robotics: The Marriage of Computers and Machines*. New York: Facts on File. ISBN 978-0-8160-2628-9.

Turing, Alan (October 1950), "Computing Machinery and Intelligence", *Mind*, LIX (236): 433–460, doi:10.1093/mind/LIX.236.433, ISSN 0026-4423, retrieved 2008-08-18.

van der Walt, Christiaan; Bernard, Etienne (2006). "Data characteristics that determine classifier performance" (PDF). Archived from the original (PDF) on 25 March 2009. Retrieved 5 August 2017.

Vinge, Vernor (1993). "The Coming Technological Singularity: How to Survive in the Post-Human Era".

Wason, P. C.; Shapiro, D. (1966). "Reasoning". In Foss, B. M. *New horizons in psychology*. Harmondsworth: Penguin.

Weizenbaum, Joseph (1976). *Computer Power and Human Reason*. San Francisco: W.H. Freeman & Company. ISBN 0-7167-0464-1.

Weng, J.; McClelland; Pentland, A.; Sporns, O.; Stockman, I.; Sur, M.; Thelen, E. (2001). "Autonomous mental development by robots and animals" (PDF). *Science*. 291: 599–600. doi:10.1126/science.291.5504.599 – via msu.edu.

SECTION TWO

MACHINE LEARNING

Contents

1 Overview

Machine learning is a field of computer science that gives computers the ability to learn without being explicitly programmed.

Introduction

Machine learning (ML) explores the study and construction of algorithms that can learn from and make predictions on data Kohavi (1998) – such algorithms, overcome following strictly static program instructions, by making data-driven predictions or decisions, through building a model from sample inputs. Machine learning is employed in a range of computing tasks where *designing and programming explicit algorithms with good performance is difficult*; example applications include email filtering, detection of network intruders or malicious insiders working towards a data breach, Dickson (2017), Optical Character Recognition (OCR), Werwick, etal (2010) learning to rank, and computer vision.

Chapter Learning Outcomes

▢ Outlines the study of machine learning.

▢ Demonstrates the purpose of algorithms in ML.

▢ The use of instructions.

▢ Introduces the variety of tasks that ML can be applied .

▢ Having successfully completed the module, you will be able to:

▢ 1. Critically assess ML basics.

▢ 2. Assess the tools of (ML) in today's world.

☐ Having completed the module, you will be able to:

☐ 1. Understand the variety of (ML) applications and their uses.

• 2. Be able to explain the principal goals of each in (ML).

Critical thinking

Having successfully completed this topic, you will be able to:1. Critically evaluate the variety of techniques used in (ML) .2. Understand and debate the areas of (ML) to management.

OBJECTIVES

The chapter endeavours to explain machine learning and outline the issues facing this area of technology.

1.1 Types of problems and tasks

Machine learning is a subject of computer science that gives computers the ability to learn without being obviously programmed. Arthur Samuel an American pioneer in the field of computer gaming and artificial intelligence, created the term "Machine Learning" in 1959 while at IBM (Kohavi etal,1998). Advanced from the study of pattern recognition and computational Learning Theory in artificial intelligence, machine learning discovers the study and construction of algorithms that can learn from and make forecasts on data , such algorithms follow exact static program instructions by making data-driven predictions or decisions, through developing a model from sample inputs. Machine learning is employed in a range of computing tasks where designing and programming explicit algorithms with good performance is problematic or not practical; example applications include in marketing email filtering, detection of network intruders or malicious insiders working towards a data breach, Dickson (2017) optical character recognition (OCR), learning to rank, and computer vision.

Machine learning is narrowly related to (and often overlaps with) computational statistics, which also focuses on prediction-making through the use of computers which is used in marketing models and scenario work.

It has strong binds to mathematical optimization, which delivers methods, theory and application domains to the field. Machine learning is sometimes confused with data mining commonly used in marketing, Mannila (1996) where the second subfield focuses more on *exploratory data analysis* and is known as unsupervised learning. Machine learning can also be unsupervised and be used to learn and establish baseline behavioural profiles for various entities and then used to find meaningful anomalies.

Within the field of marketing data analytics, machine learning is a technique used to develop complex models and algorithms that lend themselves to prediction analysis used in marketing forecasting; in commercial use, this is known *as predictive analytics.*

These analytical models allow marketers, researchers, data scientists, engineers, and analysts to "produce reliable, repeatable decisions and results" and uncover "hidden insights" through learning from historical relationships and 'trends' in the data.

Effective machine learning is difficult because finding patterns is hard, and often not enough training data is available; as a result, machine-learning programs often fail to deliver value. Among other categories of machine learning problems ' learning to learn' learns its own inductive bias based on *previous experience.* Developmental learning, expounded for robot learning, generates its own sequences (also called curriculum) of learning situations to cumulatively develop repertoires of novel skills through autonomous self-exploration and social interaction with human teachers and using guidance mechanisms such as active learning, maturation, motor synergies, and imitation.

Another categorization of machine learning tasks arises when one considers the desired *output* of a machine-learned system in marketing:

- In *classification*, inputs are divided into two or more classes, and the learner must produce a model that assigns unseen inputs to one or more (multi-label classification) of these classes. This is typically tackled in a supervised way. Spam filtering is an example of classification, where the inputs are email (or other) messages and the classes are "spam" and "not spam".
- In *regression*, also a supervised problem, the outputs are continuous rather than discrete.
- In *clustering*, a set of inputs is to be divided into groups. Unlike in classification, the groups are not known beforehand, making this typically an unsupervised task.
- *Density estimation* finds the distribution of inputs in some space.
- *Dimensionality reduction* simplifies inputs by mapping them into a lower-dimensional space.
- *Topic Modelling* is a related problem, where a program is given a list of human language documents and is tasked to find out which documents cover similar topics

Applications for machine learning in marketing include:

- Automated theorem proving
  Automated theorem proving (also known as ATP or automated deduction) is a subfield of automated reasoning and mathematical logic trading with verifying mathematical theorems by computer programs. Automated reasoning over mathematical proof was a major motivation for the progress of computer science.

- Adaptive websites
  An adaptive website is a website that shapes a replica of user activity and modifies the information and/or presentation of information to the user in order to enhance and tackle the user's needs.

- Affective computing
  Affective computing (occasionally called artificial emotional intelligence, or emotion AI) is the education and development of systems and devices that can acknowledge, understand, practise, and simulate human affects.

- Brain Interfaces
  A brain computer interface (BCI), occasionally called a mind-machine interface (MMI), direct neural interface (DNI), or brain–machine interface (BMI), is a straight contact corridor between an heightened or wired brain and an external device. BCIs are often focused at researching, mapping, assisting, augmenting, or repairing human cognitive or sensory-motor functions.

- Computer vision, including object recognition

  Computer vision is an interdisciplinary subject that deals with how computers can be made for increasing high-level understanding from digital images or videos. From the perspective of engineering, it seeks to automate everyday jobs that the human systems can do.

- Detecting credit-card fraud

  Credit card fraud is a wide-ranging word for theft and fraud performed using or entailing a payment card, such as a credit card or debit card, as a fraudulent cause of moneys in a transaction. The intention may be to obtain goods without paying, or to obtain illegal funds from an account. Credit card fraud is also an adjunct to identity theft.

- General game playing

  General game playing (GGP) is the enterprise of artificial intelligence programs to be able to perform more than one game effectively. For many games like chess, computers are encoded to play these games using a particularly designed algorithm, which cannot be relocated to another framework.

- Information Retrieval

  Information retrieval (IR) is the action of procurement information resources pertinent to a data need from a collection of information resources. Searches can be founded on full-text or other content-based indexing. Information retrieval is the science of examining for information in a document, searching for documents themselves, and also searching for metadata that define data, and for databases of texts, images or sounds.

- Internet fraud detection

  Internet fraud is a category of fraud which causes the use of the Internet. This form of fraud differs significantly and emerges in many arrangements. It ranges from E-mail spam to online scams. Internet fraud can happen even if partly based on the use of internet facilities, however it is mostly or completely based on the use of the internet.

- Linguistics

  Linguistics is the scientific study of language, and entails an analysis of language form, language meaning, and language in context. Linguists conventionally analyse human language by detecting an inter play between sound and meaning. Phonetics is the study of speech and non-speech sounds, and investigates into their acoustic and articulatory properties.

- Machine perception

  Machine perception is the competence of a computer system to interpret data in a manner that is comparable to the way humans practice their senses to re-count the world close to them. The rudimentary method that the computers take in and act in response to their environment is through the attached hardware. Up to recently input was limited to a keyboard, or a mouse, but developments in technology, both in hardware and software, have permitted computers to take in sensory input in a way similar to humans.

- Natural language processing

  Natural language processing (NLP) is a subject of computer science, artificial intelligence and computational linguistics involved with the interactions between computers and human (natural) languages, and, in particular, concerned with programming computers to productively process large natural language.

- Natural language understanding

  Natural language understanding (NLU) is a subtopic of NLP in artificial intelligence that exchanges with machine reading comprehension. NLU is considered an AI-hard problem.

- Optimization and metaheuristic

  In mathematics, computer science and operations research, mathematical optimization or mathematical programming, alternatively spelled optimisation, is the assortment of a suitable element (with regard to some criterion) from some set of obtainable substitutes.

- Online advertising

  Online advertising, also termed online marketing or Internet advertising or web advertising, is a method of marketing and advertising which uses the Internet to transport promotional marketing messages to consumers.

- Recommender systems

  A recommender system or a recommendation system (sometimes replacing "system" with a synonym such as platform or engine) is a subclass of information filtering system that seeks to forecast the "rating" or "preference" that a user would give to an item. Recommender systems have become progressively widespread in recent years, and are utilized in a variety of subjects including movies, music, news, books, research articles, search queries, social tags, and products in general. There are also recommender systems for experts, collaborators, jokes, restaurants, garments, financial services, life insurance, romantic partners (online dating), and Twitter pages.

- Search engines

  A web search engine is a software technique that is designed to search for information on the World Wide Web. The search results are commonly presented in a boundary of results often referred to as search engine results pages (SERPs). The information may be a mix of web pages, images, and other types of files. Some search engines also mine data available in databases or open directories.

- Sentiment analysis (or opinion mining)

  Sentiment analysis (sometimes known as opinion mining or emotion AI) refers to the use of natural language processing, text analysis, computational linguistics, and biometrics to methodically identify, extract, quantify, and study affective states and subjective information. Sentiment analysis is extensively used to voice of the customer materials such as evaluations and assessment responses, online and social media, and healthcare materials for functions that range from marketing to customer service to clinical medicine.

- Sequence mining

  Sequential pattern mining is a theme of data mining bothered with finding statistically pertinent patterns between data examples where the values are delivered in a sequence. It is regularly presumed that the values are discrete, and thus time series mining is carefully related, but usually considered a different activity. Sequential pattern mining is an exclusive case of structured data mining.

- Speech and handwriting recognition

  Speech recognition is the inter-disciplinary sub-field of computational linguistics that creates methodologies and technologies that empowers the recognition and translation of spoken language into text by processors. It is also known as "automatic speech recognition" (ASR), "computer speech recognition", or just "speech to text" (STT). It incorporates knowledge and research in the linguistics, computer science, and electrical engineering fields.

- Syntactic pattern recognition

Syntactic pattern recognition or structural pattern recognition is a method of pattern recognition, in which each object can be characterised by a variable-cardinality set of symbolic, nominal topographies. This allows for representing pattern structures, taking into interpretation more complex interrelationships between qualities than is possible in the case of flat, numerical feature vectors of fixed dimensionality, that are used in statistical classification. Syntactic pattern recognition can be used as an alternative of statistical pattern recognition if there is well-defined structure in the patterns. One way to present such structure is by means of a strings of symbols from a formal language. In this case the consistencies in the structures of the sets are encoded as different grammars.

- Time series forecasting

A time series is a series of data points indexed (or listed or graphed) in time order. Most frequently, a time series is a sequence taken at sequential evenly spaced points in time. Thus it is a sequence of discrete-time data. Examples of time series are heights of ocean tides, counts of sunspots, and the daily closing value of the Dow Jones Industrial Average. Time series are commonly plotted via line charts. Time series are used in statistics, signal processing, pattern recognition, econometrics, mathematical finance, weather forecasting, earthquake prediction, electroencephalography, control engineering, astronomy, communications engineering, and principally in any domain of applied science and engineering which engages temporal measurements.

- User behaviour analytics

User behaviour analytics ("UBA") as a cybersecurity procedure is about detection of insider threats, targeted attacks, and financial fraud. UBA solutions observe patterns of human behaviour, and then apply algorithms and statistical analysis to detect meaningful anomalies from those arrangements—anomalies that indicate potential threats. Instead of tracking devices or security events, UBA tracks a system's users.
Big data platforms like Apache Hadoop are enlarging UBA functionality by allowing them to analyse petabytes worth of data to detect insider threats and advanced persistent threats.

- Translation

  Translation is the communication of the connotation of a source-language text by means of an equivalent target-language text. Even though interpreting the enabling of oral or sign-language communication between operators of different languages, antedates writing, translation started only after the arrival of written literature.

2 History and relationships to other fields

Introduction

As a scientific endeavour, machine learning grew out of the quest for artificial intelligence. Already in the early days of AI as an academic discipline, some researchers were interested in having machines learn from data. They attempted to approach the problem with various symbolic methods, as well as what were then termed "neural networks"; these were mostly perceptron's and other models that were later found to be reinventions of the generalized linear models of statistics. Probabilistic reasoning was also employed, especially in automated medical diagnosis

Chapter Learning Outcomes

⦿ What is the history behind ML.?

⦿ Understanding that ML and statistics are closely related field.

⦿ The methods used in ML.

⦿ A basic knowledge of optimization through ML.

⦿ Having successfully completed the module, you will be able to:

⦿ 1. Critically assess the history a relationship of (ML) in marketing.

⦿ 2. Assess the application tools of (ML) in today's world.

⦿ Having completed the module, you will be able to:

⦿ 1. Understand the variety of (ML) applications and their uses.

• 2. Be able to explain the principal goals of each in (ML).

Critical thinking

Having successfully completed this topic, you will be able to:1. Critically evaluate the variety of area covered in (ML) .2. Understand and debate the areas of (ML) to management.

OBJECTIVES

To provide the reader with a basic knowledge of the background to ML development and its relationship to other scientific fields.

2.1 Relation to statistics

Machine learning and statistics are closely related fields. According to Michael I. Jordan, the ideas of machine learning, from methodological principles to theoretical tools, have had a long pre-history in statistics. He also suggested the term data science as a placeholder to call the overall field (Jordan, 2014). Leo Breiman distinguished two statistical modelling paradigms: data model and algorithmic model, wherein "algorithmic model" means more or less the machine learning algorithms like Random forest. Some statisticians have adopted methods from machine learning, leading to a combined field that they call *statistical learning* (James etal, 2013).

In my experience, there is little distinction between statistics and machine learning. Also, I rarely find it useful in discussion to differentiate the two between theory and practice; their interplay is already considerate and will only increase the debate in literature as the two methods and their problems we grow more complex.

Think of the marketing problem of 'building a product.' There's a whole chain of ideas from history through marketing theory that allow one to design a new product, build them, give guarantees that they will not fail under certain conditions, tune them to specific settings, etc, etc. I suspect that there are few people involved in this chain who don't make use of "theoretical concepts" and " marketing know-how". It took decades (centuries really) for all of this to be developed. Those ideas are both theoretical and practical in nature. We have a similar challenge in statistics and ML, how do we take core inferential ideas and turn them into marketing systems that can work under whatever requirements that one has in mind (time, accuracy, cost, etc), that reflect assumptions that are *appropriate for the domain*, that are clear on what inferences and what decisions are to be made (does one want causes, predictions, variable selection, model selection, ranking, A/B tests, etc, etc), can allow interactions with humans (input of expert knowledge, visualization, personalization, privacy, ethical issues, etc, etc), that scale, that are easy to use and are robust.

Indeed, with all due respect to product marketing builders (and rocket builders, etc), there is a domain here that is more complex than any ever confronted in human society, just look at the new product failure rate.

I don't know what to call the overall field here (it's fine to use "data science" as a placeholder), but the main point is that most people who were trained in statistics or in machine learning obliquely understood themselves as *working in this overall field*; they do not say "I'm not interested in principles having to do with randomization in data collection, or with how to merge data, or with uncertainty in my predictions, or with evaluating models, or with visualization". Yes, they work on *subsets of the overall problem*, but they are certainly aware of the *overall problem* also.

Different collections of people in communities often tend to have different application domains in mind and that makes some of the details of their current work look superficially different, but there's no actual underlying intellectual distinction, and many of the seeming distinctions are historical accidents.

Take issue with the phrase 'methods more squarely in the realm of machine learning' found in textbooks. I have no idea what this means, or could possibly mean. Throughout the eighties and nineties, it was prominent how many times people working within the "ML community" realized that their ideas had had a *lengthy pre-history in statistics*. Decision trees, nearest neighbour, logistic regression, kernels, PCA, canonical correlation, graphical models, K means, and discriminant analysis come to mind, and also many general methodological principles (e.g., method of moments, which is having a mini renaissance.)

 Bayesian inference methods come in all kinds, estimation, bootstrap, cross-validation, EM, ROC, and of course stochastic gradient descent, whose pre-history goes back to the 50s and beyond), and many theoretical tools (large deviations, concentrations, empirical processes, Bernstein-von Mises, U statistics, etc).

Of course, the "statistics community" was also not ever that well classified, and while ideas such as Kalman filters, HMMs and factor analysis originated outside of the "statistics community" are narrowly defined, they were absorbed within statistics because they're clearly about inference. Similarly, layered neural networks can and should be viewed as nonparametric function estimators, objects to be analysed statistically.

In general, "statistics" refers in part to an *analysis style*---a statistician is happy to analyse the performance of any system, e.g., a logic-based system, if it takes in data that can be considered random and outputs decisions that can be considered uncertain. A "statistical method" doesn't have to have any probabilities in it per se. (Consider computing the median).

When Leo Breiman developed random forests, was he being a statistician or a machine learner? Are the SVM and boosting machine learning while logistic regression is statistics, even though they are solving essentially the same optimization problems up to slightly different shapes in a loss function? Why does anyone think that these are meaningful distinctions?

The "ML community" has developed many new inferential principles or many new optimization principles but I do think that the community has been exceptionally creative at taking existing ideas across many fields, and mixing and matching them to solve problems.

The ML community has excelled at making creative use of new computing architectures. Most would view all of this as the proto emergence of an engineering counterpart to the more purely theoretical investigations that have classically taken place within statistics and optimization.

But one should not definitely equate statistics or optimization with theory and machine learning with applications. The "statistics community" has also been very applied, it's just that for historical reasons their collaborations have tended to focus on science, medicine and policy rather than engineering. The emergence of the "ML community" has (inter alia) helped to enlarge the scope of "applied statistical inference".

It has begun to break down some barriers between engineering thinking (e.g., computer systems thinking) and inferential thinking. And of course, it has engendered many new theoretical questions.

In a marketing context it could be argued that the descriptor of ML is "the process of what machines learn on their own using the data provided to them. It is the machine learning from the data as it progresses along a process path. There is no question the machine has statistical analysis in its DNA (algorithms) however there is no external input to the output in progress." (Seligman, 2016).

In marketing we collect data, lots of it, in fact it is a problem, ML enables tasks to be completed without human supervision or intervention, it automatically takes the data and builds outputs to a pre-defined format that become ' usable knowledge.'

Take an example of ML, we have a till in a supermarket, its records sales of items for the day, we can slice and dice this information using ML which can predict on historical data the potential sales and item mix for tomorrow. However, we have 20 tills per store and 500 stores, ML can assist in the analysis of one till to the whole lot and provide data with projections, scenarios for the business without human input.

Revision

- Outline in 250 words the history of machine learning
- Discuss the difference between ML and statistics
- In 100 words outline why ML could be useful in a marketing context, show examples

3 Theory

Introduction

In computer science, computational learning theory (or just learning theory) is a subfield of Artificial Intelligence devoted to studying the design and analysis of machine learning algorithms.

☐ The concept of inductive learning.

☐ To understand the measure of performance on new tasks and data input.

☐ To appreciate the concepts of positive and negative results.

☐ Having successfully completed the module, you will be able to:

☐ 1. Critically assess the concept of theory of (ML) in marketing.

☐ 2. Assess the accuracy tools and measures of (ML) in today's world.

☐ Having completed the module, you will be able to:

☐ 1. Understand the variety of (ML) complexities and their uses.

• 2. Be able to explain the principal goals of each in (ML).

Critical thinking

Having successfully completed this topic, you will be able to:1. Critically evaluate the variety of processes used in (ML) .2. Understand and debate the areas of (ML) to management.

OBJECTIVES

A core objective of a student is to generalize from its experience. Generalization in this context is the aptitude of a learning machine to function accurately on new, invisible examples/tasks after having experienced a learning data set (Bishop,2006).

A core objective of learning is to generalize from its experience (Mohri et al, 2012). Generalization in this context is the capability of a learning machine to perform accurately on new, unseen examples/tasks after having experienced a learning data set.

Machine Learning Theory, also known as Computational Learning Theory, aims to under- stand the fundamental principles of learning as a computational process. This field seeks to understand at a precise mathematical level what capabilities and information are fundamentally needed to learn different kinds of tasks successfully, and to understand the basic algorithmic principles involved in getting computers to learn from data and to improve performance with feedback. The goals of this theory are both to aid in the design of better automated learning methods and to understand fundamental issues in the learning process itself.

Machine Learning Theory draws elements from both the Theory of Computation and Statistics and involves tasks such as:

- Creating mathematical models that capture key aspects of machine learning, in which one can analyse the inherent ease or difficulty of different types of learning problems.
- Proving guarantees for algorithms (under what conditions will they succeed, how much data and computation time is needed) and developing machine learning algorithms that provably meet desired criteria.
- Mathematically analysing general issues, such as: "Why is Occam's Razor a good idea?", "When can one be confident about predictions made from limited data?", "How much power does active participation add over passive observation for learning?", and "What kinds of methods can learn even in the presence of large quantities of distracting information?".

Another highlight of Computational Learning Theory is the development of algorithms that are able to quickly learn even in the presence of large amounts of distracting information. Typically, a machine learning algorithm represents its data in terms of features: for example, a document might be represented by the set of words it contains, and an image might be represented by a list of various properties it has. The learning algorithm processes this information to make some prediction.

Machine Learning Theory also has a number of fundamental connections to other disciplines. In cryptography, one of the key goals is to enable users to communicate so that an eavesdropper cannot acquire any information about what is being said.

Machine Learning can be viewed in this setting as developing algorithms for the eavesdropper. In particular, provably good cryptosystems can be converted to problems one cannot hope to learn, and hard learning problems can be converted into proposed cryptosystems.

Moreover, at the technical level, there are strong connections between important techniques in Machine Learning and techniques developed in Cryptography. For example, Boosting, a machine learning method designed to extract as much power as possible out of a given learning algorithm, has close connections to methods for amplifying cryptosystems developed in cryptography.

Research in Machine Learning Theory is a combination of attacking established fundamental questions, and developing new frameworks for modelling the needs of new machine learning applications. While it is impossible to know where the next breakthroughs will come, a few topics one can expect the future to hold include:

Better understanding how auxiliary information, such as un-labelled data, hints from a user, or previously learned tasks, can best be used by a machine learning algorithm to improve its ability to learn new things. Traditionally, Machine Learning Theory has focused on problems of learning a task (say, identifying spam) from labelled examples (email labelled as spam or not). However, often there is additional information available. One might have access to large quantities of un-labelled data (email messages not labelled by their type, or discussion-group transcripts on the web) that could potentially provide useful information. One might have other hints from the user besides just labels, e.g., highlighting relevant portions of the email message. Or, one might have previously learned similar tasks and want to transfer some of that experience to the job at hand. These are all issues for which a solid theory is only beginning to be developed.

Further developing connections to economic theory. As software agents based on ma- chine learning is used in competitive settings, "strategic" issues become increasingly important. Most algorithms and models to date have focused on the case of a single learning algorithm operating in an environment that, while it may be changing, does not have its own motivations and strategies. However, if learning algorithms are to operate in settings dominated by other adaptive algorithms acting in their own users' interests, such as bidding on items or performing various kinds of negotiations, then we have a true merging of computer science and economic models. In this combination, many of the fundamental issues are still wide open.

Development of learning algorithms with an eye towards the use of learning as part of a larger system. Most machine learning models view learning as a standalone pro- cess, focusing on prediction accuracy as the measure of performance. However, when a learning algorithm is placed in a larger system, other issues may come into play. For example, one would like algorithms that have more powerful models of their own confidence or that can optimize multiple objectives. One would like models that capture the process of deciding what to learn, in addition to how to learn it. There has been some theoretical work on these issues, but there is certainly is much more to be done.

The ML training examples come from some generally unknown probability distribution (reflected representative of the space of occurrences) and the learner has to develop a general model about this space that enables it to produce appropriately accurate predictions in new cases.

The computational analysis of machine learning algorithms and their functioning is a branch of theoretical computer science known as computational learning theory. Because training sets are finite and the future is uncertain, learning theory usually does not yield guarantees of the performance of algorithms.

As an alternative, probabilistic bounds on the performance are quite common. The bias–variance decomposition is one way to quantify generalization error.

For the best performance in the context of generalization, the complication of the hypothesis should match the complexity of the function underlying the data. If the hypothesis is less complex than the function, then the model is less than the data. If the complexity of the model is increased in response, then the training error decreases. But if the hypothesis is too complex, then the model is subject to over fitting and generalization will be inferior (Alpaydin, 2010).

In supplement to performance bounds, computational learning theorists study the time complexity and feasibility of learning. In computational learning theory, a computation is thought practicable if it can be done in polynomial time.

There are two kinds of time complexity results. *Positive results* show that a certain class of functions can be learned in polynomial time. *Negative results* show that certain classes cannot be learned in polynomial time.

Theoretical results in machine learning mainly deal with a type of inductive learning called supervised learning. In supervised learning, an algorithm is given samples that are labelled in some useful way. For example, the samples might be descriptions of mushrooms, and the labels could be whether or not the mushrooms are edible. The algorithm takes these previously labelled samples and uses them to induce a classifier. This classifier is a function that assigns labels to samples including samples that have never been previously seen by the algorithm. The goal of the supervised learning algorithm is to optimize some measure of performance such as minimizing the number of mistakes made on new samples. In addition to performance bounds, computational learning theory studies the time complexity and feasibility of learning. In computational learning theory, a computation is considered feasible if it can be done in polynomial time. There are two kinds of time complexity results:

- Positive results – Showing that a certain class of functions is learnable in polynomial time.
- Negative results – Showing that certain classes cannot be learned in polynomial time.

Negative results often rely on commonly believed, but yet unproven assumptions, such as:

- Computational complexity – P ≠ NP (the P versus NP problem);
- Cryptographic – One-way functions exist.

There are several different approaches to computational learning theory. These differences are based on making assumptions about the inference principles used to generalize from limited data. This includes different definitions of probability (see frequency probability, Bayesian probability) and different assumptions on the generation of samples. The different approaches include:

- Exact learning, proposed by Dana Angluin;
- Probably approximately correct learning (PAC learning), proposed by Leslie Valiant;
- VC theory, proposed by Vladimir Vapnik and Alexey Chervonenkis;
- Bayesian inference;
- Algorithmic learning theory, from the work of E. Mark Gold;
- Online machine learning, from the work of Nick Littlestone.

Computational learning theory has led to several practical algorithms. For example, PAC theory inspired boosting, VC theory led to support vector machines, and Bayesian inference led to belief networks (by Judea Pearl).

Machine Learning Theory is both a fundamental theory with many basic and compelling foundational questions, and a topic of practical importance that helps to advance the state of the art in software by providing mathematical frameworks for designing new machine learning algorithms. It is an exciting time for the field, as connections to many other areas are being discovered and explored, and as new machine learning applications bring new questions to be modelled and studied. It is safe to say that the potential of Machine Learning and its theory lie beyond the frontiers of our imagination.

When do we need machine learning rather than directly program our computers to carry out the task at hand? Two aspects of a given problem may call for the use of programs that learn and improve on the basis of their "experience": the problem's complexity and the need for adaptivity.

Tasks That Are Too Complex to Program

• Tasks Performed by Animals/Humans: There are numerous tasks that we human beings perform routinely, yet our introspection concerning how we do them is not sufficiently elaborate to extract a well-defined program. Examples of such tasks include driving, speech recognition, and image understanding. In all of these tasks, state of the art machine learning programs, programs that "learn from their experience," achieve quite satisfactory results, once exposed to sufficiently many training examples.

• Tasks beyond Human Capabilities: Another wide family of tasks that benefit from machine learning techniques are related to the analysis of very large and complex data sets: astronomical data, turning medical archives into medical knowledge, weather prediction, analysis of genomic data, Web search engines, and electronic commerce. With more and more available digitally recorded data, it becomes obvious that there are treasures of meaningful information buried in data archives that are way too large and too complex for humans to make sense of. Learning to detect meaningful patterns in large and complex data sets is a promising domain in which the combi- nation of programs that learn with the almost unlimited memory capacity and ever-increasing processing speed of computers opens up new horizons.

Adaptivity. One limiting feature of programmed tools is their rigidity – once the program has been written down and installed, it stays unchanged. However, many tasks change over time or from one user to another.

Machine learning tools – programs whose behaviour adapts to their input data – offer a solution to such issues; they are, by nature, adaptive to changes in the environment they interact with. Typical successful applications of machine learning to such problems include programs that decode handwritten text, where a fixed program can adapt to variations between the handwriting of different users; spam detection programs, adapting automatically to changes in the nature of spam e-mails; and speech recognition programs.

1.3 Types of Learning

Learning is, of course, a very wide domain. Consequently, the field of machine learning has branched into several subfields dealing with different types of learning tasks. We give a rough taxonomy of learning paradigms, aiming to provide some perspective of where the content of this book sits within the wide field of machine learning.

We describe four parameters along which learning paradigms can be classified.

Supervised versus Unsupervised

Since learning involves an interaction between the learner and the environment, one can divide learning tasks according to the nature of that interaction. The first distinction to note is the difference between supervised and unsupervised learning. As an illustrative example, consider the task of learning to detect spam e-mail versus the task of anomaly detection. For the spam detection task, we consider a setting in which the learner receives training e-mails for which the label spam/not-spam is provided. On the basis of such training the learner should figure out a rule for labelling a newly arriving e-mail message. In contrast, for the task of anomaly detection, all the learner gets as training is a large body of e-mail messages (with no labels) and the learner's task is to detect "unusual" messages.

More abstractly, viewing learning as a process of "using experience to gain expertise," supervised learning describes a scenario in which the "experience," a training example, contains significant information (say, the spam/not-spam labels) that is missing in the unseen "test examples" to which the learned expertise is to be applied. In this setting, the acquired expertise is aimed to predict that missing information for the test data. In such cases, we can think of the environment as a teacher that "supervises" the learner by providing the extra information (labels). In unsupervised learning, however, there is no distinction between training and test data. The learner processes input data with the goal of coming up with some summary, or compressed version of that data. Clustering a data set into subsets of similar objects is a typical example of such a task. There is also an intermediate learning setting in which, while the training examples contain more information than the test examples, the learner is required to predict even more information for the test examples. For example, one may try to learn a value function that describes for each setting of a chess board the degree by which White's position is better than the Black's.

Yet, the only information available to the learner at training time is positions that occurred throughout actual chess games, labelled by who eventually won that game. Such learning frameworks are mainly investigated under the title of reinforcement learning.

Active versus Passive Learners Learning paradigms can vary by the role played by the learner. We distinguish between "active" and "passive" learners. An active learner interacts with the environment at training time, say, by posing queries or performing experiments, while a passive learner only observes the information provided by the environment (or the teacher) without influencing or directing it. Note that the learner of a spam filter is usually passive – waiting for users to mark the e-mails coming to them. In an active setting, one could imagine asking users to label specific e-mails chosen by the learner, or even composed by the learner, to enhance its understanding of what spam is.

Helpfulness of the Teacher When one thinks about human learning, of a baby at home or a student at school, the process often involves a helpful teacher, who is trying to feed the learner with the information most useful for achieving the learning goal. In contrast, when a scientist learns about nature, the environment, playing the role of the teacher, can be best thought of as passive – apples drop, stars shine, and the rain falls without regard to the needs of the learner. We model such learning scenarios by postulating that the training data (or the learner's experience) is generated by some random process. This is the basic building block in the branch of "statistical learning." Finally, learning also occurs when the learner's input is generated by an adversarial "teacher." This may be the case in the spam filtering example (if the spammer tries to mislead the spam filtering designer) or in learning to detect fraud. One also uses an adversarial teacher model as a worst-case scenario, when no milder setup can be safely assumed. If you can learn against an adversarial teacher, you are guaranteed to succeed interacting any odd teacher.

Online versus Batch Learning Protocol The last parameter we mention is the distinction between situations in which the learner has to respond online, throughout the learning process, and settings in which the learner has to engage the acquired expertise only after having a chance to process large amounts of data. For example, a stockbroker has to make daily decisions, based on the experience collected so far. He may become an expert over time, but might have made costly mistakes in the process. In contrast, in many data mining settings, the learner – the data miner – has large amounts of training data to play with before having to output conclusions.

Let us consider some examples of different learning tasks.

Multiclass Classification Our classification does not have to be binary. Take, for example, the task of document classification: We wish to design a program that will be able to classify given documents according to topics (e.g., news, sports, biology, medicine).

A learning algorithm for such a task will have access to examples of correctly classified documents and, on the basis of these examples, should output a program that can take as input a new document and output a topic classification for that document. Here, the domain set is the set of all potential documents. Once again, we would usually represent documents by a set of features that could include counts of different key words in the document, as well as other possibly relevant features like the size of the document or its origin. The label set in this task will be the set of possible document topics (so Y will be some large finite set). Once we determine our domain and label sets, the other components of our framework look exactly the same as in the papaya tasting example; Our training sample will be a finite sequence of (feature vector, label) pairs, the learner's output will be a function from the domain set to the label set, and, finally, for our measure of success, we can use the probability, over (document, topic) pairs, of the event that our predictor suggests a wrong label.

Regression In this task, one wishes to find some simple pattern in the data – a functional relationship between the X and Y components of the data. For example, one wishes to find a linear function that best predicts a baby's birth weight on the basis of ultrasound measures of his head circumference, abdominal circumference, and femur length. Here, our domain set X is some subset of R^3 (the three ultrasound measurements), and the set of "labels," Y, is the set of real numbers (the weight in grams). In this context, it is more adequate to call Y the target set. Our training data as well as the learner's output are as before (a finite sequence of (x,y) pairs, and a function from X to Y respectively).

Revision

- Outline in 250 words the theory of ML

4 Approaches

Introduction

Machine learning is a subfield of computer science (more particularly soft computing) that evolved from the study of pattern recognition and computational learning theory in artificial intelligence. In 1959, Arthur Samuel defined machine learning as a "Field of study that gives computers the ability to learn without being explicitly programmed"

Chapter Learning Outcomes

⯀ The various types and applications of ML.

⯀ Review of pattern recognition in ML.

⯀ Learning about computational learning theory in ML.

⯀ Concepts of algorithms and types of learning .

⯀ Having successfully completed the module, you will be able to:

⯀ 1. Critically assess the theory of (ML) in marketing.

⯀ 2. Assess the wide range of processes of (ML) in today's world.

⯀ Having completed the module, you will be able to:

⯀ 1. Understand the variety of (ML) applications and their uses.

• 2. Be able to explain the principal goals of each in (ML).

Critical thinking

Having successfully completed this topic, you will be able to:1. Critically evaluate the theory used in (ML).2. Understand and debate the key areas of (ML) to management.

OBJECTIVES

To gain appreciation of the various applications of ML in the market today, and their objectives and function.

4.1 Decision tree learning

Decision tree learning employs a decision tree (as a predictive model) to go from interpretations about an item (represented in the branches) to conclusions about the item's target value (represented in the leaves). It is one of the predictive modelling approaches used in marketing statistics, data mining and machine learning. Tree models where the target variable can take a discrete set of values are called classification trees; in these tree structures, leaves signify class labels and branches represent aggregations of features that lead to those class labels. Decision trees where the target variable can take continuous values (typically real numbers) are called regression trees.

In decision analysis, a decision tree can be used to visually and unambiguously represent decisions and decision making. In data mining, a decision tree describes data (but the resulting classification tree can be an input for decision making). This section deals with decision trees in data mining.

Decision tree learning is a method commonly used in data mining (Rockach etal, 2008). The objective is to create a model that forecasts the value of a target variable based on several input variables.

A decision tree is a simple depiction for classifying examples. For this section, assume that all of the input features have finite discrete domains, and there is a single target feature called the "classification". Each element of the domain of the classification is called a class. A decision tree or a classification tree is a tree in which each internal (non-leaf) node is labelled with an input feature. The arcs coming from a node labelled with an input feature, and are labelled with each of the possible values of the target or output feature or the arc leads to a subordinate decision node on a different input feature. Each leaf of the tree is labelled with a class or a probability distribution over the classes.

Decision trees used in data mining are of two main types:

- Classification tree analysis is when the predicted outcome is the class to which the data belongs.
- Regression tree analysis is when the predicted outcome can be considered a real number (e.g. the price of a house, or a patient's length of stay in a hospital).

The term Classification And Regression Tree (CART) analysis is an umbrella term used to refer to both of the above procedures, first introduced by (Breiman et al, 1984).

Trees used for regression and trees used for classification have some similarities - but also some differences, such as the procedure used to determine where to split.

Some techniques, often called *ensemble* methods, construct more than one decision tree:

- Boosted trees Incrementally build an ensemble by training each new instance to emphasize the training instances previously miss modelled. A typical example is AdaBoost. These can be used for regression-type and classification-type problems (Friedman,1999).
- Bootstrap aggregated (or bagged) decision trees, an early ensemble method, builds multiple decision trees by repeatedly resampling training data with replacement, and voting the trees for a consensus prediction (Brieman,1996) A random forest classifier is a specific type of bootstrap aggregating
- Rotation forest - in which every decision tree is trained by first applying principal component analysis (PCA) on a random subset of the input features (Rodreguiz etal, 2006).

For example, Customer segmentation stems for a basic need to appropriately classify clients so as to target and manage them better. Most products and services are purchased by a wide variety of customers, with different characteristics. Even for highly personalized products, uniquely made for specific customers, there is the need to figure out their characteristics in order to anticipate and meet customer needs, and have the needed skills and materials available to do it.

In order to gain a better understanding of customer segmentation, it is useful to review the basic segmentation variables that are used. In his book, 'Marketing Management', Kotler (2006) identifies the main segmentation variables for the US consumer market as follows: geographic region, size of the city, area type (urban, suburban and rural), clime, age, family size, lifecycle stage (bachelor, married without children, etc), gender, income, profession, education, religion, race, generation, social class, lifestyle, personality, usage behaviour, features sought after in a product or service, usage proficiency, frequency of use, loyalty, attitudes towards products, etc.

This is a rather exhaustive list, and very often detailed information for customers is not available, or just not relevant. In some cases, no one has ever though collecting information about their customers, or this was just not feasible. In other cases, the information is not reliable.

Let's take the example of subscriber information for cell phone customers. In my case, I remember never having to do an update of my personal information except for my billing address, so data gathered from my initial contract might have changed quite a bit (income, employment, marital status, etc.). Then, apart from assuming that everything about me was unchanged except for a different address, how could the cell phone company profile me and get a picture of what are my characteristics as a customer?

4.2 Association rule learning

Association rule learning is a rule-based machine learning method for discovering interesting relations between variables in large databases. It is intended to identify strong rules discovered in databases using some measures of interestingness (Piatetsky-Shapiro,1991)
Based on the concept of strong rules, Agrawal etal (1993), introduced association rules for discovering regularities between products in large-scale transaction data recorded by point-of-sale (POS) systems in supermarkets. In the sales data of a supermarket could indicate that if a customer buys washing powder and conditioner together, they are likely to also buy softener. Such information can be used as the basis for decisions about marketing activities such as, e.g., promotional pricing or product placements. In addition to the above example from market basket analysis association rules are employed today in many application areas including Web usage mining, intrusion detection, continuous production, and bioinformatics. In contrast with sequence mining, association rule learning typically does not consider the order of items either within a transaction or across transactions.

Association rules are usually required to satisfy a user-specified minimum support and a user-specified minimum confidence at the same time. Association rule generation is usually split up into two separate steps:

1. A minimum support threshold is applied to find all *frequent item sets* in a database.
2. A minimum confidence constraint is applied to these frequent item sets in order to form rules.

While the second step is straightforward, the first step needs more attention.

Finding all frequent itemsets in a database is difficult since it involves searching all possible itemsets (item combinations).

The concept of association rules was popularised particularly due to the 1993 article of Agrawal et al., (1993), and is thus one of the most cited papers in the Data Mining field.

However, it is possible that what is now called "association rules" is similar to what appears in the 1966 paper[l] on GUHA, a general data mining method developed by Hajek et al, (1996). Listed below are some other associations:

Multi-Relation Association Rules: Multi-Relation Association Rules (MRAR) are association rules where each item may have several relations. These relations indicate indirect relationship between the entities. Consider the following MRAR where the first item consists of three relations *live in*, *nearby* and *humid*: "Those who *live in* a place which is *nearby* a city with *humid* climate type and also are *younger* than 20 -> their *health condition* is good". Such association rules are extractable from RDBMS data or semantic web data (Ramezani etal, 2014).

Context Based Association Rules: are a form of association rule. Context Based Association Rules claims more accuracy in association rule mining by considering a hidden variable named context variable which changes the final set of association rules depending upon the value of context variables.

For example, the baskets orientation in market basket analysis reflects an odd pattern in the early days of month. This might be because of abnormal context i.e. salary is drawn at the start of the month (Shaheen etal, 2013).

Contrast set learning is a form of associative learning. Contrast set learners use rules that differ meaningfully in their distribution across subsets (Webb etal, 2003)

Weighted class learning is another form of associative learning in which weight may be assigned to classes to give focus to a particular issue of concern for the consumer of the data mining results.

High-order pattern discovery facilitate the capture of high-order (polythetic) patterns or event associations that are intrinsic to complex real-world data (Wong & Wang, 1997)

K-optimal pattern discovery provides an alternative to the standard approach to association rule learning that requires that each pattern appear frequently in the data.

Approximate Frequent Item set mining is a relaxed version of Frequent Itemset mining that allows some of the items in some of the rows to be 0 (Jinze et al, 2006).

Generalized Association Rules hierarchical taxonomy (concept hierarchy)

Quantitative Association Rules categorical and quantitative data (Salleb-Aouissi, 2007)

Interval Data Association Rules e.g. partition the age into 5-year-increment ranged.

Sequential pattern mining discovers subsequence's that are common to more than minsup sequences in a sequence database, where minsup is set by the user. A sequence is an ordered list of transactions (Zaki et al,2001)

Subspace Clustering, a specific type of Clustering high-dimensional data, is in many variants also based on the downward-closure property for specific clustering models (Zimek et al, 2014).

Warmr is shipped as part of the ACE data mining suite. It allows association rule learning for first order relational rules.

Associated rule learning in marketing encompasses a broad set of analytics techniques aimed at uncovering the associations and connections between specific objects: these might be visitors to your website (customers or audience), products in your store, or content items on your media site. Of these, "market basket analysis" is perhaps the most famous example. In a market basket analysis, you look to see if there are combinations of products that frequently co-occur in transactions. For example, maybe people who buy flour and casting sugar, also tend to buy eggs (because a high proportion of them are planning on baking a cake). A retailer can use this information to inform:

- Store layout (put products that co-occur together close to one another, to improve the customer shopping experience).
- Marketing (e.g. target customers who buy flour with offers on eggs, to encourage them to spend more on their shopping basket).

Online retailers and publishers can use this type of analysis to:

- Inform the placement of content items on their media sites, or products in their catalogue.
- Drive recommendation engines (like Amazon's *customers who bought this product also bought these products...*).
- Deliver targeted marketing (e.g. emailing customers who bought products specific products with other products and offers on those products that are likely to be interesting to them.)

There are a wide range of algorithms, available on a wide variety of platforms, for performing market basket analysis. In this introductory recipe, we will cover:

1. Market basket analysis: the basics.
2. Performing basket analysis.
3. Managing large result sets: visualizing rules using the arulesViz package.
4. Interpreting the results: using the analysis to drive business decision-making.
5. Expanding on the analysis: zooming out from the basket to look a customer behaviour.

4.3 Artificial neural networks

Artificial neural networks (ANNs), a form of connectionism, are computing systems inspired by the biological neural networks that constitute animal brains. Such systems learn (progressively improve performance) to do tasks by considering examples, generally without task-specific programming. For example, in image recognition, they might learn to identify images that contain cats by analysing example images that have been manually labelled as "cat" or "no cat" and using the analytic results to identify cats in other images. They have found most use in applications difficult to express in a traditional computer algorithm using rule-based programming. An ANN is based on a collection of connected units called artificial neurons(analogous to biological neurons in an animal brain). Each connection (synapse) between neurons can transmit a signal to another neuron. The receiving (postsynaptic) neuron can process the signal(s) and then signal downstream neurons connected to it, Johnson (2017).

Neurons and synapses may also have a weight that varies as learning proceeds, which can increase or decrease the strength of the signal that it sends downstream. Further, they may have a threshold such that only if the aggregate signal is below (or above) that level is the downstream signal sent.

Typically, neurons are organized in layers. Different layers may perform different kinds of transformations on their inputs. Signals travel from the first (input), to the last (output) layer, possibly after traversing the layers multiple times. In artificial networks with multiple hidden layers, the initial layers might detect primitives (e.g. the pupil in an eye, the iris, eyelashes, etc.) and their output is fed forward to deeper layers who perform more abstract generalizations (e.g. eye, mouth).... and so on until the final layers perform the complex object recognition (e.g. face).

The original goal of the neural network approach was to solve problems in the same way that a human brain would. Over time, attention focused on matching specific mental abilities, leading to deviations from biology such as back propagation, or passing information in the reverse direction and adjusting the network to reflect that information. Neural networks have been used on a variety of tasks, including computer vision, speech recognition, machine translation, social network filtering, playing board and video games, medical diagnosis and in many other domains.

Most search engines have some form of artificial neural network models, which is important in learning clicks from users in relation to search terms and predicting the best results for future searchers. It is believed that the number of queries fed into this model will be instrumental in determining its effectiveness in producing the best search results or websites for users. As users click, the algorithm studies their preferences and reorders the search results page accordingly to ensure the next user finds the most relevant website. Let's say you ran a search for 'basketballs London' and 10 websites are organically generated on the search engine result page.

The top two organic results are websites that sell basketball products whilst the third website focuses on basketball clubs. Assuming most users with a similar search all visit the basketball, club website and ignore product sites such as Sports Direct., the artificial neural network ranking algorithms of Google will promote the 'Getactivelondon.com' website above that of 'Argos' and 'Sports Direct'.

Right now, there are vast databases and powerful technologies crunching numbers about your lifestyle and the lifestyles of millions of others. They know the value of your home, the type of car you drive, the ages of your children, your credit rating and more. This data is being mathematically processed to determine if you are the best target for the latest gadget to hit the market. While this sounds like something from a George Orwell novel, it describes the predictive modelling power behind neural networks and modern data mining technologies. While data mining conducted at this magnitude is limited to certain government agencies, the price of this technology has dropped substantially due to new mathematical discoveries, lower technology costs and improved processing power. As a result, many corporations are now embracing the power of predictive data mining to gain competitive advantages through customer segmentation strategies, predicting customer behaviour and by making projections about the future. Here are a few additional ways that predictive data mining is being used today.

Marketing Predictions

Producing accurate sales forecasts is an important part of measuring your marketing strategy. Inaccurate forecasts lead to missed opportunities, avoidable costs, inefficiencies and many other problems.

Although Microsoft Excel provides certain forecasting tools, its forecasting tools fail when non-linear relationships and missing data are present, this is often the case when analysing marketing data. In these cases, neural networks provide superior forecasting accuracy.

Market Segmentation

When neural networks are correctly designed and deployed, they can accurately identify people who will be most receptive to a product, promotion or advertising campaign. Some of the most frequent methods of segmentation with neural networks combine metrics such as recent purchase, frequency of purchases and amount spent. Other factors include age, sex, income, location, education level, occupation and household status. Today neural networks are a primary method for highly predictive marketing segmentation.

Prediction and Classification

Neural networks are a proven technology for solving complex classification problems. Credit companies often deploy neural networks to spot fraudulent credit card activity and identity theft. Other companies deploy neural networks to identify defecting customers in order to maximize their customer retention.

4.4 Deep learning

Deep learning (also known as deep structured learning or hierarchical learning) is part of a broader family of machine learning methods based on learning data representations, as opposed to task-specific algorithms. Learning can be supervised, partially supervised or unsupervised (Bengio et al, 2013).

Some representations are loosely based on interpretation of information processing and communication patterns in a biological nervous system, such as neural coding that attempts to define a relationship between various stimuli and associated neuronal responses in the brain (Olshausen,1996). Research attempts to create efficient systems to learn these representations from large-scale, unlabelled data sets.
Deep learning architectures such as deep neural networks, deep belief networks and recurrent neural networks have been applied to fields including computer vision, speech recognition, natural language processing, audio recognition, social network filtering, machine translation, bioinformatics and drug design (Ghazemi et al, 2017) where they produced results comparable to and in some cases superior to human experts (Krizhevsky,2012).

Deep learning is closely related to a class of theories of brain development (specifically, neocortical development) proposed by cognitive neuroscientists in the early 1990s (Utgolf, 2002) These developmental theories were instantiated in computational models, making them predecessors of deep learning systems. These developmental models share the property that various proposed learning dynamics in the brain (e.g., a wave of nerve growth factor) support the self-organization somewhat analogous to the neural networks utilized in deep learning models.

Like the neocortex, neural networks employ a hierarchy of layered filters in which each layer considers information from a prior layer (or the operating environment), and then passes its output (and possibly the original input), to other layers. This process yields a self-organizing stack of transducers, well-tuned to their operating environment. A 1995 description stated, "...the infant's brain seems to organize itself under the influence of waves of so-called trophic-factors ... different regions of the brain become connected sequentially, with one layer of tissue maturing before another and so on until the whole brain is mature (Blakeslee, 1995).

The application of big data is enabling us to reveal deeper marketing insights all the time. Whether its open data revealing predictive patterns in consumer behaviour or hyper-personalisation creating a bespoke online shopping experience, big data in action is revolutionising the way we gather and act on business intelligence.

This in-depth data insight is made possible by machines; clever programs and algorithms that can process data at speeds no human could match, and derive meaning it would take us a lot longer to uncover. This is the power of artificial intelligence (AI), machine learning and deep learning; three industry buzzwords continuing to make a huge impact in the world of data marketing.

Much of what deep learning is thought to be able to do is yet to be realized. Relatively speaking, the technology is still in its infancy yet developing constantly, so all it may be capable of very much remains to be seen. Already though, the technology that could power uses such as self-driving cars or medicines custom-made to an individual's genome – previously the stuff of science fiction – is on the horizon.
In terms of marketing, deep learning has the potential to help us find *patterns inside of patterns*. As programs are exposed to more and more data and become more adept at interpreting it and learning from it, marketers can turn to deep learning to reveal ever-more complex data relationships.

Deep-learning algorithms will bring order out of chaos, and hone in on data attributes like sentiment, emphasis and intent, the subtleties of human interaction that machines have so far failed to grasp. The marketing applications for this kind of intelligence are ever-growing: clustering and consumer classification; user preference recommendation systems; analysis of unstructured data (e.g. social media insight); advanced chatbots with personality; and reactive content generation are but a few. AI highlights some of the ways deep learning is already being use by some of the biggest names in tech, and these applications are continuing to develop at an astonishing rate. The only thing we can really be sure of is that deep learning is only just beginning to make its presence felt when it comes to marketing, so it'll be fascinating to see where it takes us next.

4.5 Inductive logic programming

Inductive logic programming (ILP) is a subfield of machine learning which uses logic programming as a uniform representation for examples, background knowledge and hypotheses. Given an encoding of the known background knowledge and a set of examples represented as a logical database of facts, an ILP system will derive a hypothesised logic program which entails all the positive and none of the negative examples.

Inductive logic programming is particularly useful in bioinformatics and natural language processing. Gordon Plotkin and Ehud Shapiro laid the initial theoretical foundation for inductive machine learning in a logical setting (Plotkin,1970. Shapiro 1981) built its first implementation (Model Inference System, a Prolog program that inductively inferred logic programs from positive and negative examples. The term *Inductive Logic Programming* was first introduced De Raedt (1999) in a paper by Stephen Muggleton in 1991.

Muggleton (1995) also founded the annual international conference on Inductive Logic Programming, introduced the theoretical ideas of Predicate Invention, Inverse resolution, and Inverse entailment. Muggleton implemented Inverse entailment first in the PROGOL system. The term *"inductive"* here refers to philosophical (i.e. suggesting a theory to explain observed facts) rather than mathematical (i.e. proving a property for all members of a well-ordered set) induction.

4.6 Support vector machines

Support vector machines (SVMs, also support vector networks) are supervised learning models with associated learning algorithms that analyse data used for classification and regression analysis. Given a set of training examples, each marked as belonging to one or the other of two categories, an SVM training algorithm builds a model that assigns new examples to one category or the other, making it a non-probabilistic binary linear classifier (although methods such as scaling exist to use SVM in a probabilistic classification setting). An SVM model is a representation of the examples as points in space, mapped so that the examples of the separate categories are divided by a clear gap that is as wide as possible. New examples are then mapped into that same space and predicted to belong to a category based on which side of the gap they fall. In addition to performing linear classification, SVMs can efficiently perform a non-linear classification using what is called the kernel trick, implicitly mapping their inputs into high-dimensional feature spaces. When data are not labelled, supervised learning is not possible, and an unsupervised learning approach is required, which attempts to find natural clustering of the data to groups, and then map new data to these formed groups.

The clustering algorithm which provides an improvement to the support vector machines is called support vector clustering Kohavi and F. Provost (1998)and is often used in industrial applications either when data are not labelled or when only some data are labelled as a pre-processing for a classification pass.

Many marketing problems require accurately predicting the outcome of a process or the future state of a system. The ability of the support vector machine to predict outcomes in emerging environments in marketing are defined as, automated modelling, mass-produced models, intelligent software agents, and data mining. The support vector machine (SVM) is a semiparametric technique with origins in the machine-learning literature of computer science. Its approach to prediction differs markedly from that of standard parametric models. We explore these differences and benchmark the SVM's prediction hit rates against those from the multinomial logit model.

4.7 Clustering

Cluster analysis or clustering is the task of grouping a set of objects in such a way that objects in the same group (called a cluster) are more similar (in some sense or another) to each other than to those in other groups (clusters). It is a main task of exploratory data mining, and a common technique for statistical data analysis, used in many fields, including machine learning, pattern recognition, image analysis, information retrieval, bioinformatics, data compression, and computer graphics.

Cluster analysis itself is not one specific algorithm, but the general task to be solved. It can be achieved by various algorithms that differ significantly in their notion of what constitutes a cluster and how to efficiently find them. Popular notions of clusters include groups with small distances among the cluster members, dense areas of the data space, intervals or particular statistical distributions. Clustering can therefore be formulated as a multi-objective optimization problem.

The appropriate clustering algorithm and parameter settings (including values such as the distance function to use, a density threshold or the number of expected clusters) depend on the individual data set and intended use of the results. Cluster analysis as such is not an automatic task, but an iterative process of knowledge discovery or interactive multi-objective optimization that involves trial and failure. It is often necessary to modify data pre-processing and model parameters until the result achieves the desired properties.

Besides the term *clustering*, there are a number of terms with similar meanings, including *automatic classification, numerical taxonomy, botryology* (from Greek βότρυς "grape") and *typological analysis*. The subtle differences are often in the usage of the results: while in data mining, the resulting groups are the matter of interest, in automatic classification the resulting discriminative power is of interest.

Cluster analysis was originated in anthropology by Driver and Kroeber in 1932 and introduced to psychology by Zubin (1938) and Tryon (1939) and famously used by Cattell beginning in 1943 for trait theory classification in personality psychology.

Cluster analysis is a convenient method for identifying homogenous groups of objects called clusters. Objects (or cases, observations) in a specific cluster share many characteristics, but are very dissimilar to objects not belonging to that cluster.

Let's try to gain a basic understanding of the cluster analysis procedure by looking at a simple example. Imagine that you are interested in segmenting your customer base in order to better target them through, for example, pricing strategies.

- The first step is to decide on the characteristics that you will use to segment your customers. In other words, you must decide which clustering variables will be included in the analysis. For example, you may want to segment a market based on customers' price consciousness (x) and brand loyalty (y). These two variables can be measured on a 7-point scale with higher values denoting a higher degree of price consciousness and brand loyalty. The objective of cluster analysis is to identify groups of objects (in this case, customers) that are very similar with regard to their price consciousness and brand loyalty and assign them into clusters. After having decided on the clustering variables (brand loyalty and price consciousness), we need to decide on the clustering procedure to form our groups of objects. This step is crucial for the analysis, as different procedures require different decisions prior to analysis computed using SPSS. These approaches are the following:
- Hierarchical methods,
- Partitioning methods (more precisely, k-means), and
- Two-step clustering.

Each of these procedures follows a different approach to grouping the most similar objects into clusters. Specifically, whereas an object in a certain cluster should be as similar as possible to all the other objects in the same cluster, it should likewise be as distinct as possible from objects in different clusters. But how do we measure similarity? Most methods calculate measures of (dis) similarity by estimating the distance between pairs of objects. Objects with smaller distances between one another are more similar, whereas objects with larger distances are more dissimilar.

An important problem in the application of cluster analysis is the decision regarding how many clusters should be derived from the data. At the beginning of the clustering process, we have to select appropriate variables for clustering. Even though this choice is of utmost importance, it is rarely treated as such and, instead, a mixture of intuition and data availability guide most analyses in marketing practice. However, faulty assumptions may lead to improper market segments and, consequently, to deficient marketing strategies. Thus, great care should be taken when selecting the clustering variables!

There are several types of clustering variables and these can be classified as follows:

⬚ General vs. specific, and

⬚ Observable vs. unobservable.

General clustering variables are independent of products, services or circumstances whereas specific variables relate to both the customer and the product, service and/or particular circumstance.

Furthermore, observable clustering variables can be measured directly while unobservable ones are inferred, for example, through observation or respondents' self-assessments.

In some cases, the choice of clustering variables is apparent because of the task at hand. For example, a managerial problem regarding corporate communications will have a well-defined set of clustering variables, including contenders such as awareness, attitudes, perceptions, and media habits. However, this is not always the case and researchers have to choose from a set of candidate variables. But how do we make this decision? To facilitate the choice of clustering variables, you should consider the following guiding questions:

⬚ Do the variables sufficiently differentiate the segments?

⬚ Are the clustering variables highly correlated?

• Is the relation between sample size and number of clustering variable reasonable?

▪ Are the data underlying the clustering variables of high quality?

4.8 Bayesian networks

A Bayesian network, Bayes network, belief network, Bayes(ian) model or probabilistic directed acyclic graphical model is a probabilistic graphical model (a type of statistical model) that represents a set of random variables and their conditional dependencies via a directed acyclic graph (DAG). For example, a Bayesian network could represent the probabilistic relationships between problem and result. Given the problem, the network can be used to compute the probabilities of the presence of various options.

Formally, Bayesian networks are DAGs whose nodes represent random variables in the Bayesian sense: they may be observable quantities, latent variables, unknown parameters or hypotheses.

Edges represent conditional dependencies; nodes that are not connected (there is no path from one of the variables to the other in the Bayesian network) represent variables that are conditionally independent of each other. Each node is associated with a probability function that takes, as input, a particular set of values for the node's parent variables, and gives (as output) the probability (or probability distribution, if applicable) of the variable represented by the node.

Efficient algorithms exist that perform inference and learning in Bayesian networks. Bayesian networks that model sequences of variables (*e.g.* speech signals or protein sequences) are called dynamic Bayesian networks. Generalizations of Bayesian networks that can represent and solve decision problems under uncertainty are called influence diagrams.

Connected modeling is an analytical modeling process that uses both data and human knowledge sources, and can handle explanatory, causation, and prediction goals to drive business actions that move the needle. It should be an approach that is intuitive, transparent, and user-friendly, but it's difficult to achieve in conventional, sequence-based modeling approaches. There are modeling frameworks and tools that lend themselves to *connected research*. Bayesian network (or Bayes Net) modeling is a perfect example. But before getting into Bayes Net, let's talk about more "conventional" modeling.

Conventional modeling involves connecting multiple results, often from different stages of the project. You may have tables to describe markets and products, segmentation solutions, sales forecasts, or interesting knowledge you've discovered through data mining. Each of these, in its own way, helps you understand both the data and the solution, but it's up to you to connect these results in a cogent and meaningful way, and even when you do, it is difficult to explain and lay out for your audience.

Figure:

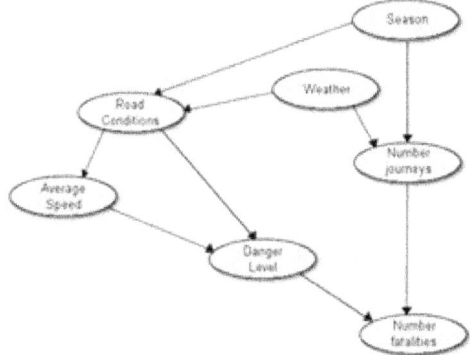

This is where Bayes Net is useful as it shows the relationship among variables by connecting *"nodes"* (variables) together using directional *"arcs."* For example, let's look at predicting the risk of driving. The season affects the road condition and weather. The number of journeys is affected by both season and weather. The number of road fatalities is affected by the number of journeys and danger level, which is influenced by both road conditions and average driving speed. Even without this explanation, you can intuitively understand what this figure means and how the nodes are connected. The arcs show the causal relationships between variables, literally visualizing how variables link together and which ones, if acted on, will affect others.

But the most useful thing about this network? You can *play* with it by updating any part of it. This allows you to use this network to immediately *see* and *answer* what-if questions, providing "on-the-fly" simulation and personalization of results.

So how do you get there? Bayesian networks can be built in one of three ways:

- structured based on your own theory;
- structured solely by the data itself;
- or structured by combining the two, letting your own theory (e.g., by imposing some constraints and/or predefining relationships) and the algorithm work together.

Figure:

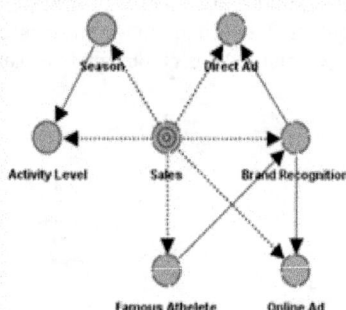

Obviously, this third option is most appealing. Bayesian networks work best when they integrate expert knowledge with the natural patterns in the data.

Typical regression models ignore the relationships among predictors (e.g., a brand recognition to online and direct ad budgets). With Bayes Net you can specify elements you can control (e.g., online or direct ad budget) or cannot control (e.g., season) to optimize your ad budget between online and direct channels. All parts are *connected,* and you can even use it as a market simulator to find the optimal solution to maximize market share.

To really get them to optimized connect results, Bayesian Net is a winner in performing *connected* research, by bringing data, knowledge, models, and client business objectives together all at once.

4.9 Reinforcement learning

Reinforcement learning (RL) is an area of machine learning inspired by behaviourist psychology, concerned with how software agents ought to take *actions* in an *environment* so as to maximize some notion of cumulative *reward*.

The problem, due to its generality, is studied in many other disciplines, such as game theory, control theory, operations research, information theory, simulation-based optimization, multi-agent systems, swarm intelligence, statistics and genetic algorithms. In the operations research and control literature, the field where reinforcement learning methods are studied is called *approximate dynamic programming*.

The problem has been studied in the theory of optimal control, though most studies are concerned with the existence of optimal solutions and their characterization, and not with the learning or approximation aspects. In economics and game theory, reinforcement learning may be used to explain how equilibrium may arise under bounded rationality.

In machine learning, the environment is typically formulated as a Markov decision process (MDP), as many reinforcement learning algorithms for this context utilize dynamic programming techniques Otterlo & Wiering, (2012).

The main difference between the classical techniques and reinforcement learning algorithms is that the latter do not need knowledge about the MDP and they target large MDPs where exact methods become infeasible.

Reinforcement learning differs from standard supervised learning in that correct input/output pairs are never presented, nor sub-optimal actions explicitly corrected. Instead the focus is on on-line performance, which involves finding a balance between exploration (of uncharted territory) and exploitation (of current knowledge),(Kaelbling 1996). The exploration vs. exploitation trade-off in reinforcement learning has been most thoroughly studied through the multi-armed bandit problem and in finite MDPs.

Reinforcement learning (RL) is an area of machine learning inspired by behaviorist psychology, concerned with how software agents ought to take actions in an environment to maximize some notion of cumulative reward -Wikipedia Reinforcement Learning is one of the most important areas of Artificial Intelligence that has been successfully used to achieve super-human performance levels in several fields. It aims at finding a competitive strategy for taking the most suitable action in each state by using an associated reward with every 'action and state' pair. It is based on the behavioral psychology where an organism tends to repeat those actions which lead to a positive reward and tries to avoid actions associated with punishment. Hence, the organism can be trained to display desired behavior by giving it an appropriate reward and punishment each time it takes an action.

Similarly, in Artificial Intelligence, Reinforcement Learning is used to find an appropriate strategy in each state by associating a reward with every action taken by the agent.

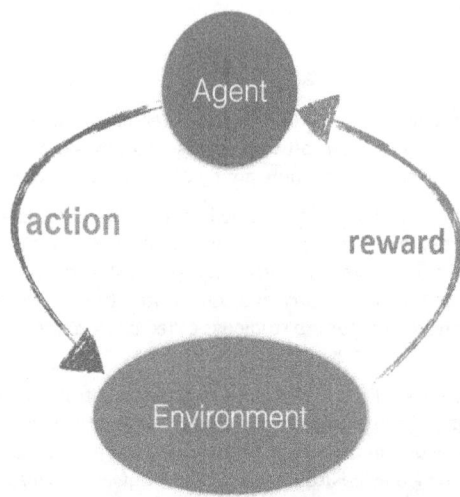

Formally, an agent observes a state and takes a certain action. Based on the current state and action taken, the environment provides a certain reward and changes the state of the agent. The agent uses reward as a guiding signal to learn the appropriate action in order to maximize the accumulated future rewards. One of the most successful applications is teaching a robot how to walk, how to play a game, etc. The exact same concept can be used in marketing. Owing to recent advancements in algorithms/tools, marketers have moved beyond manually created rule-based systems to more sophisticated and automated systems. However, marketing is still not personalized enough at a 1:1 user level and relies heavily on aggregate behavior.

With the introduction of RL, users' specific behavior can be learned over a period which will then lead to much sharpened personalized messaging. Brands can use this to get the order of channel/message for a user right, through which they can drive up marketing ROI significantly.

4.10 Representation learning

In machine learning, feature learning or representation learning Bengio etal, is a set of techniques that allows a system to automatically discover the representations needed for feature detection or classification from raw data. This replaces manual feature engineering and allows a machine to both learn the features and use them to perform a specific task.

Feature learning is motivated by the fact that machine learning tasks such as classification often require input that is mathematically and computationally convenient to process.

However, real-world data such as images, video, and sensor data has not yielded to attempts to algorithmically define specific features. An alternative is to discover such features or representations through examination, without relying on explicit algorithms.

Feature learning can be either supervised or unsupervised.

- In supervised feature learning, features are learned using labelled input data. Examples include supervised neural networks, multilayer perceptron and (supervised) dictionary learning.
- In unsupervised feature learning, features are learned with unlabelled input data. Examples include dictionary learning, independent component analysis, auto encoders, matrix factorization and various forms of clustering (Coates etal,2013).

Features form the basis for much of our preference modeling. When asked to explain one's preferences, features are typically accepted as appropriate reasons: this job paid more, that candidate supports tax reform, or it was closer to home. We believe that features must be the drivers since they so easily serve as rationales for past behavior. Choice modeling formalizes this belief by assuming that products and services are feature bundles with the value of the bundle calculated directly from the utilities of its separate features. All that we need to know about a product or service can be represented as the intersection of its features, which is why it is called conjoint analysis.

At first, this approach seems to work, but it does not scale well. We create hypothetical products and services defined by the cells in a factorial experimental design (see the book Stated Preference Methods Using R). The number of cells increases quickly with each additional feature so that we need to turn to optimal designs in R in order to limit the number of possible combinations. We have reduced the number of hypothetical descriptions, while the number of estimated parameters remains unchanged. Overall preference continues to be an additive function of the values attributed to each of the separate components.

Representation learning, on the other hand, is associated with deep neural networks, such as the h2o package discussed by John Chambers at the user! 2014 conference. According to Yoshua Bengio (see his new chapter on Distributed Representations), "a good representation is one that makes further learning tasks easy." The process is described in his first chapter on Deep Learning. As shown in this figure from Wikipedia, the observed features are visible units and the product representation is a transformation contained in hidden units.

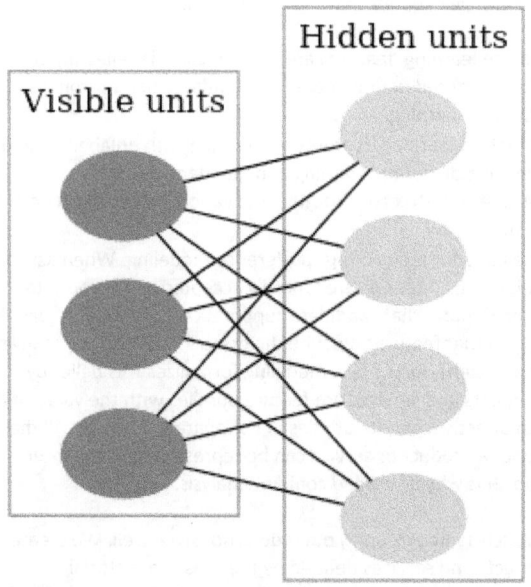

Visible units

Hidden units

What do consumers learn before deciding to buy? They learn a representational structure that reduces the complexity of the purchase process. This learning comes relatively easy with so many sources telling us what to look for and what to buy (e.g., marketing communications, professional reviews, social media and of course, friends and family). Bengio speaks of evolving culture vs. local minima as the process for "brain to brain transfer of information." Others refer to it as a meeting of minds or shared conceptualizations.

Are you thinking about a Smart Watch? Representation learning would suggest that the first step is "getting a lay of the land" or untangling the sources of variation accounting for differences among the offerings. I outlined such an approach in my last post on precursors to preference construction. It is possible to go online and request side-by-side feature comparisons that look like what one might find in choice modeling. However, that step is often late in the process after you have decided to purchase and have narrowed your consideration set. Before that, one looks at pictures, scans specifications, reads reviews and learns from others through user comments. One discovers what is available and what benefits are delivered. As you learn what if offered, you come to understand what you might want and be willing to spend.

The purchase task is somewhat easier than language translation or facial recognition because product categories are marketing creations with a deliberately simplified structure.

Products and services are simple by design with benefits and features linked together and set to music with a logo and a tagline. Product and service features are observed (red in the above figure); benefits are latent or hidden features (the blue) and can be extracted with deep neural networks or nonnegative matrix factorization. That is, we can think of representation learning as the relatively slow unsupervised learning that occurs early in the decision process and makes later learning and decision making easier and faster. Utility theory lacks the expressive power to transform the input into new ways of seeing. Both deep neural networks and nonnegative matrix factorization free us to go beyond the information given.

Finally, what happens when the consumer is pulled out of the purchase context and presented feature lists constructed according to a fractional factorial or optimal design? The norms of the marketplace are violated, yet respondents get through the task the best they can using the only information that you have provided them. Unfortunately, you do not learn much about bears in the wild when they are confined in cages.

4.11 Similarity and metric learning

Similarity learning is an area of supervised machine learning in artificial intelligence. It is closely related to regression and classification, but the goal is to learn from examples a similarity function that measures how similar or related two objects are. It has applications in ranking, in recommendation systems, visual identity tracking, face verification, and speaker verification. Similarity learning is used in information retrieval for learning to rank, in face verification or face identification, Guillaumin (2009) and in recommendation systems. Also, many machine learning approaches rely on some metric. This includes unsupervised learning such as clustering, which groups together close or similar objects. It also includes supervised approaches like K nearest neighbour algorithm which rely on labels of nearby objects to decide on the label of a new object. Metric learning has been proposed as a pre-processing step for many of these approaches (King et al, 2002).

Although its origins can be traced back to some earlier work (e.g., Short and Fukunaga, 1981; Fukunaga, 1990; Friedman, 1994; Hastie and Tibshirani, 1996; Baxter and Bartlett, 1997), metric learning really emerged in 2002 with the pioneering work of Xing et al. (2002) that formulates it as a convex optimization problem A metric learning algorithm basically aims at finding the parameters of the metric such that it best agrees with these constraints, in an effort to approximate the underlying semantic metric. Metric learning can potentially be beneficial whenever the notion of metric between in- stances plays an important role.

Recently, it has been applied to problems as diverse as link prediction in networks (Shaw et al., 2011), state representation in reinforcement learning (Taylor et al., 2011), music recommendation (McFee et al., 2012), partitioning problems (Lajugie et al., 2014), identity verification (Ben et al., 2012), webpage archiving (Law et al., 2012), cartoon synthesis (Yu et al., 2012) and even assessing the efficacy of acupuncture (Liang et al., 2012), to name a few.

In the following, listed below three large marketing fields of application where metric learning has been shown to be very useful.

Computer vision There is a great need of appropriate metrics in computer vision, not only to compare images or videos in ad-hoc representations—such as bags-of-visual-words (Li and Perona, 2005)—but also in the pre-processing step consisting in building this very representation (for instance, visual words are usually obtained by means of clustering). For this reason, there exists a large body of metric learning literature dealing specifically with computer vision problems, such as image classification (Mensink et al., 2012), object recognition (Frome et al., 2007; Verma et al., 2012), face recognition (Guillaumin et al., 2009b; Lu et al., 2012), visual tracking (Li et al., 2012; Jiang et al., 2012) or image annotation (Guillaumin et al., 2009a).

Information retrieval The objective of many information retrieval systems, such as search engines, is to provide the user with the most relevant documents according to his/her query. This ranking is often achieved by using a metric between two documents or between a document and a query. Applications of metric learning to these settings include the work of Lebanon (2006); Lee et al. (2008); McFee and Lanckriet (2010); Lim et al. (2013).

Bioinformatics Many problems in bioinformatics involve comparing sequences such as DNA, protein or temporal series. These comparisons are based on structured metrics such as edit distance measures (or related string alignment scores) for strings or Dynamic Time Warping distance for temporal series. Learning these metrics to adapt them to the task of interest can greatly improve the results. Examples include the work of Xiong and Chen (2006); Saigo et al. (2006); Kato and Nagano (2010); Wang et al. (2012a).

4.12 Sparse dictionary learning

Sparse dictionary learning is a representation learning method which aims at finding a sparse representation of the input data (also known as *sparse coding*) in the form of a linear combination of basic elements as well as those basic elements themselves. These elements are called *atoms* and they compose a *dictionary*. Atoms in the dictionary are not required to be orthogonal, and they may be an over-complete spanning set. This problem setup also allows the dimensionality of the signals being represented to be higher than the one of the signals being observed. The above two properties lead to having seemingly redundant atoms that allow multiple representations of the same signal but also provide an improvement in sparsity and flexibility of the representation.

One of the key principles of dictionary learning is that the dictionary has to be inferred from the input data. The emergence of sparse dictionary learning methods was stimulated by the fact that in signal processing one typically wants to represent the input data using as few components as possible. Before this approach the general practice was to use predefined dictionaries (such as fourier or wavelet transforms).

However, in certain cases a dictionary that is trained to fit the input data can significantly improve the sparsity, which has applications in data decomposition, compression and analysis and has been used in the fields of image denoising and classification, video and audio processing. Sparsity and over complete dictionaries have immense applications in image compression, image fusion and inpainting (Tillmann,2013).

4.13 Genetic algorithms

In computer science and operations research, a genetic algorithm (GA) is a metaheuristic inspired by the process of natural selection that belongs to the larger class of evolutionary algorithms (EA). Genetic algorithms are commonly used to generate high-quality solutions to optimization and search problems by relying on bio-inspired operators such as mutation, crossover and selection (Mitchell,1996).

In a genetic algorithm, a population of candidate solutions (called individuals, creatures, or phenotypes) to an optimization problem is evolved toward better solutions. Each candidate solution has a set of properties (its chromosomes or genotype) which can be mutated and altered; traditionally, solutions are represented in binary as strings of 0s and 1s, but other encodings are also possible (Whitley,1994)

The evolution usually starts from a population of randomly generated individuals, and is an iterative process, with the population in each iteration called a *generation*. In each generation, the fitness of every individual in the population is evaluated; the fitness is usually the value of the objective function in the optimization problem being solved. The more fit individuals are stochastically selected from the current population, and each individual's genome is modified (recombined and possibly randomly mutated) to form a new generation. The new generation of candidate solutions is then used in the next iteration of the algorithm. Commonly, the algorithm terminates when either a maximum number of generations has been produced, or a satisfactory fitness level has been reached for the population.

A typical genetic algorithm requires:

1. a genetic representation of the solution domain,
2. a fitness function to evaluate the solution domain.

A standard representation of each candidate solution is as an array of bits. Arrays of other types and structures can be used in essentially the same way. The main property that makes these genetic representations convenient is that their parts are easily aligned due to their fixed size, which facilitates simple crossover operations.

Variable length representations may also be used, but crossover implementation is more complex in this case. Tree-like representations are explored in genetic programming and graph-form representations are explored in evolutionary programming; a mix of both linear chromosomes and trees is explored in gene expression programming.

Once the genetic representation and the fitness function are defined, a GA proceeds to initialize a population of solutions and then to improve it through repetitive application of the mutation, crossover, inversion and selection operators. Here is an example in marketing:

For the brand manager, optimizing a new products positioning is a critical and difficult decision. Addressing this issue, Shocker and Srinivasan (1979) developed a framework for identifying optimal new product concepts using joint space models of consumer perceptions and preferences. Joint space analysis entails mapping the locations of existing products and ideal points for each individual (or market segment) using multi- dimensional scaling (MDS) of consumer perceptions via factor analysis, discriminant analysis or similarity scaling. Using this joint mapping of ideal points and product locations, a manager can model consumers choices of existing products, predict their responses to new products, and identify optimal new product concepts. In the ensuing time period, there have been a number of algorithms developed to identify optimal new product positions from MDS-based maps of consumer perceptions and preferences. In their review, Shocker and Srinivasan (1979) formalized the process of identifying optimal new product concepts using input from consumers at every stage from defining the market to predicting the success of a new product.

Since then, a number of algorithms have been developed for MDS-based product positioning. In 1987, SMS presented a new product positioning algorithm called PRODSRCH which incorporated a probabilistic model of consumer choice. In their formulation, demand from an ideal point is distributed to a product in inverse proportion its relative distance from the ideal point so long as the product is within the fixed size choice set of the ideal point. Otherwise, the product captures no demand share from that ideal point.

4.14 Rule-based machine learning

Rule-based machine learning is a general term for any machine learning method that identifies, learns, or evolves `rules to store, manipulate or apply, knowledge. The defining characteristic of a rule-based machine learner is the identification and utilization of a set of relational rules that collectively represent the knowledge captured by the system. This is in contrast to other machine learners that commonly identify a singular model that can be universally applied to any instance in order to make a prediction.

Rule-based machine learning approaches include learning classifier systems, association rule learning, and artificial immune systems (Bassell et al, 2011).

4.14.1 Learning classifier systems

Learning classifier systems, or LCS, are a paradigm of rule-based machine learning methods that combine a discovery component (e.g. typically a genetic algorithm) with a learning component (performing either supervised learning, reinforcement learning, or unsupervised learning), (Urbanowicz etal, 2009).

Learning classifier systems seek to identify a set of context-dependent rules that collectively store and apply knowledge in a piecewise manner in order to make predictions (e.g. behaviour modelling, classification, data mining, regression, function approximation, or game strategy). This approach allows complex solution spaces to be broken up into smaller, simpler parts.

The founding concepts behind learning classifier systems came from attempts to model complex adaptive systems, using rule-based agents to form an artificial cognitive system (i.e. artificial intelligence).

The architecture and components of a given learning classifier system can be quite variable. It is useful to think of an LCS as a machine consisting of several interacting components. Components may be added or removed, or existing components modified/exchanged to suit the demands of a given problem domain (like algorithmic building blocks) or to make the algorithm flexible enough to function in many different problem domains. As a result, the LCS paradigm can be flexibly applied to many problem domains that call for machine learning. The major divisions among LCS implementations are as follows:
(1) Michigan-style architecture vs. Pittsburgh-style architecture
(2) reinforcement learning vs. supervised learning,
(3) incremental learning vs. batch learning
(4) online learning vs. offline learning,
(5) strength-based fitness vs. accuracy-based fitness
(6) complete action mapping vs. best action mapping.

These divisions are not necessarily mutually exclusive. For example, XCS,[10] the best known and best studied LCS algorithm, is Michigan-style, was designed for reinforcement learning but can also perform supervised learning, applies incremental learning that can be either online or offline, applies accuracy-based fitness, and seeks to generate a complete action mapping (Urbanowicz,2015).

Machine learning can be used by companies and marketing teams of all sizes. In this blog post, I'll share the two main ways you should be thinking about machine learning for your marketing: machine learning for your digital experiences, and machine learning for you (the marketer). Let's dive right in.

1. Machine learning for your digital experiences

First, marketers can use machine learning to power digital experiences. When many think of website personalization, a rule-based approach comes to mind first. Rule-based personalization refers to the ability to manually set up business rules to deliver specific experiences to different segments of people. For example, you could use rules to ensure that only visitors within the US see references to free US shipping throughout your site, or that only visitors from a certain industry are invited to join a webinar.

In these situations, rule-based personalization lets you target a specific message or experience to a group of people (i.e. segments) that fit a few specific criteria. But it is *not* ideal for one-to-one communication.

If you want to create individualized experiences based on the preferences of each individual, you would have to set up and manage hundreds or even thousands of rules. That is just not scalable.

Machine-learning algorithms represent a more scalable way to achieve unique experiences for individuals (i.e. 1:1 personalization), rather than segments of people. You are probably already familiar with this type of personalization in the form of recommendations for products or content. But machine-learning personalization can also be leveraged to recommend other aspects of your website, such as categories, subcategories, brands, promotions and more. You could also use them to dynamically modify site navigation, search results and list sorting.

Essentially, every aspect of your website can be driven by machine-learning algorithms. How does it work? Every time a visitor engages with your site, you learn more about him. You learn the categories and brands he engages with most. You learn his favourite colours and his preferred price point. You learn his favourite blog topics or authors. Machine-learning algorithms leverage all of this information to select the right experiences and recommended items for each individual. And by showing him the most relevant content across your site, you can help him more easily find what he's looking for, leading to more conversions and improved loyalty.

E-Commerce Example

A shoe retailer could choose to show trending products on its homepage, recommending shoes that are most popular at a given time. To personalize those recommendations, it could boost the brands and price points each visitor prefers. One visitor may see primarily Vans shoes while another may see Steve Madden — based on which brands each visitor has shopped on the site. This helps shoppers quickly and easily find new shoes they are more likely to be interested in, rather than show all new shoes to them whether they are interested or not.

B2B Content Example

Now let's explore a content example. Assume a person landed for the first time on a site for team productivity solutions. She navigates to the resources section of the website and begins to search for a general term related to the space. In the search results, the site could prioritize resources related to her industry, product interest, challenge and her stage of the journey to surface results that are more likely to be relevant to her. So even though her search is general, the search results can help her find appropriate resources more quickly.

2. Machine learning for you (the marketer)

Beyond using machine learning to fuel the experience for your visitors and customers, you can also use it to help you focus your attention on the highest priorities for your business. Marketers have so much data available to them from many different sources (often only accessible by different members of the team).

It's impossible to stay on top of all this data at all times, and it's not always easy to prioritize the biggest opportunities or the biggest threats.

Machine learning can be used to cut through the noise. It can make sense of all the signals in the data to help you identify patterns, opportunities, or problems based on your key business metrics, and alert you to a shift so you can respond quickly.

Use machine learning to analyse which of your campaigns is providing the highest business impact, to recognize where opportunities exist on your site to help you plan future campaigns, or even to identify when a problem arises with your existing campaigns or general site performance.

E-Commerce Example

A retailer could use machine learning and predictive analytics to analyse typical inventory levels, taking into consideration seasonality, day of week, and general variation. Machine learning can recognize when shoppers are seeing more out of stock items than is expected, helping the retailer to quickly identify the problem and act immediately.

B2B Content Example

A site focused on demand generation could use machine learning to analyse content downloads on the site, to identify when the number of leads generated is lower than predicted. The marketing team could dig into that information to identify when an important link is broken to correct it before too much damage occurs.

Final Thoughts

Machine learning is quickly becoming a hot topic in the marketing industry, but many marketers are still working to figure out the best way to leverage it in their own strategies. As you explore machine learning, think about it on two fronts:

1. How it can impact your digital experience, providing highly personalized, relevant

   content to customers when they need it;

2. How it can help you better do your job by identifying your best opportunities and

   helping you to take quickly advantage of them.

5 Applications

Introduction

There are currently over 50 application areas of ML in the market today and this number is rising as new ways are discovered to apply ML to tasks from computing to translation software.

Chapter Learning Outcomes

▢ What ML applications are in use and why.

▢ The range of industries and areas using ML.

▢ The flexibility and adaptability of ML.

▢ How ML could be applied in a range of marketing areas.

▢ Having successfully completed the module, you will be able to:

▢ 1. Critically assess the applications of (ML) in marketing.

▢ 2. Assess the various uses and tools of (ML) in today's world.

⊡ Having completed the module, you will be able to:

⊡ 1. Understand the variety of (ML) applications and their uses.

• 2. Be able to explain the principal goals of each in (ML).

Critical thinking

Having successfully completed this topic, you will be able to:1. Critically evaluate the variety of applications used in (ML) .2. Understand and debate the areas of (ML) to management.

OBJECTIVES

The chapter will provide insight into the various approaches developed for ML to date providing the reader with a clear understanding of each and the application in a marketing context.

The Internet and the World Wide Web have made the process of collecting data easier, adding to the volume of data available to businesses. On the one hand, many organizations have realized that the knowledge in these huge databases are key to sup- porting the various organizational decisions. Particularly, the knowledge about customers from these databases is critical for the marketing function.

Data mining is the process of searching and analyzing data in order to find implicit, but potentially useful, information w3,8,9x. It involves selecting, exploring and modeling large amounts of data to un- cover previously unknown patterns, and ultimately comprehensible information, from large databases. Data mining uses a broad family of computational methods that include statistical analysis, decision trees, neural networks, rule induction and refinement, and graphic visualization. Although, data mining tools have been available for a long time, the advances in computer hardware and software, particularly exploratory tools like data visualization and neural networks, have made data mining more attractive and practical. Pattern extraction is an important component of any data mining activity and it deals with relation- ships between subsets of data.

Dependency knowledge is the association between sets of items stated with some minimum specified confidence w1x. This is also called Amarket basket analysisB w3x and gives us the relationship between different products purchased by a customer. This type of knowledge can be useful in developing marketing strategies for promoting products that have dependency relationships in the minds of the customers. For example, rules that have P e.g., A sausage and in the antecedent and Q e.g.,

A mustard in the consequent may help determine the additional items that have to be sold together with P i.e., sausage., in order to make it highly likely that Q i.e. mustard. will also be sold.

Class identification groups customers into classes, which are defined in advance. There are two types of class identification tasks — mathematical taxonomy and concept clustering. Mathematical taxonomy algorithms produce classes that maximize similarity within classes but minimize similarity between classes. For example, a food store can classify its customers based on their income or past purchase amounts and then target its marketing efforts accordingly. A drawback of this task is its inability to use background information, such as domain knowledge, to facilitate clustering. Concept clustering over- comes this limitation and determines clusters according to attribute similarity as well as conceptual cohesiveness as defined by domain knowledge. Users provide the domain knowledge by identifying useful clustering characteristics. For example, based on the session log data of Internet users, an Internet based company can classify the web users into 'email only', 'users', 'serious surfers', and 'fun and entertainment surfers. '

Concept description is a technique to group customers based on domain knowledge and the database, without forced definitions of the groups. Concept description can be used for summarization, discrimination, or comparison of marketing and customer knowledge.

Data summarization is the process of deriving a characteristic summary of a data subset that is interesting with respect to domain knowledge and the full data file. Technically, summarization of a concept A is performed by scanning all tuples that satisfy A and computing for all fields, in parallel, statistics on their values w23x. Using summarization, a marketer can learn about customer characteristics by grouping them according to their occupation, income, spending patterns and types of purchases, and build customer profiles. Discrimination describes qualities enough to differentiate records of one class from another w9x. For example, the color of the car might be used to distinguish whether a salesperson is from the Midwest. It can be done by a discrimination algorithm. Comparison describes the class in a way that facilitates comparison and analysis with other records.

A taxonomy of data mining tasks

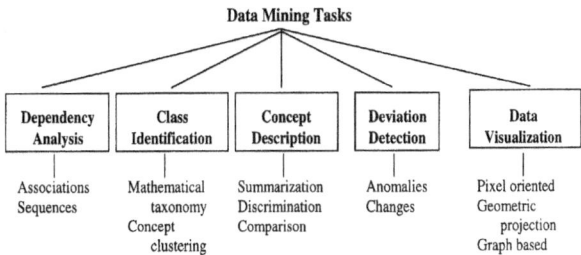

Deviations are useful for the discovery of anomaly and changes. Anomalies are different from the normal. For example, compare a group of similar salespeople and identify those who stand apart from the average, either in a positive or a negative way. Note that we need to adjust the various factors of the group before comparison. Anomalies can be detected by analysis of the means, standard deviations, and volatility measures from the data. In addition to anomalies, variables or attributes may have significantly different values from the previous transactions for the same customer or group of customers. A credit card company may find a sudden increase in the credit purchases of an individual customer. This change in behavior can be a result of a change in the status of the customer, and not necessarily a fraud.

Data visualization software allows marketers to view complex patterns in their customer data as visual objects complete in three dimensions and colours. They also provide advanced manipulation capabilities to slice, rotate or zoom the objects to provide varying levels of details of the patterns observed. To explore the knowledge in database, data visualization can be used alone or in association with other tasks such as dependency analysis, class identification, concept description and deviation detection.

Keim (1996) provides an elaborate analysis of visualization techniques for mining large databases and classifies visualization techniques into pixel-oriented, geometric projection and graph-based. The pixel-oriented technique maps each data value to a colored pixel and presents the data values belonging to each at- tribute in separate windows. Geometric projection techniques aim at finding 'interesting ' projections of multidimensional data set. The basic idea of the graph-based technique is to effectively present a large graph using specific layout algorithms, query languages, and abstraction techniques. Examples of graph based, representations are 2-dimensional graphs, 3-dimensional graphs, Hygraphs.

Knowledge discovery and learning is an iterative process that extends the collection of data mining techniques into a knowledge management framework. Though data mining techniques are usually applied to the complete database, it is possible to mine a statistically representative sample of the data. The outcome of the data mining efforts is evaluated to identify the usefulness of the resulting patterns to the solution of the marketing problem and the accuracy of prediction of future customer behavior from a known set of data. This assessment gives further insights into the data set and helps the marketer to refine the data mining model. The iterative learning process continues until the model is acceptable. One of the important issues in knowledge management is the organization, distribution and refinement of knowledge. Knowledge can be generated by data mining tools, can be acquired from third parties, or can be refined or refreshed knowledge. The collected knowledge can then be organized by indexing the knowledge elements, filtering based on content and establishing linkages and relationships among the elements. This knowledge is then integrated into a knowledge base and distributed to the decision support applications. The insights gained by the decision support applications are used to refine the existing knowledge and feedback into knowledge organization.

Marketing decisions, such as promotions, distribution channels and advertising media, based on traditional segmentation approaches result in poor response rate and increased cost. Today's customers have such varied tastes and preferences that it is not possible to group them into large homogenous populations to develop marketing strategies. In fact, each customer wants to be served according to her individual and unique needs. Database marketing characterized by marketing strategies based on the great deal of information available from the transaction databases and customer databases became popular Holtz (1992) and most organizations have built up massive databases about their customers and their purchase transactions. But, due to lack of appropriate tools and techniques to analyze these huge databases, a wealth of customer information and buying patterns is permanently hidden and unutilized in such databases. Knowledge-based marketing, which uses appropriate data mining tools and knowledge management framework, addresses this need and helps leverage knowledge hidden in databases. There are three major areas of application of data mining for knowledge-based marketing 1. customer profiling, deviation analysis, and 3. trend analysis.

Customer profiling

One of the useful knowledges about a customer is her profile, which is used to make several important marketing decisions. A customer profile is a model of the customer, based on which the marketer decides on the right strategies and tactics to meet the needs of that customer. Fig. 5 presents a customer profiling system that uses data mining tasks.

While learning customer profiles, a marketer is interested in the customer demographic details as well as the characteristics of the purchase transactions of the customer. The data mining tasks used in customer profiling can be dependency analysis, class identification and concept description, and we present a list of transaction characteristics that can help the marketer construct useful customer profiles.

Frequency of purchases

How often does the customer buy your product or visit your shop? By knowing this, the marketer can build targeted promotions such as 'frequent buyer programs.'

Size of purchases

How much does the customer spend on a typical transaction? This information helps the marketer de- vote appropriate resources to the customer who spends more.

Recency of purchases

How long has it been since this customer last placed an order? The marketer may investigate the reasons a customer or a group has not purchased over a long period of time and take appropriate steps. Many times, this could be due to the customer having moved from that location or having shifted loyalty.

Identifying typical customer groups

The characteristics of each group can be obtained by class identification or concept description. For example, a profile indicating that the customer has purchased a new house may lead to the marketer offering a special deal for home furnishings. Knowing the customer and targeting the right deal gets a far better response rate than a general message.

Computing customer lifetime Values

With customer profiling supported by data mining and knowledge discovery systems, several marketing activities can be enhanced, such as computing customer lifetime values, prospecting and success or failure of marketing programs.Customer lifetime values, a measure to understand what is happening to the size and value of a customer base, can be computed by using the customer profile information combined with the product and promotional statistics. Customer lifetime values are asset measures that can help marketers judge their expenditures by measuring a plan's efficiency in producing assets.

Prospecting

Customer profiles, especially their buying patterns, give clues to the marketer on prospective customers. For example, consider the pattern purchase of toys for age group 3 – 5 years, is followed by purchase of kid's bicycle within 6 months about 90% of the time by high income customers discovered by data mining. A marketer who has knowledge about the above pattern can identify the prospective customers for kid's bicycle based on toy purchase details and tailor the mail catalog accordingly, thus, increasing the prospect of sales.

Decision Support System

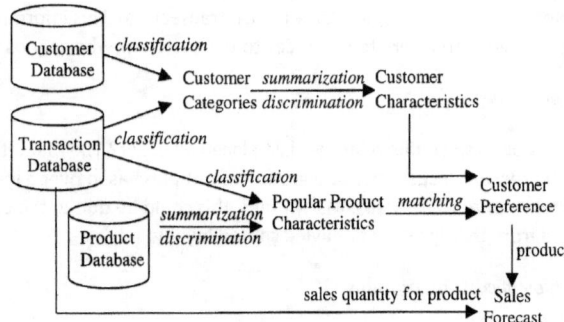

M.J. Shaw et al (2001) 127–137

Success or *failure of marketing programs*

Customer databases provide accurate information on the results of marketing programs. The marketer can use the patterns of purchase discovered from the database and the related marketing programs to measure the short-term and long-term effects of the programs.

4.2. Deviation analysis

Knowledge of deviations from normal is extremely important to a marketer. A deviation can be an anomaly or fraud or a change. In the past, such deviations were difficult to detect in time to take corrective action. Data mining tools provide powerful means such as neural networks for detecting and classifying such deviations. For example, a higher than normal credit purchase on a credit card can be a fraud (anomaly) or a genuine purchase by the customer (change).

Once a deviation has been discovered as a fraud, the marketer takes steps to prevent such frauds and initiates corrective action. If the deviation has been discovered as a change, further information collection is necessary. For example, a change can be that a customer got a new job and moved to a new house.

In this case, the marketer must update the knowledge about the customer. A marketer can use the deviation detection capability to query changes that occurred as a result of recent price changes or pro- motions.

Trend analysis

Trends are patterns that persist over a period. Trends could be short-term trends like the immediate increase and subsequent slow decrease of sales following a sales campaign. Or, trends could be long-term, like the slow flattening of sales of a product over a few years. Data mining tools, such as visualization, help us detect trends, sometimes very subtle and hidden in the database, which would have been missed using traditional analysis tools like scatter plots. In marketing decisions, trends can be used for evaluating marketing programs or to forecast future sales.

Evaluate performance of products or marketing programs

The customer database provides an accurate record of the transactions. Marketers can use visualization tools to identify trends in sales, costs and profits by products, regions or markets in order to understand the impact of, say, a sales promotion. Data mining also provides statistical tools to precisely measure the performance of the various parameters of interest.

Forecast future sales

One of the popular uses of trends is forecasting future sales. Marketers are interested in knowing how various marketing programs affect future sales of their products. Data mining allows discovery of subtle relationships like a peak in sales of a product associated with a change in the profile of a group of customers.

The recent emphasis on customer relationship management has put the focus back on the customer. The four key steps for customer relationship management

1. identifying the right customers,

2. differentiating among them,

3. interacting with and learning from existing customers

4. customizing the product or service to the needs of individual customers are based on knowing customers better (Pepper and Rogers, 1999).

Current efforts on customer relationship management are focused on the customer interface and managing customer interactions. But inadequate knowledge about customers and the lack of a systematic knowledge management framework continue to hinder the efforts of organizations, particularly the marketing function, to manage their customer relationships.

The knowledge management framework described can provide the basis for organizations to effectively integrate the discovery of customer knowledge with their relationship management strategies.

Though data mining techniques are used in several areas such as fraud detection, bankruptcy prediction, medical diagnosis, and scientific discoveries, their use for marketing decision support highlights unique and interesting issues such as *customer relationship management, real-time interactive marketing, customer profiling and cross-organizational management of knowledge.* In the current customer- centric business environment, it is my firm belief that there is a need for deeper understanding of use of data mining and knowledge management for marketing decision support. Towards that end, I have shown how data mining can be integrated into a marketing knowledge management framework. With the availability of large volume of data, made possible by modern information technology, a major problem is to filter, sort, process, analyze and manage this data in order to extract the information relevant to the user. The growth in the size and number of existing databases far exceeds human abilities to analyze such data using traditional tools and thus creates both a need and an opportunity for data mining tools. With the shift from mass marketing to one-to-one relationship marketing, one area that could greatly benefit from data mining is the marketing function itself. A systematic application of data mining techniques will enhance the knowledge management process and arm the marketers with better knowledge of their customers leading to better service to customers. It is also clear that the Web technology will have a major impact on the practice of data mining and knowledge management using machine learning and applications, and that this should present interesting challenges for future information systems research.

Let us now look at some of the software that is used in marketing applications:

In today's knowledge economy, the marketing landscape for businesses has changed dramatically. Companies that hope to effectively spread the word about their offerings, attract customers, engage with them and ultimately retain them, need to adapt to these changes. Those that fail to do so will fall behind. Below are 15 great marketing software's that can help companies remain relevant and master marketing in the digital age.

The data is from company websites:

1) Marketo
Marketo is one of the biggest and most established marketing automation companies, which makes it easy to launch and manage marketing campaigns. Marketo offers everything marketers need including tools for automating inbound marketing, lead management, social media marketing, sales management dashboards as well as analytics.

2) Vocus
Vocus **VOCS +0%** is a leading cloud-based marketing software which helps with customer acquisition and retention by making it easier for marketers to reach out via social media and other online media channels.
Vocus offers a comprehensive suite of tools which integrate social media marketing, search marketing, email marketing as well as effective PR.

3) HubSpot
HubSpot offers a powerful inbound marketing solution as a personalized and more effective alternative to traditional marketing strategies which can tend to harass consumers. It has developed a host of marketing apps which include tools for blogging, social media, lead management and even marketing analytics that people love and respond to.

4) Yesware
Yesware is an email platform which makes it easier for salespeople to manage and track emails and thus close more deals. The platform tracks email opens provide in-email analytics as well as data on user engagement. Yesware syncs seamlessly with CRMs like Salesforce, Microsoft MSFT -0.98% Dynamics and Oracle ORCL +NaN% CRM saving time and increasing efficiency.

5) Sailthru
Sailthru aims to increase user engagement and conversion through smart data which marketers can use to better understand and respond to users in real time. This results in a personalized user experience in the form of targeted emails, for example, or a homepage tailored to an individual's interests. Sailthru's clients include Business Insider, AOL **AOL +0%**. Huffington Post and Newsweek among others.

6) Optimove
Optimove's retention automation platform leverages proprietary customer modeling technology to help marketers at online companies maximize the value of every customer. The software helps Internet businesses convert more leads, increase customer spend and engagement, reduce churn and win back more lost customers. By affecting customer behavior through highly relevant, personalized offers and incentives, Optimove helps businesses -- including clients like Conduit and GetTaxi -- understand customers and maximize revenue.

7) LocalVox

LocalVox is a platform for local, social and mobile marketing for businesses, helping them generate news and engage local customers across the web, a network of local publishers, mobile, social media, email newsletters and search.

8) Mail Chimp

Mail Chimp makes it easy to customize emails to suit a particular marketing campaign. Other features include analytics, the option to A/B test and geo-target as well as spam filter diagnostics. Mail Chimp has more than 2 million users and is growing at rate of about 6,000 users a day.

9) Infusionsoft

Infusionsoft provides comprehensive and cost-effective marketing and sales software for small businesses. As part of its marketing suite, Infusionsoft offers marketing automation and e-commerce tools as well as CRM. Infusionsoft makes it easier for small businesses to convert leads with its all-in-one solution.

10) ThriveHive

ThriveHive provides small businesses with all the tools they need to excel at marketing. This includes building a custom marketing plan tailored to suit the company's unique needs. Thrive Hive's services range from marketing consultation to SEO optimization.

11) Demand base

Demand base aims to give B2B marketers the tools they need to improve conversion rates and turn website traffic into sales. This software works by identifying a website's traffic and tailoring the site's content to those visitors thus providing an experience which is personalized and relevant.

12) Word Stream

Word Stream aims to optimize search engine marketing and helps marketers get better results out of their SEO and PPC campaigns. It lets marketers effectively manage and create paid as well as organic campaigns.

13) Act-On

Act-On is a cloud-based marketing solution which is designed to automate marketing tasks increasing efficiency. Act-On offers tools for organizing marketing campaigns, converting leads and integrating marketing efforts into sales systems. It has over 1000 customers.

14) CAKE

CAKE provides real-time analytics and tracking for efficient marketing campaigns. CAKE organizes all information in one place and lets the marketer control everything from location, device and even traffic source to be targeted. Launched in 2007, the company has a client base which includes Score Big, Convert 2 Media and Life script among others.

15) Optify

Optify is a cloud-based service which gives a marketer complete control over lead generation programs. With Optify it's possible to generate new leads, nurture existing leads and even measure the success of marketing efforts.

Existing office suites contain wide range of various components. Most typically, the base components include:

- Word Processor
- Presentation program

Other components of office suites include:

- Database software
- Graphics suite (raster graphics editor, vector graphics editor, image viewer)
- Desktop publishing software
- Formula editor
- Diagramming software
- Email client
- Communication software
- Personal information manager
- Notetaking software
- Groupware
- Project management software
- Web log analysis software

Internet suites

- Arachne
- Cybercop
- Mozilla Application Suite and Sea Monkey internet suite
- Gnuzilla
- K Desktop Environment
- MSN Explorer
- Netscape Communicator
- Netscape
- Opera (version 12.17 and earlier)

Graphic suites

- Adobe graphics suite
- CorelDRAW Graphics Suite
- Microsoft Expression Studio

Proprietary software

- Amazon Web Service
 A subsidiary of Amazon.com that provides on-demand cloud computing platforms to individuals, companies and governments, on a paid subscription basis with a free-tier option available for 12 months. The technology allows subscribers to have at their disposal a full-fledged virtual cluster of computers, available all the time, through the internet. AWS's version of virtual computers have most of the attributes of a real computer including hardware (CPU(s) & GPU(s) for processing, local/RAM memory, hard-disk/SSD storage); a choice of operating systems; networking; and pre-loaded application software such as web servers, databases, CRM, etc

- Angoss Knowledge Studio
A provider of predictive analytics systems, through software licensing and services. Angoss' customers represent industries including finance, insurance, mutual funds, retail, health sciences, telecom and technology.

- Ayasdi
A machine intelligence software company that offers a software platform and applications to organizations looking to analyse and build predictive models using big data or highly dimensional data sets. Organizations and governments have deployed Ayasdi's software across a variety of use cases including the development of clinical pathways for hospitals, anti-money laundering, fraud detection, trading strategies, customer segmentation, oil and gas well development, drug development, disease research, information security, anomaly detection, and national security applications.

- IBM Data Science Experience

IBM's platform for data science, a one-stop workspace that offers all the collaboration and open-source tools data scientists need and use every day. It was created for data scientists who like working with open source tools, collaborating with their peers and accessing their data tools and data sets in one place. In DSX, data scientists can create projects with a group of collaborators, all with access to a host of analytics models and support for various languages (R/Python/Scala). DSx brings together staple open source tools like RStudio, Spark and Python in an integrated environment - along with IBM value-adds like a managed Spark service and data shaping capabilities, all in a secure and governed environment.

Data Science Experience provides access to data sets that are available through Watson Data Platform, on-premises or on the cloud. The platform also has a large community and embedded resources like articles on the latest developments from the data science world and public data sets. DSx is available on-premises, on the cloud and on desktop.

- Google Prediction API

A set of application programming interfaces (APIs) developed by Google which allow communication with Google Services and their integration to other services. Examples of these include Search, Gmail, Translate or Google Maps. Third-party apps can use these APIs to take advantage of or extend the functionality of the existing services. The APIs provide functionality like analytics, machine learning as a service (the Prediction API) or access to user data (when permission to read the data is given). Another important example is an embedded Google map on a website, which can be achieved using the Static mps API, Places API or Google Earth API.

- IBM SPSS Modeler

A data mining and text analytics software application from IBM. It is used to build predictive models and conduct other analytic tasks. It has a visual interface which allows users to leverage statistical and data mining algorithms without programming. One of its main aims from the outset was to get rid of unnecessary complexity in data transformations, and to make complex predictive models very easy to use. The first version incorporated decision trees (ID3), and neural networks (backprop), which could both be trained without underlying knowledge of how those techniques worked.

- KXEN Modeler
  A predictive modelling suite developed by KXEN that assists analytic professionals, and business executives to extract information from data. Among other functions, Infinite Insight is used for variable importance, classification, regression, segmentation, time series, product recommendation, as described and expressed by the Java Data Mining interface, and for social network analysis. Infinite Insight allows prediction of a behaviour or a value, the forecast of a time series or the understanding of a group of individuals with similar behaviour. Advanced functions include behavioural modelling, exporting the model code into different target environments or building predictive models on top of SAS or SPSS data files. Competitors are SAS Enterprise Miner, IBM SPSS Modeler, and Statistica. Open source predictive tools like the R package or Weka are also competitors, since they provide similar features free of charge.

- LION solver

  LION solver is an integrated software for data mining, business intelligence, analytics, and modelingLearning and Intelligent OptimizatioN and reactive business intelligence approach. A non-profit version is available as LIONoso. LION solver can be used to build models, visualize them, and improve business and engineering processes. It is a tool for decision making based on data and quantitative models, it can be connected to most databases and external programs.

  It is fully integrated with the Grapheur business intelligence software and intended for more advanced users, interested in designing business logic and processes and not only in simple analytics and visualization tasks.

- Mathematica
  A mathematical symbolic computation program, sometimes termed a computer algebra system or program, used in many scientific, engineering, mathematical, and computing fields. It was conceived by Stephen Wolfram and is developed by Wolfram Research of Champaign, Illinois. The Wolfram Language is the programming language used in Mathematica.

- MATLAB
  A multi-paradigm numerical computing environment. A proprietary programming language developed by MathWorks, MATLAB allows **matrix manipulations**, plotting of functions and data, implementation of algorithms, creation of user interfaces, and interfacing with programs written in other languages, including C, C++, C#, Java, Fortran and Python. Although MATLAB is intended primarily for numerical computing, an optional toolbox uses the MuPAD symbolic engine, allowing access to symbolic computing abilities.

An additional package, Simulink, adds graphical multi-domain simulation and model-based design for dynamic and embedded systems.

- Microsoft Azure Machine Learning

  A cloud computing service created by Microsoft for building, testing, deploying, and managing applications and services through a global network of Microsoft-managed centres. It provides software as a service (SaaS), platform as a service and infrastructure as a service and supports many different programming languages, tools and frameworks, including both Microsoft-specific and third-party software and systems. Azure was announced in October 2008 and released on February 1, 2010 as "Windows Azure" before being renamed "Microsoft Azure" on March 25, 2014.

- Neural Designer
  A software tool for data analytics based on neural networks, a main area of artificial intelligence research. It has been developed from the open source library OpenNN, and contains a graphical user interface which simplifies data entry and interpretation of results.

- NeuroSolutions
  A neural network development environment developed by Neuro Dimension. It combines a modular, icon-based (component-based) network design interface with an implementation of advanced learning procedures, such as conjugate gradients, Levenberg-Marquardt and back propagation through time.

  The software is used to design, train and deploy neural network (supervised learning and unsupervised learning) models to perform a wide variety of tasks such as data mining, classification, function approximation, multivariate regression and time-series prediction.

- Oracle Data Mining
  It contains several data mining and data analysis algorithms for classification, prediction, regression, associations, feature selection, anomaly detection, feature extraction, and specialized analytics. It provides means for the creation, management and operational deployment of data mining models inside the database environment.

- Oracle AI Platform Cloud Service

  The company specializes primarily in developing and marketing database software and technology, cloud engineered systems and enterprise software products — particularly its own brands of database management systems. In 2015, Oracle was the second-largest software maker by revenue, after Microsoft.

The company also develops and builds tools for database development and systems of middle-tier software, enterprise resource planning (ERP) software, customer relationship management (CRM) software and supply chain management (SCM) software.

- RCASE

  A proprietary algorithm developed from research originally at the Warwick Manufacturing Group (WMG) at Warwick University. RCASE development commenced in 2003 to provide an automated version of root cause analysis, the method of problem solving that tries to identify the root causes of faults or problems.

- SAS Enterprize Miner

  A software suite developed by SAS Institute for advanced analytics, multivariate analyses, business intelligence, data management, and predictive analytics.

- Sky mind

  Sky mind's deep neural networks can be applied to use cases such as fraud and anomaly detection, recommender systems, machine vision, machine translation, machine transcription, face and voice recognition, time series predictions, business intelligence and econometric analytics. They are able to perform dimensionality reduction, classification, regression, collaborative filtering, feature learning and topic modelling.

- Splunk

  Splunk (the product) captures, indexes, and correlates real-time data in a searchable repository from which it can generate graphs, reports, alerts, dashboards, and visualizations.

  Splunk's mission is to make machine data accessible across an organization by identifying data patterns, providing metrics, diagnosing problems, and providing intelligence for business operations. Splunk is a horizontal technology used for application management, security and compliance, as well as business and Web analytics.

- Statistica Data Miner

  Statistica is a suite of analytics software products and solutions originally developed by Stat Soft and acquired by Dell in March 2014. The software includes an array of data analysis, data management, data visualization, and data mining procedures; as well as a variety of predictive modelling, clustering, classification, and exploratory techniques. Additional techniques are available through integration with the free, open source Reprogramming environment. Different packages of analytical techniques are available in six product lines

Revision

- Using 100 words discuss decision tree learning.
- Explain in 50 words a decision support system, what are the components?
- AS a task of 200 words ' how would you profile a Toothpaste user?'
- In 25 words outline what is 'support vector machines.

6 Model assessments

Introduction

Classification machine learning models can be validated by accuracy estimation techniques like the Holdout method, which splits the data in a training and test set (conventionally 2/3 training set and 1/3 test set designation) and evaluates the performance of the training model on the test set.

Chapter Learning Outcomes

⍰ Provide an insight into ML model assessment.

⍰ Outline the various assessment techniques.

⍰ Review positive and negative rates.

⍰ Understand the concepts .

⍰ Having successfully completed the module, you will be able to:

⍰ 1. Critically assess the various models of assessment of (ML) in marketing.

⍰ 2. Assess the classifications of (ML) in today's world.

⍰ Having completed the module, you will be able to:

⍰ 1. Understand the variety of (ML) model assessments and their uses.

• 2. Be able to explain the principal goals of each in (ML).

Critical thinking

Having successfully completed this topic, you will be able to:1. Critically evaluate the variety of philosophies and ethics used in (AI) .2. Understand and debate the two areas of (AI) to management.

OBJECTIVES

The assessment of ML applications is a key factor in their outcomes achieving their desired objectives. By validating their performance marketers can measure their positive and negative rates.

Machine learning has become a central part of our life – as consumers, customers, and hopefully as researchers and practitioners! Whether we are applying predictive modelling techniques to our research or business problems, I believe we have one thing in common: We want to make "good" predictions! Fitting a model to our training data is one thing, but how do we know that it generalizes well to unseen data? How do we know that it doesn't simply memorize the data we fed it and fails to make good predictions on future samples, samples that it hasn't seen before? And how do we select a good model in the first place? Maybe a different learning algorithm could be better suited for the problem at hand?

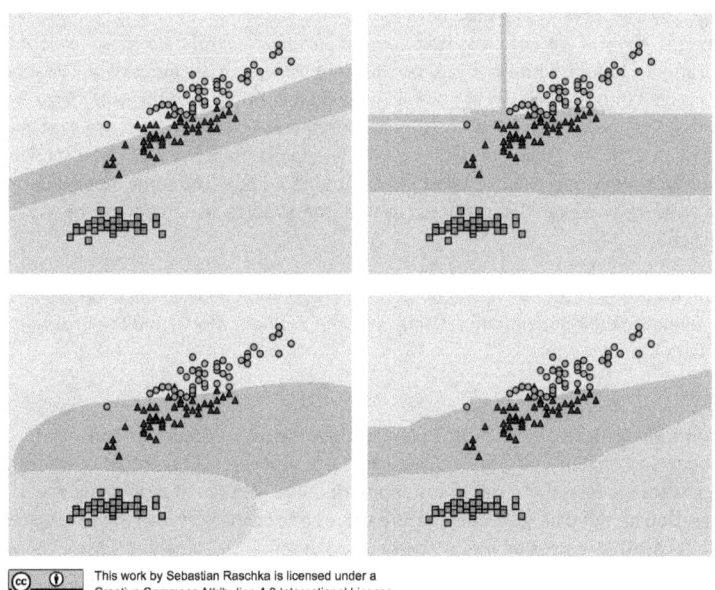

Model evaluation is certainly not just the end point of our machine learning pipeline. Before we handle any data, we want to plan ahead and use techniques that are suited for our purposes. We will go over a selection of these *techniques*, and we will see how they fit into the bigger picture, a typical machine learning workflow.

Evaluating the performance of a model is one of the core stages in the data science process. It indicates how successful the scoring (predictions) of a dataset has been by a trained model.

Azure Machine Learning supports model evaluation through two of its main machine learning modules: Evaluate Model and Cross-Validate Model. These modules allow you to see how your model performs in terms of several metrics that are commonly used in machine learning and statistics (Microsoft Azure, 2017).

Evaluation vs. Cross Validation

Evaluation and cross validation are standard ways to measure the performance of your model. They both generate evaluation metrics that you can inspect or compare against those of other models.

Evaluate Model expects a scored dataset as input (or 2 in case you would like to compare the performance of 2 different models). This means that you need to train your model using the Train Model module and make predictions on some dataset using the Score Model module, before you can evaluate the results. The evaluation is based on the scored labels/probabilities along with the true labels, all of which are output by the Score Model module.

Alternatively, you can use cross validation to perform several train-score-evaluate operations (10 folds) automatically on different subsets of the input data. The input data is split into 10 parts, where one is reserved for testing, and the other 9 for training. This process is repeated 10 times and the evaluation metrics are averaged. This helps in determining how well a model would generalize to new datasets. The Cross-Validate Model module takes in an untrained model and some labeled dataset and outputs the evaluation results of each of the 10 folds, in addition to the averaged results.

In the following sections, we will build simple regression and classification models and evaluate their performance, using both the Evaluate Model and the Cross-Validate Model modules.

Evaluating a Regression Model

Assume we want to predict a car's price using some features such as dimensions, horsepower, engine specs, and so on. This is a typical regression problem, where the target variable (price) is a continuous numeric value. We can fit a simple linear regression model that, given the feature values of a certain car, can predict the price of that car. This regression model can be used to score the same dataset we trained on. Once we have the predicted prices for all the cars, we can evaluate the performance of the model by looking at how much the predictions deviate from the actual prices on average. To illustrate this, we use the Automobile price data (Raw) dataset available in the Saved Datasets section in Azure Machine Learning Studio.

Creating the Experiment

Add the following modules to your workspace in Azure Machine Learning Studio:

- ▢ Automobile price data (Raw)
- ▢ Linear Regression
- ▢ Train Model
- ▢ Score Model
- ▢ Evaluate Model

Connect the ports as shown below in Figure 1 and set the Label column of the Train Model module to price (Microsoft Azure,2017).

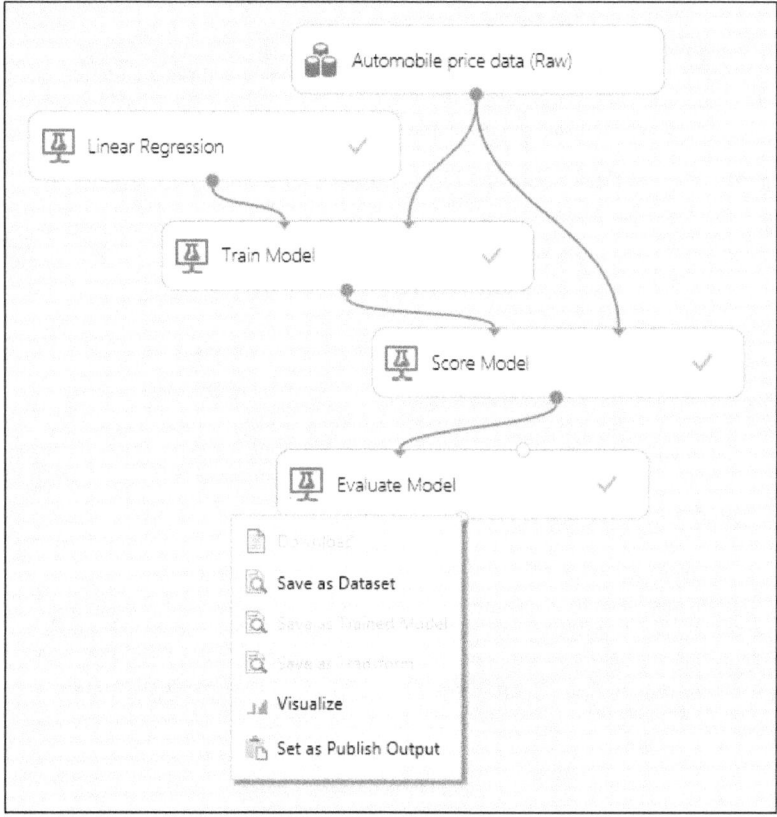

Figure 1. Evaluating a Regression Model.

Inspecting the Evaluation Results
After running the experiment, you can click on the output port of the Evaluate Model module and select Visualize to see the evaluation results. The evaluation metrics available for regression models are: Mean Absolute Error, Root Mean Absolute Error, Relative Absolute Error, Relative Squared Error, and the Coefficient of Determination.

The term "error" here represents the difference between the predicted value and the true value. The absolute value or the square of this difference are usually computed to capture the total magnitude of error across all instances, as the difference between the predicted and true value could be negative in some cases.

The error metrics measure the predictive performance of a regression model in terms of the mean deviation of its predictions from the true values. Lower error values mean the model is more accurate in making predictions. An overall error metric of 0 means that the model fits the data perfectly.

The coefficient of determination, which is also known as R squared, is also a standard way of measuring how well the model fits the data. It can be interpreted as the proportion of variation explained by the model. A higher proportion is better in this case, where 1 indicates a perfect fit.

◢ Metrics	
Mean Absolute Error	747.975254
Root Mean Squared Error	955.587783
Relative Absolute Error	0.163528
Relative Squared Error	0.026598
Coefficient of Determination	0.973402

Figure 2. Linear Regression Evaluation Metrics.

Using Cross Validation
As mentioned earlier, you can perform repeated training, scoring and evaluations automatically using the Cross-Validate Model module. All you need in this case is a dataset, an untrained model, and a Cross-Validate Model module (see figure below). Note that you need to set the label column to price in the Cross-Validate Model module's properties.

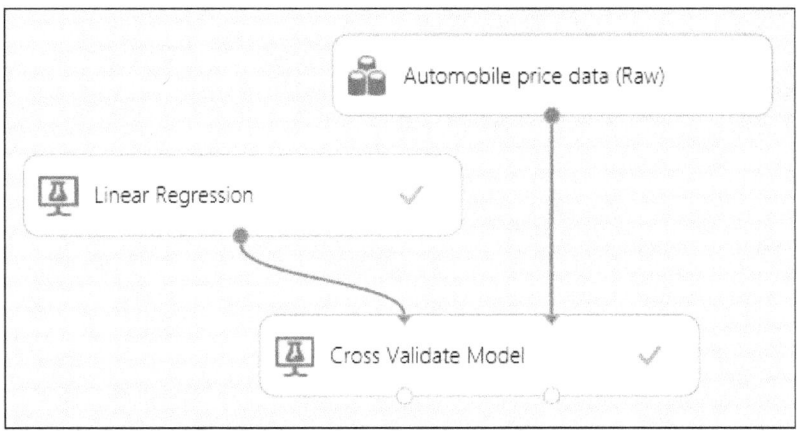

Figure 3. Cross Validating a Regression Model.

After running the experiment, you can inspect the evaluation results by clicking on the right output port of the Cross-Validate Model module. This will provide a detailed view of the metrics for each iteration (fold), and the averaged results of each of the metrics (Figure 4).

Fold Number	Number of examples in fold	Model	Mean Absolute Error	Root Mean Squared Error	Relative Absolute Error	Relative Squared Error	Coefficient of Determination
0	20	Microsoft.Analytics.Machi neLearning.Local.BatchLin earRegressor	1975.890000	2868.853475	0.318462	0.261852	0.738148
1	21	Microsoft.Analytics.Machi neLearning.Local.BatchLin earRegressor	1204.367667	1736.360322	0.259077	0.101772	0.898228
2	20	Microsoft.Analytics.Machi neLearning.Local.BatchLin earRegressor	1275.525323	1565.686411	0.148945	0.021472	0.978528
3	21	Microsoft.Analytics.Machi neLearning.Local.BatchLin earRegressor	1180.795629	1479.619128	0.150116	0.024304	0.975696
4	20	Microsoft.Analytics.Machi neLearning.Local.BatchLin earRegressor	672.068144	902.187494	0.091132	0.010176	0.989824
5	20	Microsoft.Analytics.Machi neLearning.Local.BatchLin earRegressor	1166.036215	1492.147079	0.227148	0.055168	0.944832
6	21	Microsoft.Analytics.Machi neLearning.Local.BatchLin earRegressor	1544.193782	1936.495628	0.272313	0.07162	0.92838
7	21	Microsoft.Analytics.Machi neLearning.Local.BatchLin earRegressor	1435.049593	2035.841829	0.17445	0.042546	0.957454
8	20	Microsoft.Analytics.Machi neLearning.Local.BatchLin earRegressor	1583.894079	2032.621829	0.186764	0.042628	0.957322
9	21	Microsoft.Analytics.Machi neLearning.Local.BatchLin earRegressor	1069.870402	1464.412809	0.113144	0.020426	0.979574
Mean	205	Microsoft.Analytics.Machi neLearning.Local.BatchLin earRegressor	1310.740083	1777.443708	0.193857	0.065197	0.934803
Standard Deviation	205	Microsoft.Analytics.Machi neLearning.Local.BatchLin earRegressor	320.085779	332.636933	0.073523	0.07438	0.07438

Figure 4. Cross-Validation Results of a Regression Model.

Evaluating a Binary Classification Model

In a binary classification scenario, the target variable has only two possible outcomes, for example: {0, 1} {false, true}, {negative, positive}. Assume you are given a dataset of adult employees with some demographic and employment variables, and that you are asked to predict the income level, a binary variable with the values {"<=50K", ">50K"}.

In other words, the negative class represents the employees who make less than or equal to 50K per year, and the positive class represents all other employees. As in the regression scenario, we would train a model, score some data, and evaluate the results. The main difference here is the choice of metrics Azure Machine Learning computes and outputs. To illustrate the income level prediction scenario, we will use the Adult dataset to create an Azure Machine Learning experiment and evaluate the performance of a two-class logistic regression model, a commonly used binary classifier.

Creating the Experiment
Add the following modules to your workspace in Azure Machine Learning Studio:

- Adult Census Income Binary Classification dataset
- Two-Class Logistic Regression
- Train Model
- Score Model
- Evaluate Model

Connect the ports as shown below in Figure 5 and set the Label column of the Train Model module to income.

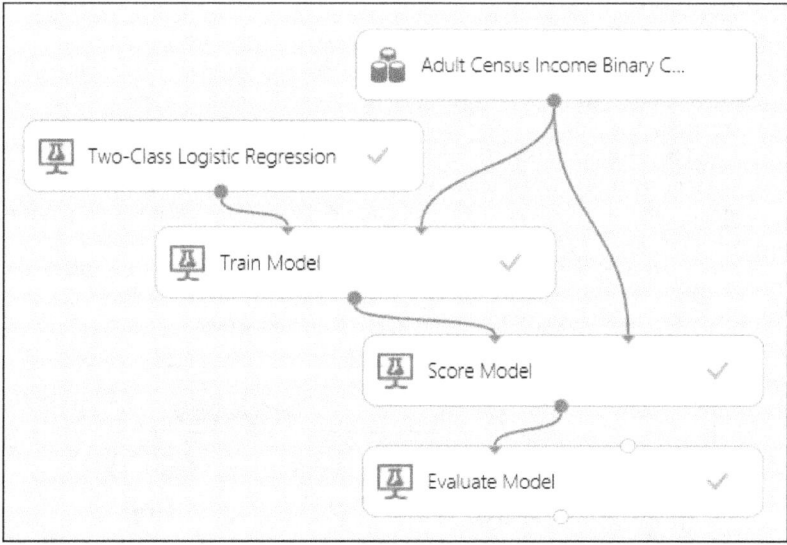

Figure 5. Evaluating a Binary Classification Model.

Inspecting the Evaluation Results
After running the experiment, you can click on the output port of the Evaluate Model module and select Visualize to see the evaluation results (Figure 7). The evaluation metrics available for binary classification models are: Accuracy, Precision, Recall, F1 Score, and AUC. In addition, the module outputs a confusion matrix showing the number of true positives, false negatives, false positives, and true negatives, as well as ROC, Precision/Recall, and Lift curves.

Accuracy is simply the proportion of correctly classified instances. It is usually the first metric you look at when evaluating a classifier. However, when the test data is unbalanced (where most of the instances belong to one of the classes), or you are more interested in the performance on either one of the classes, accuracy doesn't really capture the effectiveness of a classifier. In the income level classification scenario, assume you are testing on some data where 99% of the instances represent people who earn less than or equal to 50K per year.

It is possible to achieve a 0.99 accuracy by predicting the class "<=50K" for all instances. The classifier in this case appears to be doing a good job overall, but it fails to classify any of the high-income individuals (the 1%) correctly.

For that reason, it is helpful to compute additional metrics that capture more specific aspects of the evaluation. Before going into the details of such metrics, it is important to understand the confusion matrix of a binary classification evaluation. The class labels in the training set can take on only 2 possible values, which we usually refer to as positive or negative. The positive and negative instances that a classifier predicts correctly are called true positives (TP) and true negatives (TN), respectively. Similarly, the incorrectly classified instances are called false positives (FP) and false negatives (FN). The confusion matrix is simply a table showing the number of instances that fall under each of these 4 categories. Azure Machine Learning automatically decides which of the two classes in the dataset is the positive class. If the class labels are Boolean or integers, then the 'true' or '1' labeled instances are assigned the positive class. If the labels are strings, as in the case of the income dataset, the labels are sorted alphabetically, and the first level is chosen to be the negative class while the second level is the positive class.

	Predicted	
	Positive	Negative
Actual True	TP	FN
Actual False	FP	TN

Figure 6. Binary Classification Confusion Matrix.

Going back to the income classification problem, we would want to ask several evaluation questions that help us understand the performance of the classifier used. A very natural question is: 'Out of the individuals whom the model predicted to be earning >50K (TP+FP), how many were classified correctly (TP)?' This question can be answered by looking at the Precision of the model, which is the proportion of positives that are classified correctly: TP/(TP+FP). Another common question is "Out of all the high earning employees with income >50k (TP+FN), how many did the classifier classify correctly (TP)".

This is the Recall, or the true positive rate: TP/(TP+FN) of the classifier. You might notice that there is an obvious trade-off between precision and recall. For example, given a relatively balanced dataset, a classifier that predicts mostly positive instances, would have a high recall, but a rather low precision as many of the negative instances would be misclassified resulting in many false positives. To see a plot of how these two metrics, vary, you can click on the 'PRECISION/RECALL' curve in the evaluation result output page (top left part of Figure 7).

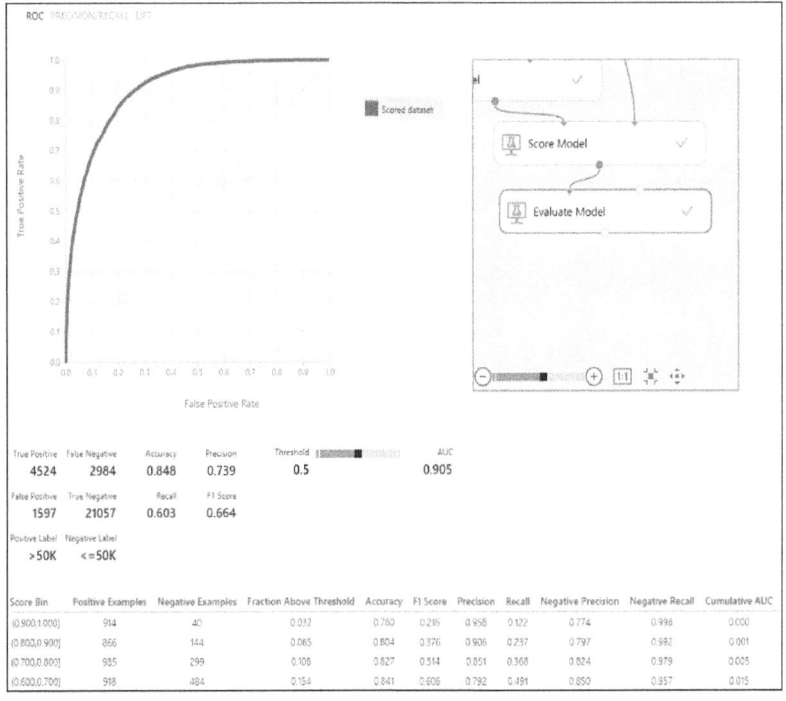

Figure 7. Binary Classification Evaluation Results.

Another related metric that is often used is the F1 Score, which takes both precision and recall into consideration. It is the harmonic mean of these 2 metrics and is computed as such: F1 = 2 (precision x recall) / (precision + recall). The F1 score is a good way to summarize the evaluation in a single number, but it's always a good practice to look at both precision and recall together to better understand how a classifier behaves.

In addition, one can inspect the true positive rate vs. the false positive rate in the Receiver Operating Characteristic (ROC) curve and the corresponding Area Under the Curve (AUC) value. The closer this curve is to the upper left corner; the better the classifier's performance is (that is maximizing the true positive rate while minimizing the false positive rate).

Curves that are close to the diagonal of the plot, result from classifiers that tend to make predictions that are close to random guessing.

Using Cross Validation
As in the regression example, we can perform cross validation to repeatedly train, score and evaluate different subsets of the data automatically. Similarly, we can use the Cross-Validate Model module, an untrained logistic regression model, and a dataset. The label column must be set to income in the Cross-Validate Model module's properties.
After running the experiment and clicking on the right output port of the Cross-Validate Model module, we can see the binary classification metric values for each fold, in addition to the mean and standard deviation of each.

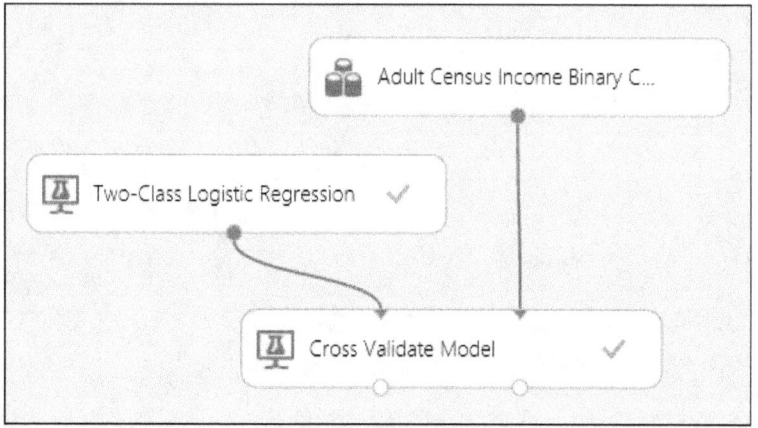

Figure 8. Cross Validating a Binary Classification Model.

rows 32	columns 10								
Fold Number	Number of examples in fold	Model	Accuracy	Precision	Recall	F-Score	AUC	Average Log Loss	Training Log Loss
0	3256	Logistic Regression	0.850359	0.737342	0.621333	0.674385	0.506809	0.325788	41.989626
1	3256	Logistic Regression	0.842245	0.707358	0.585062	0.640424	0.901871	0.32527	40.990733
2	3256	Logistic Regression	0.852583	0.767007	0.591864	0.668148	0.905203	0.32936	41.51439
3	3256	Logistic Regression	0.847333	0.729685	0.598639	0.657690	0.898848	0.333642	40.075913
4	3256	Logistic Regression	0.844305	0.741194	0.614213	0.671756	0.90969	0.332448	41.921163
5	3256	Logistic Regression	0.834601	0.716393	0.57189	0.636099	0.897829	0.339868	39.878498
6	3256	Logistic Regression	0.85	0.728188	0.598621	0.657078	0.902695	0.327404	40.596835
7	3257	Logistic Regression	0.846128	0.743464	0.599473	0.663749	0.90208	0.333052	41.153979
8	3256	Logistic Regression	0.846973	0.734861	0.601071	0.661267	0.902736	0.329349	41.259562
9	3256	Logistic Regression	0.849388	0.742718	0.607947	0.668609	0.903525	0.328219	41.623392
Mean	32561	Logistic Regression	0.846396	0.734821	0.599021	0.659921	0.902629	0.33044	41.100509
Standard Deviation	32561	Logistic Regression	0.005145	0.016276	0.014102	0.012778	0.00269	0.004408	0.725968

Figure 9. Cross-Validation Results of a Binary Classifier.

Evaluating a Multiclass Classification Model
In this experiment we will use the popular Iris dataset which contains instances of 3 different types (classes) of the iris plant. There are 4 feature values (sepal length/width and petal length/width) for each instance. In the previous experiments we trained and tested the models using the same datasets. Here, we will use the Split Data module to create 2 subsets of the data, train on the first, and score and evaluate on the second.
The Iris dataset is publicly available on the UCI Machine Learning Repository, and can be downloaded using an Import Data module.

Creating the Experiment
Add the following modules to your workspace in Azure Machine Learning Studio:

• Import Data
• Multiclass Decision Forest
• Split Data
• Train Model
• Score Model
• Evaluate Model
•
Connect the ports as shown below in Figure 10.

Set the Label column index of the Train Model module to 5. The dataset has no header row, but we know that the class labels are in the fifth column.

Click on the Import Data module and set the Data source property to Web URL via HTTP, and the URL to http://archive.ics.uci.edu/ml/machine-learning-databases/iris/iris.data.

Set the fraction of instances to be used for training in the Split Data module (0.7 for example).

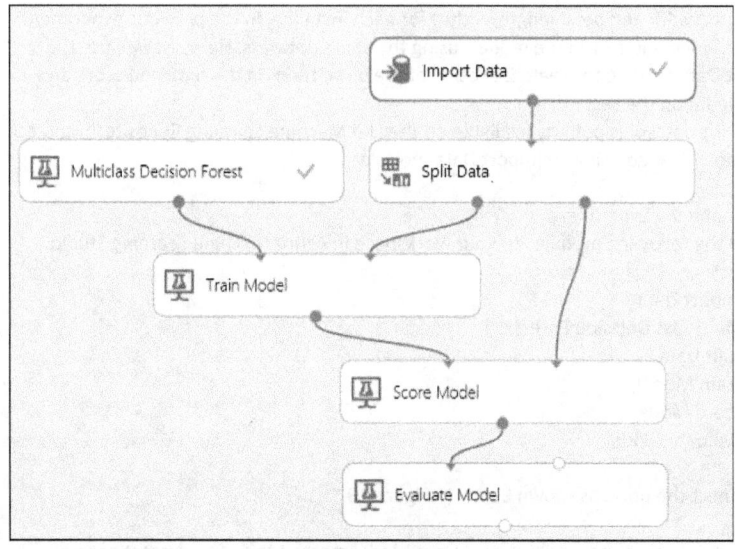

Figure 10. Evaluating a Multiclass Classifier

Inspecting the Evaluation Results
Run the experiment and click on the output port of Evaluate Model. The evaluation results are presented in the form of a confusion matrix, in this case. The matrix shows the actual vs. predicted instances for all 3 classes.

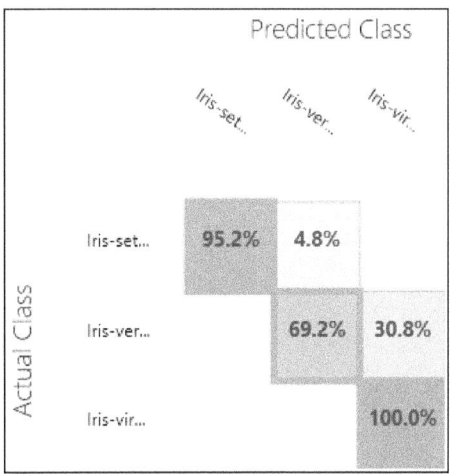

Figure 11. Multiclass Classification Evaluation Results.

Using Cross Validation
As mentioned earlier, you can perform repeated training, scoring and evaluations automatically using the Cross-Validate Model module. You would need a dataset, an untrained model, and a Cross-Validate Model module (see figure below). Again you need to set the label column of the Cross-Validate Model module (column index 5 in this case). After running the experiment and clicking the right output port of the Cross-Validate Model, you can inspect the metric values for each fold as well as the mean and standard deviation. The metrics displayed here are the like the ones discussed in the binary classification case. However, note that in multiclass classification, computing the true positives/negatives and false positives/negatives is done by counting on a per-class basis, as there is no overall positive or negative class. For example, when computing the precision or recall of the 'Iris-setosa' class, it is assumed that this is the positive class and all others as negative.

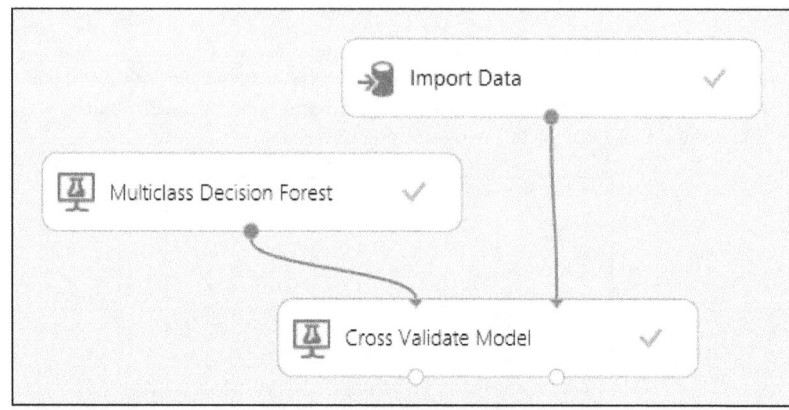

Figure 12. Cross Validating a Multiclass Classification Model.

rows 12	columns 12										
	Fold Number	Number of examples in fold	Model	Average Log Loss for Class "Iris-setosa"	Precision for Class "Iris-setosa"	Recall for Class "Iris-setosa"	Average Log Loss for Class "Iris-versicolor"	Precision for Class "Iris-versicolor"	Recall for Class "Iris-versicolor"	Average Log Loss for Class "Iris-virginica"	Precision for Class "Iris-virginica"	Recall for Class "Iris-virginica"
view as											
	0	15	Microsoft.Analytics.Modul es.Gemini.Dll.MulticlassGe mini.DecisionForestClassifi er	0	1	1	0.415868	1	0.8	0	0.857143	1
	1	15	Microsoft.Analytics.Modul es.Gemini.Dll.MulticlassGe mini.DecisionForestClassifi er	0	1	1	0.026706	0.833333	1	0.122604	1	0.875
	2	15	Microsoft.Analytics.Modul es.Gemini.Dll.MulticlassGe mini.DecisionForestClassifi er	0.057536	1	1	0.026706	1	1	0.057536	1	1

Figure 13. Cross-Validation Results of a Multiclass Classification Model.

The above data and figures 1-13 are using ' How to evaluate Model Performance in Azure Machine Learning' (docs. Microsoft.com)

In comparison, the N-fold-cross-validation method randomly splits the data in k subsets where the k-1 instances of the data are used to train the model while the kth instance is used to test the predictive ability of the training model. Cross-validation is a technique to evaluate predictive models by partitioning the original sample into a training set to train the model, and a test set to evaluate it. ... The cross-validation process is then repeated k times (the folds), with each of the k sub samples used exactly once as the validation data.
 In addition to the holdout and cross-validation methods, bootstrap, which samples n instances with replacement from the dataset, can be used to assess model accuracy (Kohavi,1995).

Bootstrapping allows assigning measures of accuracy (defined in terms of bias, variance, confidence intervals, prediction error or some other such measure) to sample estimates. This technique allows estimation of the sampling distribution of almost any statistic using random sampling methods.

In supplement to overall accuracy, investigators frequently report sensitivity and specificity meaning True Positive Rate (TPR) and True Negative Rate (TNR) respectively. Sensitivity (also called the true positive rate, the recall, or probability of detection in some fields) measures the proportion of positives that are correctly identified as such (e.g. the percentage of sick people who are correctly identified as having the condition). Specificity (also called the true negative rate) measures the proportion of negatives that are correctly identified as such (e.g. the percentage of healthy people who are correctly identified as not having the condition).

Similarly, investigators sometimes report the False Positive Rate (FPR) as well as the False Negative Rate (FNR). However, these rates are ratios that fail to reveal their numerators and denominators. The Total Operating Characteristic (TOC) is an effective method to express a model's diagnostic ability. TOC shows the numerators and denominators of the previously mentioned rates, thus TOC provides more information than the commonly used Receiver operating characteristic (ROC) and ROC's associated Area Under the Curve (AUC). In machine learning, the study and construction of algorithms that can learn from and make predictions on data Kohavi (1998) is a common task. Such algorithms work by making *data-driven predictions* or decisions through *building a mathematical model from input data*. The data used to build the final model usually comes from multiple datasets. In particular, *three data sets* are commonly used in different stages of the creation of the model.

The model is initially 'fit on a training dataset' Gareth (2013), that is a set of examples used to fit the parameters (e.g. weights of connections between neurons in artificial neural networks) of the model (Ripley, 1996). The model (e.g. a neural net or a naive Bayes classifier) is trained on the training dataset using *a supervised learning method* (e.g. gradient descent or stochastic gradient descent). In practice, the training dataset often consist of pairs of an input vector and the corresponding *answer* vector or scalar, which is commonly denoted as the *target*. The current model is run with the training dataset and produces a result, which is then compared with the *target*, for each input vector in the training dataset. Based on the result of the comparison and the specific learning algorithm being used, the parameters of the model are 'adjusted.' The model fitting can include both variable selection and parameter estimation.

Successively, the fitted model is used to predict the responses for the observations in a second dataset called the *validation dataset* (Gareth,2013). The validation dataset provides an unbiased evaluation of a model fit on the training dataset while tuning the model's hyper parameters Brownlee (2017), (e.g. the number of hidden units in a neural network).

Validation datasets can be used for regularization by early stopping: stop training when the error on the validation dataset increases, as this is a sign of over fitting to the training dataset.

This simple procedure is complicated in practice by the fact that the validation dataset's error may fluctuate during training, producing multiple local minima. This complication has led to the creation of many ad-hoc rules for deciding when over fitting has truly begun (Prechelt et al, 2012).

Finally, the test dataset is a dataset used to provide an unbiased evaluation of a *final* model fit on the training dataset.

A *training dataset* is a dataset of examples used for learning, that is to fit the parameters (e.g., weights) of, for example, a classifier. Most approaches that search through training data for empirical relationships tend to over fit the data, meaning that they can identify apparent relationships in the training data that do not hold in general. In practice, the training dataset often consist of pairs of an input vector and the corresponding *answer* vector or scalar, which is commonly denoted as the *target*. The current model is run with the training dataset and produces a result, which is then compared with the *target*, for each input vector in the training dataset. Based on the result of the comparison and the specific learning algorithm being used, the parameters of the model are adjusted. The model fitting can include both variable selection and parameter estimation.

A *test dataset* is a dataset that is independent of the training dataset, but that follows the same probability distribution as the training dataset. If a model fit to the training dataset also fits the test dataset well, minimal overfitting has taken place (see figure below). A better fitting of the training dataset as opposed to the test dataset usually points to over fitting. In statistics, overfitting is "the production of an analysis that corresponds too closely or exactly to a particular set of data, and may therefore fail to fit additional data or predict future observations reliably".

A *test set* is therefore a set of examples used only to assess the performance (i.e. generalization) of a fully specified classifier. A test set is therefore a set of examples used only to assess the performance (i.e. generalization) of a fully specified classifier.

A *validation dataset* is a set of examples used to tune the hyper parameters (i.e. the architecture) of a classifier. In artificial neural networks, an hyperparameter is, for example, the number of hidden units (Ripley,1996). In order to avoid overfitting, when any classification parameter needs to be adjusted, it is necessary to have a validation dataset in addition to the training and test datasets. For example, if the most suitable classifier for the problem is sought, the training dataset is used to train the candidate algorithms, the validation dataset is used to compare their performances and decide which one to take and, finally, the test dataset is used to obtain the performance characteristics such as accuracy, sensitivity, specificity, F-measure, and so on. The validation dataset functions as a hybrid: it is training data used by testing, but neither as part of the low-level training nor as part of the final testing.

In order to avoid over fitting, when any classification parameter needs to be adjusted, it is necessary to have a validation dataset in addition to the training and test datasets. For example, if the most suitable classifier for the problem is sought, the training dataset is used to train the candidate algorithms, the validation dataset is used to compare their performances and decide which one to take and, finally, the test dataset is used to obtain the performance characteristics such as *accuracy, sensitivity, specificity, F-measure*, and so on.
The validation dataset functions as a hybrid: it is training data used by testing, but neither as part of the low-level training nor as part of the final testing.

In statistics, when performing multiple comparisons, a false positive ratio (or false alarm ratio) is the *probability of falsely rejecting the null hypothesis* for a particular test. The false positive rate is calculated as the *ratio between the number of negative events wrongly categorized as positive (false positives) and the total number of actual negative events (regardless of classification)*.

The false positive rate (or "false alarm rate") usually refers to the *expectancy of the false positive ratio*. The false positive rate is the proportion of all negatives that still yield positive test outcomes, i.e., the conditional probability of a positive test result given an event that was not present.

The false positive rate is equal to the significance level. The specificity of the test is equal to 1 minus the false positive rate.

In statistical hypothesis testing, this fraction is given the Greek letter α, and 1−α is defined as the specificity of the test. Increasing the specificity of the test lowers the probability of type I errors, but raises the probability of type II errors (false negatives that reject the alternative hypothesis when it is true).

Complementarily, the false negative rate is the proportion of positives which yield negative test outcomes with the test, i.e., the conditional probability of a negative test result given that the condition being looked for is present.

In statistics, a receiver operating characteristic curve, i.e. ROC curve, is a *graphical plot that illustrates the diagnostic ability of a binary classifier system as its discrimination threshold is varied*. The ROC curve is created by plotting the true positive rate (TPR) against the false positive rate (FPR) at various threshold settings. The ROC curve was first developed by electrical engineers and radar engineers during World War II for detecting enemy objects in battlefields and was soon introduced to psychology to account for perceptual detection of stimuli. ROC analysis since then has been used in medicine, radiology, biometrics, forecasting of natural hazards, meteorology, *model performance assessment*, and other areas for many decades and is increasingly used *in machine learning and data mining research*.

The ROC is also known as a relative operating characteristic curve, because it is a comparison of two operating characteristics (TPR and FPR) as the criterion changes (Swets,1996).

Revision

- In 150 words outline 'Evaluate Model' and 'Cross-Validate Model'
- Discuss 'Using Cross Validation' and why it is important, 50 words
- Debate why choosing the right model at the beginning is vital, 100 words

7 Ethics

Introduction

Machine ethics (or machine morality, computational morality, or computational ethics) is a part of the ethics of artificial intelligence concerned with the *moral behaviour of AI beings* (Spyros, 2016). Machine ethics contrasts with robo-ethics, which is concerned with the moral behaviour of *humans* as they design, construct, use and treat such beings. Machine ethics should not be confused with computer ethics, which focuses on professional behaviour towards computers and information.

Chapter Learning Outcomes

⊡ The treatment of non-human information.

⊡ The three laws of robotics.

⊡ The impact on culture.

⊡ The positive and negative influences of ML.

⊡ Having successfully completed the module, you will be able to:

⊡ 1. Critically assess the philosophy and ethics of (ML) in marketing.

⊡ 2. Assess the philosophy and ethics tools of (ML) in today's world.

⊡ Having completed the module, you will be able to:

⊡ 1. Understand the variety of (ML) philosophies and ethics and their uses.

• 2. Be able to explain the principal goals of each in (ML).

Critical thinking

Having successfully completed this topic, you will be able to:1. Critically evaluate the variety of philosophies and ethics used in (ML) .2. Understand and debate the two areas of (ML) to management.

OBJECTIVES

A chapter that explains the philosophy and ethics related to ML and why this understanding is important. ML application is growing in marketing thus understanding the issues and ethics of ML by marketers will in part ensure the validity of AI in this area.

MACHINE ETHICS

The developing academic field of machine ethics seeks to make *artificial agents safer* as they become more pervasive throughout society. Motivated by planned next-generation robotic systems, machine ethics typically *explores solutions for agents with autonomous capacities intermediate between those of current artificial agents and humans, with designs developed incrementally by and embedded in a society of human agents.* These assumptions substantially simplify the problem of designing a desirable agent and reflect the near-term future well, but there are also cases in which they do not hold. In particular, they need not apply to artificial agents with human-level or greater capabilities. The potentially very large impacts of such agents suggest that advance analysis and research is valuable. Machine ethics is concerned with ensuring that the behaviour of machines toward human users, and perhaps other machines as well, is 'ethically acceptable.'

The ultimate goal of machine ethics, I believe, is to create a machine that *itself* follows an ideal ethical principle or set of principles; that is to say, it is guided by this principle or these principles in decisions it makes about possible courses of action it could take. We need to make a distinction between what James Moor has called an *"implicit ethical agent"* and an *"explicit ethical agent"* (Moor 2006). According to Moor, a machine that is an implicit ethical agent is one that has been programmed to behave ethically, or at least avoid unethical behaviour, without an explicit representation of ethical principles. It is constrained in its behaviour by its designer who is following ethical principles. A machine that is an explicit ethical agent, on the other hand, is able to calculate the best action in ethical dilemmas using ethical principles. It can "represent ethics explicitly and then operate effectively on the basis of this knowledge." Using Moor's terminology, most of those working on machine ethics would say that the ultimate goal is to *create a machine that is an explicit ethical agent.*

We are primarily concerned with the ethical decision making itself, rather than how a machine would gather the information needed to make the decision and incorporate it into its general behaviour. It is important to see this as a separate and considerable challenge. It is separate because having all the information and facility in the world will not, by itself, generate ethical behaviour in a machine.

One needs to turn to the branch of philosophy that is concerned with ethics for insight into what is considered to be ethically acceptable behaviour. It is a considerable challenge because, even among experts, ethics has not been completely codified. It is a field that is still evolving. One other point should be made in introducing the subject of machine ethics. Ethics can be seen as both easy and hard.

It appears easy because we all make ethical decisions on a daily basis. But that does not mean that we are all experts in ethics. There are at least three reasons that can be given for machine ethics. First, there are ethical ramifications to what machines currently do and are projected to do in the future.

To neglect this aspect of machine behaviour could have serious repercussions. South Korea has recently mustered more than 30 companies and 1000 scientists to the end of putting "a robot in every home by 2010" (Onishi 2006). DARPA's grand challenge to have a vehicle drive itself across 132 miles of desert terrain has been met, and a new grand challenge is in the works that will have vehicles manoeuvring in an urban setting. The United States Army's Future Combat Systems program is developing armed robotic vehicles that will support ground troops with "direct- fire" and antitank weapons. From family cars that drive themselves and machines that discharge our daily chores with little or no assistance from us, to fully autonomous robotic entities that will begin to challenge our notions of the very nature of intelligence, it is clear that machines such as these will be capable of causing harm to human beings unless this is prevented by adding an ethical component to them.

Second, it could be argued that humans' fear of the possibility of autonomous intelligent machines stems from their concern about whether these machines will behave ethically, so the future of AI may be at stake. Whether society allows AI researchers to develop any- thing like autonomous intelligent machines may hinge on whether they are able to build in safeguards against unethical behaviour. From the murderous robot uprising in the 1920 play *R.U.R.* (Capek 1921) and the deadly coup d'état perpetrated by the HAL 9000 computer in *2001: A Space Odyssey* (Clarke 1968), to *The Matrix* virtual reality simulation for the pacification and subjugation of human beings by machines, popular culture is rife with images of machines devoid of any ethical code mistreating their makers. In his widely circulated treaise, "Why the future doesn't need us," Bill Joy (2000) argues that the only antidote to such fates and worse is to "relinquish dangerous technologies." We believe that machine ethics research may offer a viable, more realistic solution.

Finally, it is possible that research in machine ethics will advance the study of ethical theory. Ethics, by its very nature, is the most practical branch of philosophy. It is concerned with how agents ought to behave when faced with ethical dilemmas. Despite the obvious applied nature of the field of ethics, too often work in ethical theory is done with little thought to actual application. When examples are discussed, they are typically artificial examples.

Research in machine ethics has the potential to discover problems with current theories, perhaps even leading to the development of better theories, as AI researchers force scrutiny of the details involved in actually applying an ethical theory to particular cases. As Daniel Dennett (2006) recently stated, AI "makes philosophy honest." Ethics must be made computable in order to make it clear exactly how agents ought to behave in ethical dilemmas.

An exception to the general rule that ethicists do not spend enough time discussing actual cases occurs in the field of biomedical ethics, a field that has arisen out of a need to resolve pressing problems faced by health-care workers, insurers, hospital ethics boards, and bio- medical researchers. As a result of their having been more discussion of actual cases in the field of biomedical ethics, a consensus is beginning to emerge as to how to evaluate ethical dilemmas in this domain, leading to the ethically correct action in many dilemmas.

A reason there might be more of a consensus in this domain than in others is that in the area of bio- medical ethics there is an ethically defensible goal (the best possible health of the patient), whereas in other areas (such as business and law) the goal may not be ethically defensible (make as much money as possible, serve the client's interest even if he or she is guilty of an offense or doesn't deserve a settlement) and ethics enters the picture as a limiting factor (the goal must be achieved within certain ethical boundaries). AI researchers working with ethicists might find it helpful to begin with this domain, discovering a general approach to computing ethics that not only works in this domain, but could be applied to other domains as well.

It does seem clear, to those who have thought about the issue, that some sort of safeguard should be in place to prevent unethical machine behaviour (and that work in this area may provide benefits for the study of ethical theory as well). This shows the need for creating at least *implicit* ethical machines; but why must we create *explicit* ethical machines, which would seem to be a much greater (perhaps even an impossible) challenge for AI researchers?

First, the goal of machine ethics, at the end, is to guarantee that programs behave according to certain rigorous (moral and ethical) requirements. The area would thus seem to be a natural target for automated formal reasoning about programs. Secondly, machine ethics can be a source of interesting problems for the formal methods community. Most recent work in software analysis is motivated by applications in system software (such as operating system code). Machine ethics, in contrast, involves reasoning about knowledge, choices, obligations, etc. in high-level decision-making.

Intelligent programs Reasoning about ethics is arguably only sensible for "intelligent" programs, but when is a program "intelligent"? There is no one answer to this question, but a reasonable requirement is that the program be able to adapt to new circumstances and learn new modes of behaviour.

For instance, a natural model for such a program is a Markov Decision Process (MDP): a dynamical system where probabilistic and nondeterministic transitions are permitted and where transitions are associated with quantitative *rewards*. Nondeterminism in an MDP can model the decision-making capacities of a program and parameters that are unknown at the time of design. The probabilistic transitions can be used to model uncertainty in the program's inputs. The rewards would associate a value on the outcome of each action. The operational semantics of the program would replace the nondeterministic choice either with determinism or with probabilistic choice, thus producing a concrete (possibly randomized) algorithm.

Ethical programs In philosophy, an ethical framework is a set of guidelines that an agent follows while making ethically significant decisions. For instance, a robot that follows a utilitarian ethics would want to maximize the aggregate well-being of every human in its environment. As computer scientists, we may view these guidelines as forming a *specification*, given either as constraints on the decision-making behaviour of the program or as a reference program. A program is then ethical if it satisfies or simulates this specification.

We have some choices in defining a specification of a program's ethics:

- Our specifications can be formalization soft traditional ethical frameworks— for example utilitarian, Kantian, or Rawlsian ethics. Note that developing such a formalization is a challenging task, as traditional ethical systems are often defined rather abstractly.
- We could define the specification as "whatever an average human follows." For instance, to define the ethics of a self-driving car, we could train a statistical model using observations about how a population of humans drives their cars. The downside of this definition is that it sets the ethics of the typical human as an upper bound on machine machines. Given that humans suffer from weaknesses such as racial prejudice, short-termism, and the instinct to survive at all costs, this choice seems arbitrary.

Utilitarian Ethics

Utilitarianism is a normative ethical theory that places the locus of right and wrong solely on the outcomes (consequences) of choosing one action/policy over other actions/policies. As such, it moves beyond the scope of one's own interests and considers the interests of others.

Utilitarianism is an ethical theory that determines right from wrong by focusing on outcomes. It is a form of <u>consequentialism.</u>

Utilitarianism holds that the most ethical choice is the one that will produce the greatest good for the greatest number. It is the only moral framework that can be used to justify military force or war. It is also the most common approach to <u>moral reasoning</u> used in business because of the way in which it accounts for costs and benefits. However, because we cannot predict the future, it's difficult to know with certainty whether the consequences of our actions will be good or bad. This is one of the limitations of utilitarianism.

Utilitarianism also has trouble accounting for values such as justice and individual rights. For example, assume a hospital has four people whose lives depend upon receiving organ transplants: a heart, lungs, a kidney, and a liver. If a healthy person wanders into the hospital, his organs could be harvested to save four lives at the expense of one life. This would arguably produce the greatest good for the greatest number. But few would consider it an acceptable course of action, let alone the most ethical one.

So, although utilitarianism is arguably the most reason-based approach to determining right and wrong, it has obvious limitations.

Kantian Ethics

Kantian ethics refers to a deontological ethical theory ascribed to the German philosopher Immanuel Kant. ... Central to Kant's construction of the moral law is the categorical imperative, which acts on all people, regardless of their interests or desires. Kant, unlike Mill, believed that certain types of actions (including murder, theft, and lying) were absolutely prohibited, even in cases where the action would bring about more happiness than the alternative. For Kantians, there are two questions that we must ask ourselves whenever we decide to act: (i) Can I rationally will that *everyone* act as I propose to act? If the answer is no, then we must not perform the action. (ii) Does my action respect the goals of human beings rather than merely using them for my own purposes? Again, if the answer is no, then we must not perform the action. (Kant believed that these questions were equivalent).

Kant's theory is an example of a deontological moral theory—according to these theories, *the rightness or wrongness of actions does not depend on their consequences* but on whether they full fill our duty. Kant believed that there was a supreme principle of morality, and he referred to it as *The Categorical Imperative*. The CI determines what our moral duties are.

The categorical imperative has three different formulations. That is to say, there are three different ways of saying what it is. Kant claims that all three do in fact say the same thing, but it is currently disputed whether this is true. The second formulation is the easiest to understand, but the first one is most clearly a categorical imperative. Here is the first formulation.

1) First formulation (*The Formula of Universal Law*): "Act only on that maxim through which you can at the same time will that it should become a universal law [of nature]."

a) What is a maxim? A maxim is the rule or principle on which you act. For example, I might make it my maxim to give at least as much to charity each year as I spend on eating out, or I might make it my maxim only to do what will benefit some member of my family.

b) Basic idea: The command states, crudely, that you are not allowed to do anything yourself that you would not be willing to allow everyone else to do as well. You are not allowed to make exceptions for yourself. For example, if you expect other people to keep their promises, then you are obligated to keep your own promises.

c) More detail: More accurately, it commands that every maxim you act on must be such that you are willing to make it the case that everyone always act on that maxim when in a similar situation.

For example, if I wanted to lie to get something I wanted, I would have to be willing to make it the case that everyone always lied to get what they wanted - but if this were to happen no one would ever believe you, so the lie would not work and you would not get what you wanted. So, if you willed that such a maxim (of lying) should become a universal law, then you would thwart your goal - thus, it is impermissible to lie, according to the categorical imperative. It is impermissible because the only way to lie is to make an exception for yourself.

Rawlsian Ethics

Contemporary philosopher John Rawls provides one example of an ethical theory that places the concept of justice at its centre. Rawls' primary concern is that we be able to *design and evaluate social institutions and practices* on the basis of principles of justice. The basis of such principles is found in a concept that Rawls termed the *original position*. Imagine a group of people representing the range of human diversity and then place them behind a veil of ignorance so that they no longer know who they are on the other side. Rawls contends that from this original position people would agree to establish a social order based on the moral standards of an egalitarian form of justice. That is, they would promote rules and institutions that would ensure their own well-being once the veil is lifted.

In its strictest sense, egalitarianism requires that all persons receive an equal distribution of certain political, social, and economic goods and rights; however, Rawls does not advocate a strict egalitarianism. He maintains that inequalities are inevitable but can be justified and minimized with at least two principles discoverable in the original position. The first is the liberty principle, which advocates that each person should have an equal right to as many basic liberties as possible and still allow a similar system of liberty for all (Munson 2004).

That is, each individual should possess as much liberty to live and seek opportunity as is possible, short of infringing on the liberty interests of others.

The second principle that Rawls identifies is termed the *difference principle* and requires that social and economic inequalities be arranged so that they benefit those who are least advantaged. In other words, differences in wealth and social position are acceptable as long as they can be shown to benefit everyone and, in particular, those who have the fewest advantages. This principle also requires that systems allow for all people to have access to goods and positions under conditions of fair equality of opportunity based on both need and merit (Munson 2004).

Some examples of concrete formal methods problems concerning machine ethics.

Reasoning about optimal strategies: consider a robot deployed in a battlefield that is required to take lethal actions. A utilitarian ethics demands that at any program state, the right action for the robot is the one that produces maximal strategic benefit while causing minimal harm to civilians.

However, the calculation of harm and benefit cannot be based on purely local criteria, as a locally optimal decision may not be globally optimal. Thus, the problem of enforcing utilitarian ethics amounts to solving a quantitative formal reasoning problem where the goal is to prove that the program takes an optimal sequence of actions while ensuring certain basic boolean criteria Swarat et al, (2014), (this definition of optimality presumes a notion of rewards associated with program actions). Given that the environment will have to be modelled probabilistically in most realistic settings, the reasoning problem would presumably also have to be stochastic.

Reasoning about fairness: Many research efforts in the formal methods community study reasoning about security and data privacy. But what about the *fairness* of decisions made by a program? Specifically, let us consider programs in charge of allocating a set of resources (for example, financial aid). Each principal has a set of fields that are morally relevant to the resource allocation problem (for example, academic ability), and a set of fields that are not (for example, morally relevant attributes, then P and P receive similar outcomes. Note that this requirement allows for affirmative action; it's just that the criteria for affirmative action are to be included among morally relevant fields.

Dwork et al. (2012)have recently posed the question of building classifiers that are fair in this sense. They show that the algorithmic ideas needed to design fair classifiers resemble that needed for differentially private data release mechanisms. A natural question for formal methods researchers is to systematically prove the fairness of a program.

It is useful to note that this question is quite similar to the question of reasoning about *robustness*, which has received attention in the verification community of late (Swarat,2011).

Logics for ethics How do we *compose* a set of ethical obligations for a program? This question necessitates the study of logics of ethics and obligations. One traditional choice here is *deontic logic*, or the class of modal logics permitting formulas O(p), meaning "The agent is obligated to ensure p".

It is well known Lennart (1984) that logics of obligation can suffer from paradoxes — for example, what if a drone in a battlefield is obligated to ensure p, but it is impossible to ensure p? Is the drone still required to fulfil its other obligations? The answer should presumably be yes.

However, note that this is a departure from classical logic, where the impossibility to meet p would amount to an inconsistency, rendering moot every other consideration. Designing logics that overcome such conceptual issues (possibly using a quantitative weighting of various obligations) can be an interesting challenge for programming language research.

Revision

- Using 150 words discuss the reasons for machine ethics
- In 50 words critic Utilitarian ethics
- Considering Kantian ethics, in 150 words discuss the three formulations
- Using 100 words discuss 'reasoning' and fairness' in ML

8 Software

Introduction

There is a growing amount of ML software suites in use today providing a variety of ML algorithms that match certain tasks. A basic understanding of these tools will enable a marketer to asses each one.

Chapter Learning Outcomes

☐ Understanding of Free and open source software.

☐ Appreciation of Proprietary software.

☐ Related functionality of each.

☐ The pluses and minuses of each type.

☐ Having successfully completed the module, you will be able to:

☐ 1. Critically assess the software of (ML) in marketing.

☐ 2. Assess the software tools of (ML) in today's world.

☐ Having completed the module, you will be able to:

☐ 1. Understand the variety of (ML) software and their uses.

• 2. Be able to explain the principal goals of each in (ML).

Critical thinking

Having successfully completed this topic, you will be able to:1. Critically evaluate the variety of software applications used in (ML) .2. Understand and debate these areas of (ML) to management.

OBJECTIVES

A discussion on ML software, and their current applications. Understand the various suites that could be applied in a marketing context.

Below is a list of frameworks for machine learning engineers and marketers:

Apache Singa: is a general distributed deep learning platform for training big deep learning models over large datasets. It is designed with an intuitive programming model based on the layer abstraction. A variety of popular deep learning models are supported, namely feed-forward models including convolutional neural networks (CNN), energy models like restricted Boltzmann machine (RBM), and recurrent neural networks (RNN). Many built-in layers are provided for users.

Amazon machine learning is a service that makes it easy for developers of all skill levels to use machine learning technology. Amazon Machine Learning provides visualization tools and wizards that guide you through the process of creating machine learning (ML) models without having to learn complex ML algorithms and technology. It connects to data stored in Amazon S3, Redshift, or RDS, and can run binary classification, multiclass categorization, or regression on said data to create a model.

Azure ml studio allows Microsoft Azure users to create and train models, then turn them into APIs that can be consumed by other services. Users get up to 10GB of storage per account for model data, although you can also connect your own Azure storage to the service for larger models. A wide range of algorithms are available, courtesy of both Microsoft and third parties. You don't even need an account to try out the service; you can log in anonymously and use Azure ML Studio for up to eight hours.

Caffe is a deep learning framework made with expression, speed, and modularity in mind. It is developed by the Berkeley Vision and Learning Centre (BVLC) and by community contributors. Yangqing Jia created the project during his PhD at UC Berkeley. Caffe is released under the BSD 2-Clause license. Models and optimization are defined by configuration without hard coding & user can switch between CPU and GPU. Speed makes Caffe perfect for research experiments and industry deployment. Caffe can process over 60M images per day with a single NVIDIA K40 GPU.

H2O makes it possible for anyone to easily apply math and predictive analytics to solve today's most challenging business problems. It intelligently combines unique features not currently found in other machine learning platforms including: Best of Breed Open Source Technology, Easy-to-use WebUI and Familiar Interfaces, Data Agnostic Support for all Common Database and File Types. With H2O, you can work with your existing languages and tools. Further, you can extend the platform seamlessly into your Hadoop environments.

Massive online analysis is the most popular open source framework for data stream mining, with a very active growing community.
It includes a collection of machine learning algorithms (classification, regression, clustering, outlier detection, concept drift detection and recommender systems) and tools for evaluation. Related to the WEKA project, MOA is also written in Java, while scaling to more demanding problems.

MLib Spark is Apache Spark's machine learning library. Its goal is to make practical machine learning scalable and easy. It consists of common learning algorithms and utilities, including classification, regression, clustering, collaborative filtering, dimensionality reduction, as well as lower-level optimization primitives and higher-level pipeline APIs.

Mlpack, a C++-based machine learning library originally rolled out in 2011 and designed for "scalability, speed, and ease-of-use," according to the library's creators. Implementing mlpack can be done through a cache of command-line executables for quick-and-dirty, "black box" operations, or with a C++ API for more sophisticated work. Mlpack provides these algorithms as simple command-line programs and C++ classes which can then be integrated into larger-scale machine learning solutions.

Pattern is a web-mining module for the Python programming language. It has tools for data mining (Google, Twitter and Wikipedia API, a web crawler, a HTML DOM parser), natural language processing (part-of-speech taggers, n-gram search, sentiment analysis, WordNet), machine learning (vector space model, clustering, SVM), network analysis and <canvas> visualization.

Scikit Learn leverages Python's breadth by building on top of several existing Python packages — NumPy, SciPy, and matplotlib — for math and science work. The resulting libraries can be used either for interactive "workbench" applications or be embedded into other software and reused. The kit is available under a BSD license, so it's fully open and reusable. Scikit-learn includes tools for many of the standard machine-learning *tasks* (such as clustering, classification, regression, etc.). And since scikit-learn is developed by a large community of developers and machine-learning experts, promising new techniques tend to be included in fairly short order.

Shogun is among the oldest most venerable of machine learning libraries, Shogun was created in 1999 and written in C++, but isn't limited to working in C++. Thanks to the SWIG library, Shogun can be used transparently in such languages and environments: as Java, Python, C#, Ruby, R, Lua, Octave, and Matlab. Shogun is designed for unified large-scale learning for a broad range of feature types and learning settings, like classification, regression, or explorative data analysis.

Tensor Flow is an open source software library for numerical computation using data flow graphs. TensorFlow implements what are called data flow graphs, where batches of data ("tensors") can be processed by a series of algorithms described by a graph.

The movements of the data through the system are called "flows" — hence, the name. Graphs can be assembled with C++ or Python and can be processed on CPUs or GPUs.

Theano is a Python library that lets you to define, optimize, and evaluate mathematical expressions, especially ones with multi-dimensional arrays (numpy.ndarray). Using Theano it is possible to attain speeds rivalling hand-crafted C implementations for problems involving large amounts of data. It was written at the LISA lab to support rapid development of efficient machine learning algorithms.
Theano is named after the Greek mathematician, who may have been Pythagoras' wife. Theano is released under a BSD license.

Torch is a scientific computing framework with wide support for machine learning algorithms that puts GPUs first. It is easy to use and efficient, thanks to an easy and fast scripting language, LuaJIT, and an underlying C/CUDA implementation. The goal of Torch is to have maximum flexibility and speed in building your scientific algorithms while making the process extremely simple. Torch comes with a large ecosystem of community-driven packages in machine learning, computer vision, signal processing, parallel processing, image, video, audio and networking among others, and builds on top of the Lua community.

Veles is a distributed platform for deep-learning applications, and it's written in C++, although it uses Python to perform automation and coordination between nodes. Datasets can be analysed and automatically normalized before being fed to the cluster, and a REST API allows the trained model to be used in production immediately.
It focuses on performance and flexibility. It has little hard-coded entities and enables training of all the widely recognized topologies, such as fully connected nets, convolutional nets, recurrent nets etc.

8.1 Free and open-source software

- CNTK
- dlib
- ELKI
- GNU Octave
- H2O
- Mahout
- Mallet
- MEPX
- mlpy
- MLPACK
- MOA (Massive Online Analysis)
- MXNet
- ND4J: ND arrays for Java
- NuPIC
- OpenAI Gym
- OpenAI Universe
- OpenNN

- Orange
- R
- scikit-learn
- Shogun
- TensorFlow
- Torch
- Yooreeka
- Weka

8.2 Proprietary software with free and open-source editions

- KNIME
- RapidMiner

8.3 Proprietary software

- Amazon Machine Learning
- Angoss KnowledgeSTUDIO
- Ayasdi
- IBM Data Science Experience
- Google Prediction API
- IBM SPSS Modeler
- KXEN Modeler
- LION solver
- Mathematica
- MATLAB
- Microsoft Azure Machine Learning
- Neural Designer
- NeuroSolutions
- Oracle Data Mining
- Oracle AI Platform Cloud Service
- RCASE
- SAP Leonardo
- SAS Enterprise Miner
- SequenceL
- Sky mind
- Splunk
- STATISTICA Data Miner

For those in the marketing profession, below under an activity heading is a list of software that may assist you. This is not a recommendation list from the author; however, it is guide to the 'off the shelf' software in the ML arena. Always remember when choosing software, is it compatible, will it achieve our objectives, what training is needed, ROI, is it scalable. The data below is from company web sites:

1) Customer Relationship Software

- Sales Force

Salesforce is much more than just a CRM solution. It brings together all your customer information in a single, integrated platform that enables you to build a customer-centred business from marketing right through to sales, customer service and business analysis.

This gives you more complete understanding of your customers to drive your business's success. That's why we call it the Customer Success Platform.

- Dynamics 365

Use digital intelligence to reimagine what's possible for your business. Dynamics 365 unifies CRM and ERP capabilities into applications that work seamlessly together across sales, customer service, field service, operations, financials, marketing, and project service automation. Start with what you need, add applications as your business grows. Rethink what's possible for your business when you: Better engage customers, Empower employees, Optimize operations, Reinvent products and business models

- Zoho

Zoho One is a revolutionary all-in-one suite to run your entire business—an unprecedented 35+ integrated applications on one account, with complete administrative control—for a price that will change the way you think about buying software. Zoho One includes more than 35 applications with complementary mobile apps so you can run your entire business on one suite. This is the real deal here: You're getting full-featured, enterprise editions of the entire Zoho suite. That means being able to reach customers, grow sales, balance your books, and work in productive and collaborative ways from any device—all with a single login and password.

- HubSpot CRM

Get an up-to-the-minute view of your entire sales funnel on a clean, visual dashboard. You can sort deals won and lost, appointments scheduled, contracts sent over, and track performance against quotas you set in one simple view. Sort deals by name, owner, amount, or stage with custom filters for actionable intel in a fraction of the time.

- Sugar CRM

SugarCRM enables businesses to create extraordinary customer relationships with the most empowering, adaptable and affordable customer relationship management (CRM) solution on the market. We are the industry's leading company focused exclusively on customer relationship management. Helping our clients build a unique customer experience through great customer relationships is our sole focus. Today, digital disruption is driving a tectonic shift in how companies deliver an extraordinary customer experience, inventing new ways to connect with and deliver value to customers. The companies that win in this era of empowered customers do so because they create better relationships with their customers. But you can't deliver a superior customer experience with the same old CRM. You need a new kind of CRM. Sugar is the solution for CRM heroes, mavericks, innovative, forward-thinking change agents. The brave, the bold, who dare to be different. Our customers look for new solutions that will give them a competitive edge. They look at the default choice, and question whether it is the best choice. They see Sugar as the chance to find a better way to grow their business and help their employees do their jobs better.

It's the CRM that does more to adapt to your business -- the easiest CRM there is to customize, extend and deploy. And it's the CRM that can enable everyone across your entire organization to become a customer expert and make a difference. Recognized by leading market analysts as a CRM visionary and innovator, Sugar is deployed by more than 2 million individuals in over 120 countries and 26 languages. Companies large and small are turning from yesterday's CRM solutions to rely on Sugar to manage customer relationships.

2) Marketing Software

- Marketo

Is considered the founder of the marketing automation software category and identifies itself as "the leading provider of engagement marketing software and solutions". In 2017, Marketo named as a leader in the Gartner Magic Quadrant for CRM Lead Management for the sixth year in a row. Marketo products are provided on a subscription basis in three editions, including Spark, tailored specifically for small businesses.

- Marketo Lead Management
- Marketo Sales Insight
- Marketo Revenue Cycle Analytics
- Marketo Social Marketing

In 2008, Marketo introduced its first product, Marketo Lead Management, followed by Marketo Sales Insight in 2009 and Marketo Revenue Cycle Analytics in 2010. In April 2012, Marketo completed its first acquisition by acquiring Crowd Factory, which enabled the company to integrate social media marketing capabilities into its application suite. In November 2012, Marketo introduced Launch Point, an app and services network for the "marketing nation" of technology partners and professional service providers.

- Outreach

Outreach is an intuitive sales automation platform. Based on "sequences", the application helps sales teams set up email campaigns & touch points based upon any number of criteria that they choose. Teams can create a sequence of emails & calls to put every single prospect through.

- Discover org

Sales and marketing teams need direct paths to the right decision makers. Accurate names, contact info, and role and responsibility data are crucial, but only the first step. Sales and marketing professionals also need context to evaluate prospects, nurture leads, and close sales. The DiscoverOrg platform is a game-changer for sales, marketing, and staffing professionals.
The feature-rich sales intelligence platform is the only one in the market that is built on a foundation of technology + human-verification.

Our data is gathered through our proprietary combination of technology, tools, integrations, and then human-verified by our research team before ever publishing – all enabling accurate, insightful intelligence that 4,000 teams today use to break ahead of the pack.

- Zoominfo

Find the prospects you're looking for based on industry, location, company size, company revenue, job title, job function, and more. ZoomInfo's database provides access to the most direct dials and email addresses than any other market intelligence provider.

- Inside View

Target your best prospects more precisely with Inside View solutions for sales, marketing, and operations. Targeted engagement strategies, such as Account Based Marketing, require a deep understanding of your prospects and customers. They also require a consistent view of — and messaging to — those targets across every marketing, sales, and customer service touch point. That's not possible when marketing uses one set of data, sales relies on another, and customer service and other teams rely on still more platforms of siloed, conflicting data.

Inside View solves that problem with our Targeting Intelligence platform. It delivers consistent, real-time access to data, insights, and connections that unify your siloed systems and align your customer engagement around a single, reliable view of the customer.

3) Conversion Software

- Google analytics

Get stronger results across all your sites, apps, and offline channels. Google Analytics Solutions offer marketing analytics products for businesses of all sizes to better understand your customers.
The Google Analytics 360 Suite gathers data from across the many touch points of today's complex customer journey. It then uses deep insights to help your enterprise measure and improve the impact of your marketing.

- Instapage
- Instapage empowers your team to create stunning landing pages at scale without having to rely on your engineering team. Use our conversion-tested templates to showcase your product and convert new users, more cost-efficiently.

- Landingi

If you are a small company or a small team that doesn't have the resources to make full use of big-name CRM's, it is a waste resources considering you could be using Landingi. It is cost effective, quick, and flexible. Landingi gives you all the templates, dropdown menus, and tools to customize your own landing pages. Click, copy and paste your way to perfection.

- Un Bounce

The Unbounce Builder empowers every member of your team to rapidly build custom landing pages and Convertibles for any campaign — without developers, coding skills or tech\ bottlenecks. Unbounce is the world's most sophisticated landing page builder. What's to like about it?
Well, marketers love the drag and drop builder and airtight integrations. Designers love the ability to match any creative vision or brand guideline. And developers love how nobody asks them to do anything.

- Exponea

Full suite of personalization & engagement solutions to drive revenue and engagement throughout the customer journey. Run effective, automated campaigns independently of your IT department. With our powerful scenario designer, clients finally gain full control over their marketing efforts. Exponea comes as a fully integrated marketing cloud, allowing you to leverage the power of deep customer analysis to drive your company to incredible business results.

Native integration with the best of breeds tools plus we built our own real-time data storage and combined it with the world's best technologies. Your customer data is safe, yet accessible, anytime and anywhere.

4) Social Media Software

- Mention

Get live updates about your brand from the web and social media. Explore how you can easily monitor the web; media monitoring lets you listen closely to the entire web. See what's said by competitors - and about them - anywhere online. Influencer marketing is a powerful strategy. It helps you boost brand awareness, improve your reputation, and reach a new audience. Take your influencer strategy to the next level with Mention.

- Buzz Somo

Discover the most shared content across all social networks and run detailed analysis reports. Find influencers in any topic area, review the content they share and amplify. Be the first to see content mentioning your keyword; or when an author or competitor publishes new content. Track your competitor's content performance and do detailed comparisons.

- Dovetail

Dovetale, claims to be the first of its kind to utilize AI-enabled image recognition to seamlessly match influencers to brands. Simply drag and drop images of the brand and Dovetale's engine scours YouTube, Instagram, Twitch and Twitter and returns results showing the influencers that are most closely aligned. The approach is a more logical way to match a brand's affinity to a potential influencer than other platforms in the marketplace that rely strictly on keywords, hashtags or other generic meta data.

- Klear

A social media analytics and intelligence platform that provides social data services for brands, agencies and enterprises. Klear serves more than 2 million monthly visitors in three core areas: Social media monitoring, Influencer marketing and competitive intelligence.

5) Digital Analytics Software

- Google Analytics; 360; Tag Manager

A data management platform announced on 15 March 2015 by google. It provides analytical data which companies can use to track ROI and marketing. There are six products in the suite; Analytics 360, Tag Manager 360, Optimize 360, 360 attribution, Audience Centre 360, and Data Studio 360.

- Exponea

Full suite of personalization & engagement solutions to drive revenue and engagement throughout the customer journey.

- Gosquared

Customers of all shapes and sizes use GoSquared every day to understand their website traffic and increase conversion from visitor to customer. GoSquared shows you every visitor on your website in real-time. Qualify them as leads with key information such as their traffic source, location, and the pages they're viewing.

- Heap

Understand your users in-depth by using heap. Add User Properties to assign custom properties that persist across sessions. You can even tie mobile and web sessions together into a single user identity using heap. Identify. Tag a user with an email address, payment plan, total revenue, age, or anything else you need to measure.

- Kissmetrics

Kissmetrics is a platform to understand, segment and engage your customers based on their behaviour. Built to help marketers and product teams increase conversions, engagement and retention. Kissmetrics Analyze tracks everything people are doing on your website or products. We provide a suite of reports so you can understand what's going on, what's working and what's not. You'll get all the insights you need to act with confidence.

6) Marketing Analytics Software
- Bizible

Bizible's measurement and planning solutions enables marketing leaders to excel in their roles. CMOs can align planning, execution, and measurement to core business objectives with multi-touch attribution and revenue planning. Marketing teams can't replicate success without knowing what's working and what's not. Bizible ties together every touch point in the customer journey, generating actionable insights for your marketing team.
Do annual and quarterly planning using machine learning, not Excel. Get forecasts based on highly detailed revenue data and run what-if scenarios to see revenue impact on channel mix changes.

- Looker

Looker makes data visualization and exploration easy for everyone. Looker is a new kind of analytics platform that lets everyone in your business make informed decisions - from anywhere. Across industries, today's most data-driven businesses use the Looker platform to do more with their data.

- Bright Funnel

Through Bright Funnel's best-of-breed, full-funnel reporting suite, your whole marketing team has visibility into what moves the needle—so they can orchestrate the entire customer journey from lead acquisition to close. Connecting marketing investments to revenue is hard and making sense of attribution data is even harder. At Bright Funnel, we believe the key to understanding and accelerating revenue is orchestrating the right sales and marketing touches at the right time in the customer journey.

- Affinie

Our Smart ethos and approach to critical communications brings together disparate technologies, devices, platforms and protocols to deliver truly smart, unified networks. Organisations across a variety of sectors, from national governments to utility providers, trust us to handle their mission-critical voice and data, as well as additional communication requirements, today and as they grow in the future.

- Ninja Cat

Think about all the current and future data sources you need to pull from (AdWords, Bing, Analytics, Facebook, DSPs, Call Tracking Providers, SEO Platforms, Email Platforms, CRMs, etc).

Imagine if all your data from those sources was automatically pulled into one location and combined in a way that made reporting and monitoring easy? Ninja Cat makes that a reality.

- Maroon

Maroon Analytics works with leading investment banks, hedge funds and corporate treasuries across Southeast Asia to implement innovative financial analytics that have a tangible P&L impact. The company enables its clients to more effectively price, trade and risk-manage their derivatives and structured products and, as a FINCAD partner, empowers them with the industry's leading tools for valuation and risk-reporting. Maroon provides front and back office derivative solutions across all asset classes that:

- Accelerate time-to-market for new structured products and strategies;
- Increase the speed of calculations;
- Improve quant team productivity;
- Validate and benchmark models;
- Enhance understanding of market and counterparty risk; and
- Reduce operating costs and risk.

Maroon Analytics has over 40 years of combined experience working directly with traders on trading floors in London, New York, Singapore and Hong Kong. Maroon represents FINCAD in Southeast Asia from its base in Singapore.

7) Business Intelligence Software

- Domo

Domo transforms your most complex data into actionable insights to help you find answers fast—and make decisions even faster—with live data that connects you directly to the pulse of your business.

- Micro Strategy

Tap into the industry's latest data sources and systems with ease. With dozens of out-of-the-box gateways and drivers, MicroStrategy makes it easy to start getting answers from the world's most challenging data sets. Eliminate roadblocks and put key metrics in the hands of thousands of users fast. Create sophisticated, personalized reports, and distil critical top-level views of your organization into compelling dashboards.

- Looker

Looker has harnessed the power of SQL to create a uniquely powerful data analytics platform that helps companies get real value from their data. Now anyone can ask sophisticated questions of the data using familiar business terms.

- SAP

Explore machine learning applications and AI software.
Build an intelligent enterprise with artificial intelligence (AI) and machine learning software to unite human expertise and computer insights. Create, run, consume, and maintain machine self-learning apps with ease by using algorithms that require no data-science skills.
The foundation connects developers, partners, and customers to machine learning technology through SAP Cloud Platform. With our latest release, we've expanded the set of capabilities – making it even simpler, and giving you more flexibility, to integrate AI into your business

- Insight Squared

Turn your CRM data into decision-quality reports and board-ready visuals with Insight Squared's sales intelligence software. Together, Tiles and Slate become the "operating system" for your sales team. It's everything you need to understand, forecast, and optimize your sales in one place.

8) Digital Advertising Campaign Software

- Kenshoo Sizmek

Kenshoo provides best-in-class solutions and an open architecture framework that adapts to your business environment and delivers actionable intelligence. With more than 100 third-party integrations completed, Kenshoo serves as your true north for channel management, optimization, and analytics.

- 4C

4c is a global leader in data science and media technology with software for multi-screen marketing, we transform the way advertising and content are measured, planned, bought and sold.

- Double Click

Digital Marketing Reach today's always-connected consumers wherever they are with DoubleClick's integrated digital marketing solutions. Revenue Management Take charge of your ad sales across screens and channels with DoubleClick's complete revenue management solutions.

9) E-Commerce Software

- Shopify

Whether you sell online, on social media, in store, or out of the trunk of your car, Shopify has you covered. Your brand, your way No design skills needed. Establish your brand online with a custom domain name and online store. With instant access to hundreds of the best looking themes, and complete control over the look and feel, you finally have a gorgeous store of your own that reflects the personality of your business.

- Netsuite

NetSuite provides you with instant access to your critical business information, when you need it and in real time. It delivers an in-depth insight to all areas of your organisation, so you can make informed business decisions with confidence. Implemented into more than 40,000 organisations worldwide, NetSuite is your first choice for cloud ERP.

- Woo Commerce

WooCommerce is an open source e-commerce plugin for WordPress. It is designed for small to large-sized online merchants using WordPress. Launched on September 27, 2011, the plugin quickly became popular for its simplicity to install and customize and free base product.

WooCommerce has been adopted by over 380,000 online retailers. It is used by a number of high-traffic websites, among them are Internet Systems Consortium and Small Press Expo.

For the 3rd week of September 2015, Trends indicated that WooCommerce ran on 30% of e-commerce sites and millions of active installs.

10) Product Management Software

- Jira

A proprietary issue tracking product, developed by Atlassian. It provides bug tracking, issue tracking, and project management functions. The product name is a truncation of *Gojira*, the Japanese name for Godzilla, itself a reference to Jira's main competitor, Bugzilla. It has been developed since 2002. According to one ranking method, as of June 2017, Jira is the most popular issue management tool.

- CA Agile

CA Agile Central shows you how strategy ties to execution and delivery—so you can make faster, smarter decisions. Use this agile software to align strategy and daily work, track and manage delivery in a predictable cadence and leverage key data to quickly and accurately measure performance.

- Pivotal Tracker

Proven project management for successful teams. With a shared view of team priorities, a process that fosters collaboration, and dynamic tools to analyse progress, your team will deliver more frequently and consistently.

- Wrike

Core Building Blocks of Work. Break large goals into manageable pieces, attach files, and set due dates. Easily track overall progress and individual contribution. Add any task into multiple folders or projects and create any combination of folder structures to meet your needs.

11) Content Management Software

- Google Drive

Google Drive is a file storage and synchronization service developed by Google. Launched on April 24, 2012, Google Drive allows users to store files in the cloud, synchronize files across devices, and share files. In addition to a website, Google Drive offers apps with offline capabilities for Windows and macOS computers, and Android and iOS smartphones and tablets. Google Drive encompasses Google Docs, Sheets and Slides, an office suite that permits collaborative editing of documents, spreadsheets, presentations, drawings, forms, and more. Files created and edited through the office suite are saved in Google Drive.

Google Drive offers users 15 gigabytes of free storage, with 100 gigabytes, 1 terabyte, 2 terabytes, 10 terabytes, 20 terabytes, and 30 terabytes offered through optional paid plans.

- Microsoft One Drive

OneDrive is a file-hosting service operated by Microsoft as part of its suite of online services. It allows users to store files as well as other personal data like Windows settings or BitLocker recovery keys in the cloud.

- Sharepoint

SharePoint is a web-based, collaborative platform that integrates with Microsoft Office. Launched in 2001, SharePoint is primarily sold as a document management and storage system, but the product is highly configurable and usage varies substantially between organizations. Microsoft states that SharePoint has 190 million users across 200,000 customer organizations.

- Box

Working with co-workers, customers and partners has never been simpler. With Box, not only can you securely share files, you can also create, edit and review documents with others in real time from anywhere, on any device. Box offers three account types: Enterprise, Business and Personal. There are official clients offered for Windows and macOS, but not for Linux. A mobile version of the service is available for Android, BlackBerry 10, iOS, WebOS, and Windows Phone devices.

- Citrix Share File

Simplify collaboration inside and outside your organization
Enable true business-class data security for mobile users while maintaining total IT control. Your team or clients can access, sync, and securely share files from anywhere, on any device. Automate feedback and approval workflows to streamline your business and maximize productivity.

In the above section we have discussed machine learning, it is a discipline focused on two interrelated questions: How can one construct computer systems that automatically improve through experience and what are the fundamental statistical-computational-information-theoretic laws that govern all learning systems, including computers, humans, and organizations? The study of machine learning in marketing is important both for addressing these fundamental scientific and engineering questions and for the highly practical computer software it has produced and fielded across many applications.

Machine learning has progressed dramatically over the past two decades, from laboratory curiosity to a practical technology in widespread commercial use. Within artificial intelligence (AI), machine learning has emerged as the method of choice for developing practical software for computer vision, speech recognition, natural language processing, robot control, and other applications. Many developers of AI systems now recognize that, for many applications, it can be far easier to train a system by showing it examples of desired input-output behaviour than to program it manually by anticipating the desired response for all possible inputs.

The past decade has seen rapid growth in the ability of networked and mobile computing systems to gather and transport vast amounts of data, a phenomenon often referred to as "Big Data." The scientists and engineers who collect such data have often turned to machine learning for solutions to the problem of obtaining useful insights, predictions, and decisions from such data sets. Indeed, the sheer size of the data makes it essential to develop scalable procedures that blend computational and statistical considerations, but the issue is more than the mere size of modern data sets; it is the granular, personalized nature of much of these data. Mobile devices and embedded computing permit large amounts of data to be gathered about individual humans, and machine-learning algorithms can learn from these data to customize their services to the needs and circumstances of each individual.

Moreover, these personalized services can be connected, so that an overall service emerges that takes advantage of the wealth and diversity of data from many individuals while still customizing to the needs and circumstances of each.

Instances of this trend toward capturing and mining large quantities of data to improve services and productivity can be found across many fields of commerce, science, and government.

Machine learning helps marketers segment customers, predict churn, forecast customer LTV and effectively personalize messaging. Machine learning and pattern recognition can help marketers in a variety of ways. One of the biggest challenges facing marketers is how to personalize messaging to individual prospects and customers so that it most strongly resonates with the recipient. The results of successful, highly relevant marketing include increased customer loyalty, engagement, and spending. Without machine learning, it is simply too difficult to compile and process the huge amounts of data coming from multiple sources (e.g., purchase behaviour, website visit flow, mobile app usage and responses to previous campaigns) required to predict what marketing offers and incentives will be most effective for each individual customer. However, when all of this data is made available to computers programmed to perform data mining and machine learning, very accurate next best action predictions can be made.

Other areas in which a machine learning application can help marketers include:

- Customer segmentation – Machine learning customer segmentation models are very effective at extracting small, homogeneous groups of customers with similar behaviours and preferences. Successful customer segmentation is a critical tool in every marketer's toolbox.
- Customer churn prediction – By discovering patterns in the data generated by many customers who churned in the past, churn prediction machine learning forecasting can accurately predict which current customers are at a high risk of churning. This allows marketers to engage in proactive churn prevention, an important way to increase revenues.
- Customer lifetime value forecasting – CRM machine learning systems are an excellent way to predict the customer lifetime value (LTV) of existing customers, both new and veteran. LTV is a valuable tool for segmenting customers, and for measuring the future value of a business and predicting growth. Implementing Machine Learning in Marketing

Pattern recognition and machine learning software have come a long way since their early days in the 1960s. New algorithms and technologies are constantly emerging, suggesting new possibilities and applications. Despite this, most marketers are not using any form of machine learning in their day-to-day efforts because it remains a complex field, requiring the involvement of data scientists and developers.

As a consequence, effective implementations of machine learning algorithms in marketing remain beyond the reach of many small- and medium-sized businesses. However, specialized applications developed specifically to address marketing challenges and to be very easy for marketers to use are now available for smaller businesses with modest budgets. This is a game changer for savvy marketers because machine learning can eliminate the guesswork involved in many of the most challenging and valuable aspects of data-driven marketing.

Revision
- Discuss in 150 words the logic behind machine learning software, what is good and bad about it
- IN 50 words outline how you would asses ML software
- Explain in 150 words how ML can be used by a marketer / team
- Provide 10-15 points /reasons why marketing teams should use ML

9. References (as they appear in the text)

Samuel, A. (1959). "Some Studies in Machine Learning Using the Game of Checkers". *IBM Journal of Research and Development*. **3** (3). doi:10.1147/rd.33.0210..Confer Koza, John R.; Bennett, Forrest H.; Andre, Keane, D. Martin A. (1996). *Automated Design of Both the Topology and Sizing of Analog Electrical Circuits Using Genetic Programming*. Artificial Intelligence in Design '96. Springer, Dordrecht. pp. 151–170. doi:10.1007/978-94-009-0279-4_9. "Paraphrasing Arthur Samuel (1959), the question is: How can computers learn to solve problems without being explicitly programmed?"

Kohavi, R. and F. Provost, \Glossary of terms," Machine Learning, vol. 30, no. 2-3, pp. 271-274, 1998 Ron Kohavi; Foster Provost (1998). "Glossary of terms". *Machine Learning*. 30: 271–274.Machine learning and pattern recognition "can be viewed as two facets of the same field."

Dickson, B. "Exploiting machine learning in cybersecurity". *TechCrunch*. Retrieved 2017-05-23

Wernick, Yang, Brankov, Yourganov and Strother, Machine Learning in Medical Imaging, *IEEE Signal Processing Magazine*, vol. 27, no. 4, July 2010, pp. 25–38

Mannila, H. (1996). *Data mining: machine learning, statistics, and databases*. Int'l Conf. Scientific and Statistical Database Management. IEEE Computer Society.

Friedman, J H. (1998). "Data Mining and Statistics: What's the connection?". *Computing Science and Statistics*. **29** (1): 3–9.

"Machine Learning: What it is and why it matters". *www.sas.com*. Retrieved 2016-03-29.

Gartner's 2016 Hype Cycle for Emerging Technologies Identifies Three Key Trends That Organizations Must Track to Gain Competitive Advantage. Retrieved 2017-04-10.

Why Machine Learning Models Often Fail to Learn: QuickTake Q&A. *Bloomberg.com*. 2016-11-10. Retrieved 2017-04-10.

Simonite, T. "Microsoft says its racist chatbot illustrates how AI isn't adaptable enough to help most businesses". *MIT Technology Review*. Retrieved 2017-04-10.

Mitchell, T. (1997). *Machine Learning*. McGraw Hill. p. 2. ISBN 0-07-042807-7.

Harnad, S. (2008), "The Annotation Game: On Turing (1950) on Computing, Machinery, and Intelligence", in Epstein, Robert; Peters, Grace, *The Turing Test Sourcebook: Philosophical and Methodological Issues in the Quest for the Thinking Computer*, Kluwer Sarle, Warren.

Neural Networks and statistical models. *CiteseerX*. CiteSeerX 10.1.1.27.699 .

Russell,S .; Norvig, P. (2003) [1995]. *Artificial Intelligence: A Modern Approach* (2nd ed.). Prentice Hall. ISBN 978-0137903955.

Langley, P. (2011). "The changing science of machine learning". *Machine Learning*. 82 (3): 275–279. doi:10.1007/s10994-011-5242-y.

Le Roux, N; Bengio, Y; Fitzgibbon, A. (2012). "Improving First and Second-Order Methods by Modeling Uncertainty". In Sra, Suvrit; Nowozin, Sebastian; Wright, Stephen J. *Optimization for Machine Learning*. MIT Press. p. 404.

Jordan M.I. (2014-09-10). "statistics and machine learning". reddit. Retrieved 2014-10-01.

Cornell University Library. "Breiman: Statistical Modeling: The Two Cultures (with comments and a rejoinder by the author)". Retrieved 8 August 2017.

Gareth J; Witten, D; Hastie, T; Tibshirani, R. (2013). *An Introduction to Statistical Learning*. Springer. p. vii.

Bishop, C. M. (2006), *Pattern Recognition and Machine Learning*, Springer, ISBN 0-387-31073-8 Mohri, Mehryar; Rostamizadeh, Afshin; Talwalkar, Ameet (2012). *Foundations of Machine Learning*. USA, Massachusetts: MIT Press. ISBN 9780262018258.

Alpaydin, E. (2010). *Introduction to Machine Learning*. London: The MIT Press. ISBN 978-0-262-01243-0. Retrieved 4 February 2017.

Lee,H ., Grosse,R.,Ranganath, R., Ng, A., Y., "Convolutional Deep Belief Networks for Scalable Unsupervised Learning of Hierarchical Representations" Proceedings of the 26th Annual International Conference on Machine Learning, 2009.

Lu, H; Plataniotis, K.N.; Venetsanopoulos, A.N. (2011). "A Survey of Multilinear Subspace Learning for Tensor Data" (PDF). *Pattern Recognition*. 44 (7): 1540–1551. doi:10.1016/j.patcog.2011.01.004.

Bengio,Y., (2009). *Learning Deep Architectures for AI*. Now Publishers Inc. pp. 1–3. ISBN 978-1-60198-294-0.

Tillmann, A., M., "On the Computational Intractability of Exact and Approximate Dictionary Learning", IEEE Signal Processing Letters 22(1), 2015: 45–49.
Aharon, M., Elad, M., and Bruckstein, A.,. (2006). "K-SVD: An Algorithm for Designing Overcomplete Dictionaries for Sparse Representation." Signal Processing, IEEE Transactions on 54 (11): 4311–4322

Goldberg, D., E.; Holland, J., H. (1988). "Genetic algorithms and machine learning". *Machine Learning*. **3** (2): 95–99. doi:10.1007/bf00113892.

Michie, D.; Spiegelhalter, D. J.; Taylor, C. C. (1994). *Machine Learning, Neural and Statistical Classification*. Ellis Horwood.

Zhang, J; Zhan, Z; Lin, Y; Chen, N; Gong, Y; Zhong, J; Chung, S.H.; Li, Y; Shi, Y (2011). "Evolutionary Computation Meets Machine Learning: A Survey" (PDF). *Computational Intelligence Magazine*. IEEE. **6** (4): 68–75. doi:10.1109/mci.2011.942584.

Bassel, G., W.; Glaab, E; Marquez, J; Holdsworth, M., J.; Bacardit, J., (2011-09-01). "Functional Network Construction in Arabidopsis Using Rule-Based Machine Learning on Large-Scale Data Sets". *The Plant Cell*. **23** (9): 3101–3116. doi:10.1105/tpc.111.088153. ISSN 1532-298X. PMC 3203449 . PMID 21896882.

Urbanowicz, R., J.; Moore, J., H. (2009-09-22). "Learning Classifier Systems: A Complete Introduction, Review, and Roadmap". *Journal of Artificial Evolution and Applications*. 2009: 1–25. doi:10.1155/2009/736398. ISSN 1687-6229.

Bridge, J., P., Holden, S., B., and Paulson L.,C.,. "Machine learning for first-order theorem proving." Journal of automated reasoning 53.2 (2014): 141-172.

Loos, S, et al. "Deep Network Guided Proof Search." arXiv preprint arXiv:1701.06972 (2017).

Finnsson, H, and Björnsson, Y.,. "Simulation-Based Approach to General Game Playing." AAAI. Vol. 8. 2008.

Sarikaya, R, Hinton, G.,E., and Deoras, A,. "Application of deep belief networks for natural language understanding." IEEE/ACM Transactions on Audio, Speech and Language Processing (TASLP) 22.4 (2014): 778-784.

AI-based translation to soon reach human levels: industry officials Yonhap news agency. Retrieved 4 Mar 2017.

BelKor Home Pageresearch.att.com

The Netflix Tech Blog: Netflix Recommendations: Beyond the 5 stars (Part 1) . Retrieved 8 August 2017.

Khosla, V., (January 10, 2012). "Do We Need Doctors or Algorithms?". Tech Crunch.

When A Machine Learning Algorithm Studied Fine Art Paintings, It Saw Things Art Historians Had Never Noticed, *The Physics at ArXiv blog*

Kohavi, R., (1995). "A Study of Cross-Validation and Bootstrap for Accuracy Estimation and Model Selection" (PDF). *International Joint Conference on Artificial Intelligence*.

Bostrom, N., (2011). "The Ethics of Artificial Intelligence" (PDF). Retrieved 11 April 2016.

Tolulope E,. "The fight against racist algorithms". *The Outline*. Retrieved 17 November 2017.

Jeffries, A,. "Machine learning is racist because the internet is racist". *The Outline*. Retrieved 17 November 2017.

Nilsson,N.,J., *Introduction to Machine Learning*.
Hastie, T., Tibshirani, R., and Friedman, J., H., (2001). *The Elements of Statistical Learning*, Springer. ISBN 0-387-95284-5.

Domingos,P ., (September 2015), The Master Algorithm, Basic Books, ISBN 978-0-465-06570-7

Witten,I ., H ., and Eibe Frank (2011). *Data Mining: Practical machine learning tools and techniques* Morgan Kaufmann, 664pp., ISBN 978-0-12-374856-0.

Alpaydin, E., (2004). Introduction to Machine Learning, MIT Press, ISBN 978-0-262-01243-0.

MacKay, D., J., C.,. *Information Theory, Inference, and Learning Algorithms* Cambridge: Cambridge University Press, 2003. ISBN 0-521-64298-1

Duda, R., O., Hart, P.,E.,Stork, D., G., (2001) *Pattern classification* (2nd edition), Wiley, New York, ISBN 0-471-05669-3.

Bishop, C., (1995). *Neural Networks for Pattern Recognition*, Oxford University Press. ISBN 0-19-853864-2.

Stuart Russell & Peter Norvig, (2002). *Artificial Intelligence - A Modern Approach.* Prentice Hall, ISBN 0-136-04259-7.

Solomonoff, R., *An Inductive Inference Machine*, IRE Convention Record, Section on Information Theory, Part 2, pp., 56-62, 1957.

Solomonoff, R., "An Inductive Inference Machine" A privately circulated report from the 1956 Dartmouth Summer Research Conference on AI.

www.ingramcontent.com/pod-product-compliance
Lightning Source LLC
Chambersburg PA
CBHW071416180526
45170CB00001B/122